高等院校国际经济与贸易专业系列教材

国际市场营销双语教程

主　编　药朝诚　江永洪

微信扫一扫

教师服务入口　　学生服务入口

南京大学出版社

图书在版编目(CIP)数据

国际市场营销双语教程 / 药朝诚，江永洪主编. -- 南京：南京大学出版社，2017.7(2020.7 重印)

ISBN 978-7-305-18888-6

Ⅰ. ①国… Ⅱ. ①药… ②江… Ⅲ. ①国际营销-双语教学-高等学校-教材 Ⅳ. ①F740.2

中国版本图书馆 CIP 数据核字(2017)第 158347 号

出版发行　南京大学出版社
社　　址　南京市汉口路 22 号　　　邮　编　210093
出 版 人　金鑫荣

书　　名　国际市场营销双语教程
主　　编　药朝诚　江永洪
责任编辑　杨洋潇燊　李　博　　　编辑热线　025-83592315

照　　排　南京南琳图文制作有限公司
印　　刷　常州市武进第三印刷有限公司
开　　本　787×1092　1/16　印张 15.75　字数 364 千
版　　次　2017 年 7 月第 1 版　2020 年 7 月第 3 次印刷
ISBN 978-7-305-18888-6
定　　价　39.00 元

网址：http://www.njupco.com
官方微博：http://weibo.com/njupco
微信服务号：njuyuexue
销售咨询热线：(025) 83594756

Preface

This *International Marketing* text book is designed for meeting the demand of bilingual teaching in China's universities, to help business students of both graduates and undergraduates learn modern concept and techniques of international marketing strategy. A founder of Hewlett-Packard, David Packard, said, "Marketing is too important to be left to the Marketing Department." Everyone in an organization has a marketing function. Marketing is not just selling, or market research, or advertising. Everyone must understand what the customer wants and needs in order to produce products and services that satisfy the customer.

This course book covers the principles of marketing and presents the latest techniques for international marketing planning, strategy, implementation, and management. The complex variations of marketing are applied to consumer, industrial, and nonprofit making operations, to domestic and international organizations of all sizes. Lots of practical examples and case studies of real-world organizations provide the students an easy-to-understand approach to learn the interactions of the many factors involved in international marketing.

Michael E. Porter of the Harvard Business School in his book—*The Competitive Advantage of Nations*, answered the question, "Why do some social groups, economic institutions, and nations advance and prosper?" This book approaches the same question and answers it in a different context.

Chapter 1 introduces the understanding the international marketing and its definition, and describing the different company orientations toward international marketing, identifying the driving forces that direct companies going international, as well as identifying obstacles preventing companies from successful marketing. The theory has a structure of static and dynamic dimensions that interconnected in many ways to meet the requirements of each type of organization, marketing environment, marketing strategy, culture environment, governmental environment, and operational paradigm. The real-world examples and cases that apply to each problem area are presented.

Chapter 2 describes the environment of the international market. The environment is a continually changing aspect of each market. As economic factors change, products and services change, laws change, plus many other factors, there is a fluid nature to every marketing environment. In an international market there are many more uncontrollable factors than in a purely domestic market.

Chapter 3 discusses the nature of cultural differences and their diverse impact on multinational business. A dimensional perspective then is developed for becoming sensitive to and thinking about cultural differences. This perspective provides a framework for discussing ways to understand, adapt to and more effectively manage cultural differences that affect the implementation of international marketing plan.

Chapter 4 addresses the complicated subject of market segmentation on a global scale. The marketers should not only understand the meaning of market segmentation, but also know the segmentation technology when doing the market segmentation. Here is where companies' current competitive situations, product and service comparisons, and other factors help determine market mix strategy. Actual cases are described that demonstrate what can happen in different situations.

Chapter 5 covers the process of international marketing research, from the initial planning of market research to consideration of information requirements and data collection and analysis. The differences between market research in a new market and research in a mature market with international dimension are examined.

Chapter 6 discusses the problems of entering foreign markets, how multinational companies are organized, and how to program for global marketing. Strategies for market entry and growth in global marketing situations are introduced.

Chapter 7 presents the determination of product policy for world markets. As each market differs, sometimes product characteristics must be modified to meet the requirements of the customers. This chapter describes how to develop different product strategies for the various market, as well as advantages / disadvantages of the different product strategies.

Chapter 8 addresses challenges that international firms face internally when setting prices. It also addresses the impact of the international competitive, political and legal, and economic and financial environment on firm pricing decisions. Finally, it evaluates pricing policies of firms for different international markets.

Chapter 9 covers distribution problems and considerations in International marketing. The many economic factors, environmental factors, and government regulations have major effects on distribution decisions. It is also discussed in the chapter the main/minor considerations for selecting channels and how could

Middlemen be managed effectively and efficiently.

Chapter 10 presents the marketing promotion considerations for an international market. The mix changes for each market as well as the product lifetimes. The chapter also examines the importance of each element within the marketing mix and how to determine the right marketing mix. Examples demonstrate the levels of importance that need to be applied to various types of products within a market mix.

Paul E. T. Jensen
Dean, Business School
Northwestern Polytechnic University, US
As at Feb. 17, 2017
In San Francisco

前 言

《国际市场营销双语教程》一书是为了帮助学习商科的研究生和本科生进一步掌握现代化的市场营销的理念与方法以及怎样将现代化的营销技术运用到国际市场营销战略之中而编写的。惠普公司的创始人大卫·帕克这样说:"因为市场营销工作太重要了,所以这项工作不能由企业的营销部所包揽。"这句话意味着,企业的每一个员工均承担着营销的职能。营销决不仅仅是销售、市场调研或者广告,为了向客户提供满意的产品与服务,企业的每一个员工都应该清醒地认识到客户需要什么,怎样才能满足客户的需求。

《国际市场营销双语教程》介绍了市场营销的原则与理念,提供了如何制定、实施和管理国际市场营销计划、营销战略的最新方法。这些颇为复杂多变的计划与战略可以适用于各类工商企业、非营利性组织以及各种规模的国内国际企业。书中还向大学生们提供了许多跨国公司的营销实例,使同学们能够更容易理解在国际市场营销中多种复杂因素是怎样有机地融合在一起的。

为什么有些社会团体、有些经济组织、有些国家会先进会繁荣?哈佛商学院的迈克·波特在其著作《国家竞争优势》中回答了这个问题。《国际市场营销双语教程》也以不同的内容回答了同样的问题。

本书的第一章节介绍了国际市场营销的定义,叙述了企业进入国际市场的不同的价值取向,什么是企业进入国际市场的驱动力,以及企业进入国际市场会面临哪些障碍。参与国际市场经营活动的组织和企业在静态和动态两个层面上与国际市场营销理论有着千丝万缕的关系,营销环境、营销策略、文化环境、政府环境并针对性地辅以案例支持。

第二章对国际市场的营销环境进行了阐述。由于经济因素在变化,产品与服务在变化,法律体系以及其他因素在变化,整个大市场以及各个单一市场的环境条件也在持续发生变化。因此可以说,每一个市场环境都具有流动特征。在国际市场中,不可控制因素远远大于单一的国内市场。

第三章主要讲述文化的特征、力量和所产生的影响,以及跨国公司管理文化差异的方法。全球市场中各个国家和地区间所存在的的文化差异会极大地困扰跨国公司实施其国际市场营销战略。

第四章介绍的是如何对全球市场进行细分。这是一个复杂的课题,在进行市场细分时,不仅要懂得市场细分的意义、掌握市场细分的方法和概念,还需要了解企业所处的竞争环境，与竞争对手的产品与服务进行比较，以确定正确的营销组合。

第五章中主要讲述如何从事国际市场调研，怎样就市场调研进行初始策划，怎样收集与分析相关信息和数据。每一个市场的性质和规模会有所不同，因此市场调研的策略和方法也应该有所不同。在本章中还介绍了在考虑国际环境因素后如何对不同的市场（如新市场、成熟市场）采用差异化调研方法。

第六章引申出了全球营销的概念，主要讨论进入海外市场可能遇到的问题、如何组建跨国公司，以及实施全球营销活动的步骤。在本章节中还就跨国公司的市场进入战略和成长战略进行了论述。

第七章是关于企业如何在国际市场中制定产品策略的。由于各个市场情势的不同，企业有时需要制定或修订差异性产品策略，以适应不同市场中客户的不同需求。本章讲述了如何就不同的市场开发不同的产品与服务，以及不同产品策略所具有的优势与劣势。

第八章主要介绍国际市场价格策略，强调了跨国企业制订价格决策时面临的内部和来自外部竞争对手的挑战，以及海外市场中的政治、法律、经济和金融环境的挑战。最后对跨国企业的价格策略的重要性进行了评价。

第九章叙述了国际市场营销中关于分销的决策，以及在分销决策时所需要考虑经济因素、环境因素、政府法规等。在本章中也介绍了在选择分销渠道时需要考虑的主要与次要因素、在每一个市场里可能存在的分销渠道以及如何对中间商实施有效的管理。

第十章主要介绍国际市场条件下的促销策略，对营销组合进行了详尽的阐释，强调了随着市场的变化，产品的生命周期会变化，企业的营销组合也要做相应调整。在本章中，对营销组合中的每一个成分及其功能和重要性都进行了讲解。最后介绍了跨国企业应该如何制定正确的营销组合。

保罗·詹森

美国西北理工大学商学院院长

2017年2月17日

于旧金山

Contents
目　录

Chapter 1 International Marketing in General

国际市场营销概述

Learning Objectives

本章学习目标

1. International marketing and its definition
   国际市场营销及其定义
2. Different company orientations toward international marketing
   企业进入国际市场的不同的价值取向
3. Driving forces directing companies going international
   企业进入国际市场的驱动力
4. Obstacles in world market preventing companies from successful marketing
   企业进入国际市场会面临的障碍

For long time, companies have been looking for success beyond their national borders, partnering with foreign firms, or entering new markets on their own. In the past, internationalization was an option for large firms that had the necessary resource to enter and develop new markets. Today, small and medium-sized businesses have access to international markets and can benefit from new venues—for example, the Internet and new markets, emerging markets worldwide for selling their products.

Companies can look at international markets as possible channels and venues for distributing over their productions. Alternatively, they can look at international markets as a source of limitless opportunity. Or, multinationals can react to competitive pressure and enter markets that initially did not consider especially attractive; when they are reactive, rather than proactive, however, companies encounter greater challenges and incur higher costs. Consider the case of Coca-Cola and FedEx.

Case Studies: Coca-Cola 可口可乐

For many decades, Coca-Cola ignored Central and Eastern Europe because the market was not especially attractive. These regions had government restrictions on repatriation of profits—for consumer products, such as Coke, these restrictions were the highest. The distribution was problematic and it did not appear to warrant the required high investment. Moreover, consumers in these countries could barely afford to purchase a Coke. Pepsi, on the other hand, decided that this market was worth the investment: it set up strategic alliances with government agencies in Central and Eastern Europe in the late 1960s. As a first move into this market—that is, the first significant company to move into a new market—Pepsi was able to secure exclusive access and effectively blocked Coca-Colas access for many years. In the 1990s, when these market opened their doors to foreign investment, Coca-Cola had to spend huge amounts of money to overtake Pepsi's lead in these markets. Eventually, it was successful.

Case Studies: FedEx 联邦快递

When assessing its growth opportunities, the FedEx states: "international sky is the limit." In spite of its slogan, however, FedEx has traditionally pursued markets only in industrialized countries. In many low-income countries (in sub-saharan Africa, for example), its competitor, DHL was the first to enter the market, securing business from the national government, to the expatriate community, and to local and international businesses operating there. When FedEx decided these markets had been potential, it had to spend large amounts of money to promote its services in these developing countries and to gain access there.

1.1 The Importance of International Marketing 国际市场营销的重要性

企业活动国际化,进行国际市场营销,乃是当今世界经济、市场和企业发展的必然要求。企业(特别是大企业)只有进入国际市场,进行国际市场营销,才能不断降低产品成本,保证企业利润;才能保持企业竞争优势;才能保持并扩大企业的市场,企业也才能生存和发展。

The United States constitutes one of the most important target markets in the world, consuming a high percentage of worldwide products and services. Over time, however, even as foreign investment in the United States continues to increase (it jumped 76.7 percent, to 161.5 billion in 2006 from the previous year), it has become evident that this target market is losing its dominant position: the percentage of consumers is getting smaller currently, less than 25 percent of the total world market. For U.S. companies to achieve their full potential and to effectively compete with foreign companies in the same league, it is crucial that they expand into international markets to take advantage of global market opportunities, to keep pace with competition, and to maximize the potential of their product mix.

Company	Global Revenues (billions)	Percent Revenues from Outside the U.S.
Walmart	$ 401.2	24.6%
Ford Motor	146.3	51.9
General Electric	182.5	53.7
CitiGroup	52.8	74.8
Hewlett-Packard	118.4	68.2
Boeing	60.9	38.9
Intel	37.6	85.4
Coca-Cola	31.9	77.0
Apple	36.5	46.0
Starbucks	10.4	20.8

Source: Annual Reports of Listed Firms, 2012

Figure 1－1 Selected U.S. Companies and Their International Sales

International companies such as General Motors, Mitsubishi, Microsoft, and Exxon earn profits greater than the GDP of many low-income countries, and their total market value is several times the size of their profits. Even successful small businesses can attribute their survival and success to international markets. Also, companies may find that, with products in the late stage of their life cycle, emerging markets can offer them a new life, such as the case of Avon.

Case Studies: Avon in China 雅芳开发中国市场

China may be the most difficult place for Avon. They have to abide by many regulations. China lifted its ban on direct sales in 2005, after being required to liberalize its retail industry according to WTO rules.

In spite of the restrictions, however, Avon has been doing well in China. S. K. Kao, President of Avon China, reports an increase in sales for the company, as it changed gears to focus primarily on store sales. As a result, the company is experiencing double-digit sales increases in China, currently 28 percent per quarter. It penetrated markets in large and small cities in even the most remote areas in China. Even an Avon store can be found in Lhasa, Tibet, in prominent central location, selling western beauty products.

To achieve their potential, companies must constantly monitor the international environment for opportunities. For the past two decades, privatization in counties previously dominated by state monopolies has made it possible for multinational companies to compete for local energy, airline, railway, and telecommunications industries, etc.

1.1.1 Levels of International Marketing Involvement 国际市场营销的范围和层面

All companies are affected by elements of the international marketing environment. In terms of international marketing involvement, however, companies have different degrees of commitment. A company engaging in domestic marketing has the least Commitment to international marketing. This company focuses solely on domestic consumers and on the home-country environment. The home-country environment, however, is affected by developments in the international environment. Furthermore, the local company is directly affected by local competition, which could come from global companies.

At the next level, export marketing, a company could be involved in exporting indirectly—the company takes orders from international clients—or directly the company actively seeks international clients. For both export marketers and domestic marketers, the international market constitutes an extension of the domestic market and is not given special consideration. Such firms have an ethnocentric(民族中心主义的) philosophy to internationalization.

International marketing activities require a substantial focus on international consumers in a particular country or particular countries, and when more countries are involved, international marketing is often referred to as multinational marketing. International marketing is thus defined as the processes involved in the creation, production, distribution, promotion, and pricing of products, services, ideas, and experiences for international markets. The international company is present in different countries with sales offices and subsidiaries or is an active partner in strategic alliances with local companies. It is important to note that, in this case, international activities are not coordinated across the different countries or across different regions. An international company, according to this definition, has a polycentric(跨区域—多中心), or regiocentric(以单一区域为中心) philosophy to internationalization.

Global marketing involves marketing activities across different countries without focusing primarily on national or regional segmentation. Global marketing is possible due to the emergence of global consumer segments and due to efficient global allocation of company talent and resources. A company engaging in global marketing has a geocentric philosophy to internationalization.

It should be noted, however, that the terms defined in the preceding paragraphs are often used interchangeably by non-business and business alike, even by international managers. "International", "global", and "multinational" are used to refer to any company crossing borders, without particular reference to the global strategy used. The descriptions of the levels of international marketing involvement should primarily guide one to understand when distinctions are made. A superior approach to distinguishing between companies' international orientation and philosophy is the ethnocentric, polycentric, regiocentric, and geocentric (EPRG) framework.

The definition of International Marketing is the performance of business activities designed to plan, price, promote and direct the flow of a company's goods and services to consumers or users in more than one nation for a profit. The only difference in the definitions of domestic and international marketing is in more than one nation. Different environments, add the complexity and diversity of international marketing, in terms of such as competition, legal restraints, government controls, weather, fickle consumers, etc.

1.1.2 The Different Concepts in Framework of International Marketing 各自不同的国际营销理念

Management's orientation toward the internationalization of the firm's operations affects each of the functional areas of the firm and, as such, has a direct effect on the marketing functions within the firm. Management's philosophy on international involvement affects decisions such as the firm's response to global threats and opportunities and related resource allocation. Companies' philosophies on international involvement can be described, on the basis of the EPRG framework, as ethnocentric, polycentric, regiocentric, and geocentric.

1.1.2.1 Ethnocentric Orientation 民族中心主义理念为导向

Eli Lilly is an ethnocentric firm. Top management at Eli Lilly places most of the emphasis on product research and development in an effort to bring to the marketplace high-performance pharmaceutical products. Firms with an ethnocentric orientation are guided by a domestic market extension concept. In general, top management of firms with an ethnocentric orientation consider that domestic strategies, techniques, and personnel are superior to foreign ones and therefore provide the most effective framework for the company's overseas involvement; consequently, international operations and customers are considered secondary to domestic operations and customers. Ethnocentric firms are likely to be highly centralized and consider that the purpose of their international operations is to identity markets that could absorb surplus domestic production; alternatively, international operations could represent a cash cow that generates revenue and necessitates only minimal attention and investment. As a result, plans for international markets are developed primarily in-house by an international division and are similar to those for the domestic market. Firms in the tobacco industry, as well as firms at the forefront of technology, tend to have an ethnocentric marketing orientation.

It should be mentioned that, often, ethnocentric firms approach globalization by internationalizing at the level of the function, rather than the firm; for example, the marketing department may have a geocentric strategy even if top management has an ethnocentric orientation.

In many cases, U.S. firms sell American brands along with their related U.S. life styles and traditions—for example, cigarettes, blue jeans, and entertainment. Hollywood movies are one example in the entertainment category. Another example is Disney, where an ethnocentric marketing approach worked well in some markets, but not in others.

Case Studies: Disney Abroad 迪斯尼在海外的境遇

Ethnocentric marketing was, traditionally, all that Disney was about: the mouse, princes and princesses, Cinderella and her castle, riding, working along with those things. Main streets in U. S. A., such as Frontierland, Adventureland, Tomorrowland—in other words, America and its present, past, and future in a cute package of several fun-packed acres.

It was a formula that worked well in the United States and in Japan at Tokyo Disney Resort. Exporting the concept to France and China Hong Kong seemed like a good idea; however, the company quickly found that an ethnocentric approach to the marketing of its entertainment parks in these two markets would not be an easy task. In Europe, consumers were unhappy with the U. S. themes resonating exclusively throughout the park, so Disneyland Resort Paris had reinvented the offering and adapt it to local preferences, creating entertainment based on European fairy tales, serving food that would appeal to European consumers, and creating a more lax approach to the dress code for the park's French staff. At the China Hong Kong Disneyland, which opened in 2005, attendance fell short of expectations, with visitors complaining of mistreatment and the number of attractions as well as size of the park being considered insufficient. Shortly after opening, during the Chinese New Year period, the park had to close due to ticketing problems, and ticket holders forced their way in by storming through gates and climbing over fences. Chinese authorities are now reluctant to work out the possibility of Disney opening yet another park in Shanghai.

1.1.2.2 Polycentric Orientation

跨区域—多中心理念为导向

Firms with a polycentric orientation are guided by a multi-domestic market concept. Managers of polycentric firms are very much aware of the importance of individual international markets to the success of their business and are likely to establish individual businesses, typically wholly owned subsidiaries or marketing subsidiaries, in each of the countries where they operate. The assumption the company makes is that each market is unique and needs to be addressed individually. Consequently, the company is fully decentralized and engages in minimal coordination with the headquarters.

Each subsidiary has its own marketing plans and objectives and operates autonomously as an independent profit center on an individual country basis to achieve its goals; all marketing activities are performed in each country independently of the company headquarters. To address local consumer needs, marketing research is conducted independently in each overseas market, and products are fully adapted to meet these needs. Alternatively, separate product lines are developed to meet the needs of the individual markets.

In the process of developing individual strategies for each market, the company does not coordinate activities across the different countries and cannot benefit from economies of scale that such coordination would allow. Furthermore, numerous functions are duplicated, and, ultimately, final product costs are higher to the end consumer. For decades, Ford used a polycentric strategy in meeting the needs of budget-conscious consumers by developing a Ford Escort automobile for the United Kingdom that looked different from the one sold in the United States or Southeast Asia. Currently, the automobile addressing the needs of the budget-conscious consumer, the Ford Focus, looks identical in each market: Ford has adopted a geocentric approach to product development.

1.1.2.3 Regiocentric Orientation

以单一区域为中心的理念导向

Firms with a regiocentric or a geocentric orientation are guided by a global marketing concept. Companies adopting a regiocentric orientation view world regions as distinct markets that share economic, political, and cultural traits such that they would be viable candidates for a region-wide marketing approach. A regiocentric orientation is now possible due to the success of regional economic and political integration that allows for implementing a uniform marketing strategy in the entire region. Member countries of the European Union, for example, are candidates for Pan-European marketing strategies, whereas signatory countries of the North American Free Trade Agreement (NAFTA) lend themselves to a successful marketing strategy aimed at the North American market. PepsiCo appears to have a regiocentric orientation: Its divisions are organized on the basis of location, with regional offices coordinating all local marketing activities. For example, Pepsi's Eastern European operations are coordinated by its Vienna (Austria) Office, which devises the company's regional objectives and oversees the implementation of the company's marketing strategy in the region.

1.1.2.4 Geocentric Orientation

以地球为中心的理念导向

Firms in which top management adopts a geocentric orientation perceive the entire world—without national and regional distinctions—as a potential market with identifiable, homogeneous segments that need to be addressed with tailored marketing strategies, regardless of geographical location or nationality. Coordinated management policies are designed to reflect the full integration among worldwide operations.

The objective of a geocentric company is most often to achieve a position as a low-cost manufacturer and marketer of its product line, such a firm achieves a strategic competitive advantage by developing manufacturing processes that add more value per unit cost to the final product than its rivals. An example of a geocentric company is McDonald's.

Case Studies: McDonald's 麦当劳

McDonald's has been successful as a result of its geocentric philosophy. The company uses local products to ultimately offer a similar service to consumers from Mexico City to Mumbay. In Europe, McDonald's uses Polish potatoes, which do not lend themselves to a thin, McDonald's-style cut French fry but are touted to be the best in the region. It also uses local beef from the European regions not affected or threatened by livestock disease. In India or Pakistan, for example, McDonald's serves lamb or vegetarian burgers. Throughout the world, it provides a uniform service that offers, in addition to the fast food it is known for, clean restrooms, air conditioning, and service with a smile-even in markets where a smile is a rare occurrence in a service encounter.

1.2 Driving Forces of International Expansion 企业国际化的驱动力

在经济全球化的背景下，极少有企业会只在封闭的市场内从事经营活动，而不受到国际市场的影响。企业所处的环境中会有很多力量驱动企业不得不走向国际化。放弃国际扩张，意味着将市场份额向竞争者拱手相让。

Few companies operate in an isolated, country-specific environment, and even fewer can effectively avoid international involvement. Local firms manufacturing for local consumers are dependent on equipment, parts, and raw materials originating abroad. They sell to clients and final consumers who have had exposure to international trade practices and to international products. A complete isolation from international influence is possible only in a closed environment such as North Korea, where for different reasons; consumers are shielded from international influence.

Increasingly, companies cannot afford to avoid involvement in international marketing. Avoiding international expansion could mean losing market share to competitors and missing numerous opportunities created by changes in the international environment. Among reactive motivations for going international is the desire to remain competitive and maintain global market share relative to competitors. In addition, evading trade barriers and other government regulations in the home country can motivate a company to go international.

Firms, however, should be proactive in their approach to internationalization. A proactive rationale for internationalization can be, among others, the search for new markets, new customers, increased market share and profits, tax advantages, or lower costs, as described in the next sections.

1.2.1 Driving Forces in the Business Environment 商务环境与驱动力

1.2.1.1 Competition 竞争驱动

Competition pressure is often a driver of internationalization. Over time, service providers and client firms develop close relationships that last as long as the firms move together into new international markets. However, the relationship is in jeopardy when the service provider does not follow the client into the new market. McCann Erickson has been, for many years, the primary advertising agency for Coca-Cola and has followed the company into new markets, as illustrated in the following example.

Case Studies: Mccann Erickson and Coca-Cola 麦肯和可口可乐

Mccann Erickson, a leading advertising agency, has followed for many years its longtime client Coca-Cola in every country where the company was present around the globe, McCann Erickson has been handling the Coca-Cola account in 129 countries since 1942. That sometimes meant McCann Erickson lost money in countries where its accounts are limited but where, nevertheless, it chose to be present to serve the advertising needs of Coke. If McCann Erickson chose not to serve its client in a market, Coca-Cola might resort to the services of a competitor, and on the basis of its experience with the competitor, Coca-Cola might replace McCann Erickson with the competing advertising firm.

1.2.1.2 Regional Economic and Political Integration
区域经济和政治一体化

In addition to cultural similarities—language and religion, for example, economic and political integration play an important part in facilitating international trade. Regional agreements such as NAFTA, and the politically and economically integrated European Union are examples of successful attempts at lowering or eliminating barriers between member countries and promoting trade within the perimeter of each common market. The benefits of integration extend to companies from nonmember states as well. It permits subsidiaries incorporated in the respective markets to benefit from free trade within the region and allows firms outside the integrated regions to conduct business within the common market without the impediments typically posed by crossing national borders-customs paperwork, separate tariffs for each country, and so on.

A company from the United States exporting products to multiple counties in the European Union, for example, will cross borders once the company will do the customs paperwork and pay the required customs duties only once, instead of applying for an import license and paying customs duties in every country where it exports products. A subsidiary of a company from the United States incorporated in any country of the European Union is a corporate citizen of the European Union. Consequently the subsidiary does not have to pay duties or foreign exchange costs when it crosses borders of European Union member states because all transactions are conducted in Euros.

1.2.1.3 Technology
科技驱动

Technology has created opportunities for firms involved in international business. In terms of media development, consumers worldwide are exposed to programming originating in other countries. The programming from the United States in particular dominates the international airways is as: Law-Order is followed by audiences worldwide, CNN is popular with business people around the world, and NBC eagerly exports its mix of late-night comedy and news magazines to the rest of the world. Advertising also crosses borders, exposing consumers to brands from other countries. The Web and the Internet have revolutionized the way many companies conduct business, offering businesses instant and unlimited international exposure—something that brick-and-mortar stores and traditional manufacturers have taken years to achieve. Such exposure offers tremendous opportunities to small businesses that do not normally have the advertising budget to communicate with the international market. For example, a Havasu-owned business in Nevada, located 2 hours by car and another 2 on horseback from Las Vegas, can advertise weekend vacation opportunities to French business people in the southern state of Languedoc-Roussillon planning to attend Las Vegas conferences or to French couples in the eastern state of Alsace looking for a unique honeymoon.

1.2.1.4 Improvements in the Infrastructure

基础设施更新

Closely linked to technology are the leaps in the area of transportation and, particularly, in the technology infrastructure. In the not-so-remote past, a Mercedes-Benz service station in Bujumbura, Burundi (Sub-Saharan East Africa), attempting to contact the company factory in Stuttgart, Germany, to order a part, would tie up an English(or German) speaking employee for most of the day for this purpose. The employee would book the telephone call with the operator early in the morning and would typically be contacted by the afternoon. The call would be facilitated by an operator in Brussels, Belgium (all calls to Burundi went via cable from Belgium to its former colonies in East Africa), who would link the factory to the service station. The quality of the connection would often be problematic, necessitating a second request for a telephone connection. An alternative would have been placing the request via telex (faxing was not an option, nor was the use of E-mail).

Today, a telephone connection to Burundi would be handled via satellite, at a significantly lower cost than previously, when it was handled via cable. The communication would be crisp and clear, especially if a cellular phone is used, analog telephones phones in Burundi are sometimes still problematic. Teleconferencing is also becoming common in international business transactions. In addition, faxing and E-mailing constitute viable options for written communication between the service station and the German factory. In fact, much of the outsourcing of customer service to developing countries, such as India and China, is largely attributed to improvements in telecommunication.

Transportation has also greatly improved since the 1980s. The introduction of containers for international inter-modal (ship, truck, train) shipping greatly facilitates the transportation of physical goods. For passenger transport, efficient and rapid air travel has become more affordable, allowing for frequent interaction between expatriate or local employees and employees from the company headquarters. Alternatively, high-speed train travel on inter-city routes allows for rapid transportation in developed countries, such as Japan, and many countries in the European Union.

1.2.1.5 Economic Growth

经济增长

Economic growth constitutes an important driver of internationalization. Economic development in general and increased buying power-attributed to the emergence of a strong middle class in large markets, such as those of Brazil and India, for example, have created great potential for international brands. Economic growth has also opened markets that were previously closed or that have limited international competition. A case in point is China, where consumers are no longer restricted with regard to their consumption and physical movement. China also welcomes foreign direct investment and supports large-scale privatization of state-owned enterprises. Emerging economies in general are more open to foreign trade and no longer severely limit international firms operating in these markets.

1.2.1.6 Transition to a Market Economy

经济体制转型

The transition of the former Eastern Bloc countries and formerly closed economies, such as that of China and Vietnam, to a market economy has led to rapid economic development in these countries and has created important new markets for international brands. Another important outcome of the transition to a market economy has been the deregulation. Opportunities exist for product manufacturers, such as Philip Morris, Whirlpool, Unilever, Procter & Gamble, Colgate-Palmolive, and other companies, to purchase or partner with local companies operating at a loss producing service providers, from Accenture to Pizza Hut, entered these markets, engaging in the highest level of commitment.

1.2.1.7 Foreign Direct Investment

外国直接投资

Currently, international companies, joint ventures between multinationals and local companies, private local businesses, as well as some remnants of the former system—for example, state-owned enterprises competing for local consumers in these transition economies. At the same time, satellite television and the Internet expose these consumers to programming, information, and advertising for international brands, shaping consumer desires and brand preferences. Companies that have, over time, ignored these markets due to the obstacles they posed (limiting operations, limiting their access to hard currency, and restricting repatriation of profits) are now embracing the many opportunities open to international investors. Investing in transition economies is a brilliant strategy for company growth. Most rewards are reaped by those companies investing in large transition economies, such as in China.

1.2.1.8 Consumer Needs
消费需求

Exposure to global brands in one's home country and, while traveling abroad, to media advertising these brands has created demand for many global products. Consumers worldwide are loyal to international brands such as Nike sneakers, Levi's jeans, Coca-Cola, Heineken beer, and Ralph Lauren shirts. Uniform consumer segments are emerging worldwide. Consumers in the United States and in Southeast Asia are loyal to the same soft-drink brands, wearing the same brands of clothing, listening to the same music, having the same idols, seeing the same television shows, and watching MTV for entertainment.

During their international travels, consumers purchase brands and services available in their home country, with which they are familiar. Most often, these offerings are successful international products and services. Alternatively, consumers traveling abroad bring with them product experiences and demand brands that may not be available in the home-country market. This would generate pulling demand, whereby consumers request the product from the retailers, who subsequently convey the information up the distribution chain to wholesalers. The wholesalers would then order the product.

Firms facing similar consumers demanding in uniform the same products have a relatively easy task in addressing the needs of these consumers, using a similar marketing strategy throughout the region. Entry in such uniform markets is facilitated by selling the same product regardless of market and by the use of the same advertising campaign to address the same generation targeted in the United States, France, Malaysia, and Salvador.

1.2.2 Firm-specific Drivers Product Life-Cycle Considerations
基于产品周期的企业内部驱动

A main driver of international expansion is a firm's attempt to prolong the life cycle of its products and thus create higher profits for the company from a larger customer base. Products that are in late maturity, or even in the decline stags, can change their position on the global product life-cycle stage by going into markets where the product is in high demand. To illustrate this point, the cigarette industry is in either the late maturity stage or in the decline stage in many industralized countries. By entering emerging markets where cigarettes are in the growth stage and consumers have increasing purchase power, such as India, China and Central and Eastern Europe, the cigarette industry is in fact prolonging its products' life cycle.

1.2.2.1 High New Product Development Costs
高昂的产品研发成本

The concept of high costs for new product development is related to the product life cycle. Companies often spend long periods and significant amounts of money to develop new products. Nike, on the average, spends close to a year to develop, test, and manufacture new product designs that then last on the shelves in the United States for only 6 months. Despite the size and purchase power of the U.S. market, it is unlikely that Nike would fully recover its product development costs and make a profit as well if it limited its sales to this country. This is especially true for companies at the forefront of technology (manufacturers of high-tech equipment and electronics, pharmaceutical firms, and others), which need to tap large markets for long periods to recoup costs and to make a profit as well; as a result, for these companies, going international is not a choice but a precondition for survival.

1.2.2.2 Standardization, Economies of Scale, and Cheap Labor
标准化、经济规模和廉价劳动力

During the maturity stage of the product life cycle the core product is likely to achieve a standard in a particular industry. Competitors, typically an oligopoly, respond to consumer needs by offering products of which components are interchangeable and which converge toward the brand experiencing the greatest consumer demand. To offer a historical illustration, standards were established in the personal computer industry, which converged on the IBM standard. Also, during the maturity stage, firms increasingly compete on price. Typically, they attempt to lower the product manufacturing costs by achieving economies of scale in production. In addition, firms with mature brands also move manufacturing operations and facilities abroad, to developing countries, in an attempt to take advantage of significantly lower labor costs.

1.2.2.3 Experience Transfers
经验转让

International companies benefit from lessons they learn in the different parts of the world. Colgate-Palmolive, for example, developed its successful Axion dishwashing paste for its Latin American market after noting that women washed dishes by hand, dunking their hands in a small tub with a few slivers of soap. The same product was then offered to consumers in Central and Eastern Europe after noting that they washed dishes using a similar method and the product was a hit. Service providers such as Pizza Hut found that they were more successful with consumers in general, but especially with younger generations of consumers in

Central and Eastern Europe if they played pop music on the rather loud side in their restaurants. As a result they started entering new markets by partnering with Radio Stations and Discos.

Such experience transfers are especially helpful to retailers in the process of internationalization. The Tesco Extra hypermarket (Superstore) in the city of Newcastle, United Kingdom, and the popular and busy Tesco hypermarket in the southern Czech Republic, are based on a Tesco hypermarket first introduced by the same U. K. retailer in Hungary. Taking advantage of experience transfers, the company is able to go to different international markets and thus reduce its dependence on any one market.

1.3 Obstacles to Internationalization 国际化进程中的障碍

企业在国际化进程中绝不会一帆风顺，一定会遇到很多困难和障碍。这些问题和障碍会来自企业的内部和外部。企业家需要懂得将这些问题和障碍转化为资本。其实，对企业家而言，最大的障碍莫过于对国际市场的恐惧。

Companies attempting to establish and maintain an international presence are likely to encounter obstacles to internationalization both from within the company and outside. Such obstacles can be financial in nature. The company might not have the finances to expand beyond national frontiers. Others are psychological. Fear of an unknown international environment or of local business practices may keep the company from international engagement. These two types of barriers, however, could equally affect the company's local expansion efforts. Companies may not have the finances to expand beyond a small regional market, or they fear going into new markets where consumers may not be familiar with their products and hence may not respond to their marketing strategy.

Some obstacles are encountered only by firms in their process of internationalization that they are unlikely to encounter in other expansion efforts. They are the self-reference criterion, government barriers, and international competition.

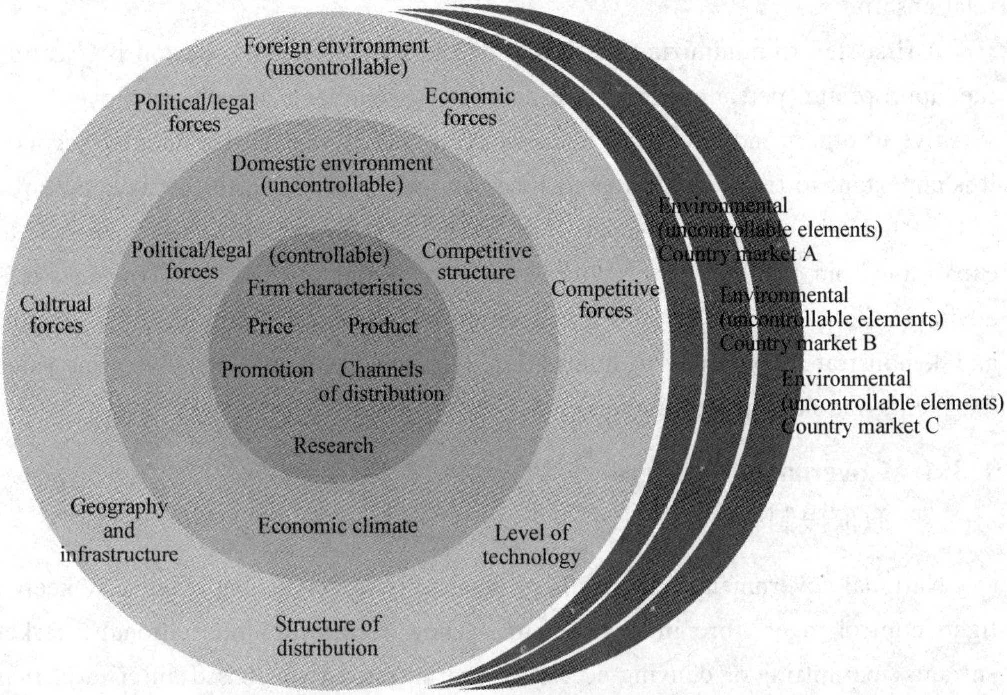

Figure 1 - 2 The International Marketing Task

Of crucial importance to international operations is the ability of the firm, and especially of its marketing program, to adapt to the local business environment to serve the needs of local consumers and to address the requirements of local government, industry and channels of distribution. An impediment to adaptation is the self-reference criterion, defined as individual conscious and unconscious reference to their own national culture and to home-country norms and values, as well as to their knowledge and experience, in the process of making decisions in the host country. At the company level, self-reference may lead the firm to fail to understand local consumers and their needs and to fail to understand the local business culture and deal effectively with local nationals.

Self-reference can lead to a breakdown in communication between parties from different cultures. For example, an employee of a large multinational company from the United States has been trained by career counselors in the United States that looking one's counterpart in the eyes conveys directness and honesty. When this individual conducts business in Japan using direct eye contact, he is likely to be perceived as abrasive and challenging. Similarly, if an employee proceeds directly to transacting the business deal in Latin America or southern Europe instead of first interacting in a social setting to establish rapport, he would be perceived as arrogant, interested only in the bottom line, rather than in a long-term working relationship.

A first step to minimizing the effect of the self-reference criterion is selecting the appropriate personnel for international assignments. Such employees are sensitive to others and have experience working in different environments. Second, it is important to train expatriates to focus on and be sensitive to the local culture, rather than limit their personal interactions to own-country nationals or to expatriate from countries with cultures that are similar to their own. In fact, it is advisable that firms institute an organization-wide general orientation that instills and demonstrates sensitivity to international environments and openly spurns value judgments and national stereotyping.

1.3.1 Government Barriers 政府限制

National governments, especially governments in developing countries, keep a tight control over foreign investment. They scrutinize international market entrants, permitting or denying access to international firms based on criteria that are deemed important for national industry and/or security considerations. Among formal methods used by national governments to restrict or impede entrance of international firms in the local market are tariffs and barriers such as import quotas. Barriers may be imposed by restrictions in import license awards, foreign exchange restrictions, local content requirements, and others. Governments may decide to devalue the currency, change commercial laws, or radically change commercial regulations.

Member countries of the WTO or members of regional economic and political integration agreements such as NAFTA and the European Union, find it difficult to use tariffs as a means of restricting international expansion of companies in the countries' territories. Increasingly, they are using nontariff barriers, such as cumbersome procedures for import paperwork processing, delays in granting licenses, or preference given to local service providers and product manufacturing for all contracting work.

1.3.2 International Competition 国际竞争

Although competition can be a driver of internationalization, competitors can also erect barriers to new entrants in a market. Competitors' arsenals of barriers include the following: blocking channels of distribution, binding retailers into exclusive agreements, slashing prices temporarily to prevent product adoption, or engaging in an advertising blitz that could hurt a company's initial sales in a market and cause it to retrench. With heavy competition from new and lesser-known brands in Asia, Central and Eastern Europe, and North Africa and the Middle East, Marlboro created a strong defensive strategy for its cigarettes: It slashed prices by as much as third and advertised heavily anywhere it was legal to do so, especially on billboards in the center of different capital cities and towns in the provinces.

As an example, sales of Marlboro in southeastern Europe were hurt by various local competitors and, in particular, by a successful regional brand, Assos, from Greece. Assos was rapidly gaining a leading position in a number of markets in the region when Marlboro went on the offensive, limiting Assos's market share to a point where the company was forced to abandon many of its markets. Marlboro effectively put in question the international expansion of many new European and Asian brands, as well as new brands from the United States. It decimated, for instance, sales of new brands of U.S. cigarettes created specifically for the Russian market by small entrepreneurs.

The Chapter's Referential Questions:
本章参考性问题

1. Define international marketing. How is it different from domestic marketing?
   请谈谈国际市场营销的定义,以及国际市场营销与国内市场营销有何不同。
2. Why is the international marketer's task more difficult than that of the domestic marketer?
   为什么说与国内市场营销相比,国际市场营销的任务会更艰巨?
3. What are the primary obstacles to access in the international market?
   企业进入国际市场会遭遇哪些主要障碍?
4. Discuss the conditions that lead to the development of global markets.
   谈谈企业开发全球市场需要具备哪些条件。
5. How do you understand the internal reasons for the evolution of international marketing concepts?
   企业在制订国际市场营销理念时,需要考虑哪些内部因素?
6. Why could the regionalization be the driving force for companies going international?
   为什么说区域一体化会成为企业国际化的驱动力?
7. Why is it said that "although competition can be a driver of internationalization,

competitors can also erect barriers to new entrants in a market"?

为什么说,"竞争既是企业国际化的推动力,又会成为企业进入国际市场的障碍"?

8. How could government set barriers for foreign companies in international marketing?

在国际市场营销中,政府通常采用哪些手段为外国公司设置障碍?

微信扫码查看

Chapter 2 International Marketing Environment

国际市场营销环境

Learning Objectives

本章学习目标

1. General Perception of the World Economic Environment
   对世界经济环境的总体认知
2. The Political Risk and How to Avoid it
   政治风险及如何规避
3. How the International Law, Home-Country Law, and Host-Country Law affect International Marketing
   国际法律、母国法律及东道国法律如何影响国际市场营销
4. The Nature and Technological Environment and Potential Limitations to International Companies
   自然环境、技术环境以及这两方面因素给跨国公司带来的限制

Case Studies: Kigali, Rwanda 卢旺达首都基加利

Kigali is a city of contrasts: internet cafes, dust, poverty, a luxurious German bakery-cum-grocery-cum-ice-cream store, persons with HIV estimated to constitute 50 percent of the local population, sporty foreigners, even better dressed locals and more dust. The city center is busy with shops selling masks, nesting baskets, and trinkets to tourists, with many bars that stay open late, restaurants, and world class hotels. Nesquik and Coca-Cola are prominently advertised, replacing joyful cigarette ads previously plastered all over the city and framing the main road to the airport. Multinationals are vying for what bringing up the past is not appropriate, as indicated in tourist guidebooks and security briefings for nongovernmental organization staff.

Kigali is the capital city of Rwanda, where 8 million people are jammed into a country smaller than Maryland, making it one of the world's most densely settled agrarian societies. In many places, nearly every patch of reddish earth is cultivated in a patchwork of fields that stretch up, and often over, Rwanda's countless hills. Just over a decade ago, Rwanda was the home of a 100-day ethnic slaughter in which most of the 800,000 victims were hacked to death with machete or beaten to death with clubs. The Belgian colonists favored the Tutsi minority and used them to run the country, creating antagonism between the Hutu majority tribe and the Tutsis. Most of the killings happened as ethnic Hutu militias rampaged through steep hillside village in search of Tutsis and those who sought to defend them.

Today, the Tutsis are in charge again. Some Hutus are being tried for their crimes. Tutsi and Hutu identity cards no longer list ethnic group information, side-by-side, at the Nyabugogo market, Tutsis and Hutu sell clothing under the metal roofs, peddle their goods in the streets, and travel crowded in the matatus—open trucks that allow people to travel standing, as they weave from hill to hill. The heart of commerce in this land try is bustling kigali, but is this city—is the country—truly ready for business again?

Countries where multiple tribes have coexisted for decades without any conflict where the president and his army have led effectively, spreading the wealth to the population and attracting in the country foreign direct investment, can still fall victim to a civil war, as in the case of Rwanda, discussed earlier. Multinational firms leave their assets open to plundering and promptly ship their expatriates to safety. This scenario is played out over and over in the world: multinational companies in Chad Rwanda, Burundi, the Congo, Sierra Leone, Haiti, Bosnia and

Herzegovina, and Croatia have all experienced losses. Multinational companies are also victims of corporate terrorism, which is on the increase worldwide. The political environment poses many challenges to businesses.

The legal environment can be problematic as well. Some companies operate in environments where everything is forbidden unless expressly allowed. Other companies operate in environments where everything is perceived as allowed unless expressly forbidden. Companies operating in legally ambiguous environments face ethical and legal challenges from host-country national governments, para-national, institutions, and the home-country government that they have to address effective to be able to survive in international markets.

The natural environment of international marketing also poses challenges to businesses: geology and the shortage of natural resources, coupled with a high population growth, can negatively affect market potential. Similarly, topography can affect access, and hydrology and climate can affect economic development. Phenomena such as a shortage of natural resources, the energy crisis, and the environmental quality crisis affect the business environment.

The technological environment of international marketing is rapidly opening international markets never before accessible to multinationals and is creating a viable future for small and medium enterprises that have never had such a broad exposure. The technological environment is also speeding the new-product development process and creating unprecedented distribution potential in industry.

This chapter focuses on elements in the environment of international marketing. We examine the effect of economic, political, legal, technology and natural environment on the international marketing operations of firms.

2.1 The Economic Environment of International Marketing 国际市场营销的经济环境

国际经济已经真正成为一个整体。大多数公司不能仅仅盯住本国或者东道国的市场,而应在世界范围内展开市场份额的争夺。因此,跨国公司的经营将不得不考虑如何面对经济全球化的现实。

2.1.1 The World Economy 全球经济

It is common today to hear that, when the United States sneezes, Europe and Japan catch a cold. This is an understatement. When the United States experiences a downturn in the economy, reverberations echo throughout the world: central and southern countries need to be rescued by the International Monetary Fund; all the Asian economies flounder; banks in developing countries default on the debt. The United States is equally affected by the world economy. The Asian crisis of the 1990s sent stock markets tumbling in the United States and in the rest of the world. In the Internet age, countries are becoming more and more connected by trade, capital markets, the flow of technology and ideas across national borders, and psychology: rather than rising and falling separately, national economies increasingly respond to the same forces. Interdependence has become the leading principle of globalization.

The rises in value of one currency and fall of another have repercussion. A weak Dollar benefits workers in the United States, and U.S. business in general. More KFC fast food restaurants are opening in China than in the United States, and more than half of the 9.1 million automobiles that General Motors produces are sold internationally. A weak Dollar makes American goods and services more competitive in foreign markets, keeps jobs at home, and depresses the trade deficit because America's workers keep more production at home and sell more goods abroad. However, if the Dollar keeps falling, it can have adverse implications for foreign economics. Germany, for example, can suffer if the Euro continues to appreciate relative to the Dollar, slowing down demand for German-made goods.

In spectral examples, an excess of steel in the world markets, attributed to overproduction in Russia and China, led to restructuring of the industry elsewhere in the world, leaving only a few players in the world steel oligopoly. And underproduction for oil attributed to the control of the organization for Petrol.

Exporting Countries (OPEC) has historically led to inflation worldwide because the price of gas is leading to the increase in price of all other goods. On the positive side, the boom in technology stocks in 1999 led to much-abeit short-lived prosperity in many industrialized countries. Technology continues to make a strong positive impact on the economics of countries that stress technical training and software design, in particular, such as India. Never in the history of mankind has there been such a degree of interdependence.

The international economy has indeed become one single unit. Major companies simply cannot afford a local, home-country focus. The market share game is played on a world scale. A one world commercial future is becoming a reality in which multinational rule. The top 100 companies in the world control about 20 percent of foreign assets, and employ 6 million workers, accounting for as much as 7 percent of total world economic activity. Multinational companies account for two-thirds of world trade, and many have economic weight, more than half of the 100 biggest economies in the world are now corporations, not nations. Mitsubishi is bigger than Indonesia, Ford is bigger than Turkey and Wal-Mart is bigger than Israel. As a result, multinationals are able to break down barriers that have withstood armies, missionaries, crusader, and politicians.

2.1.2 The Economic Development Disparity 经济发展不平衡现象

In the current economic environment, companies from high income, industrialized countries and their representative governments dominate the world economy, allocating resources worldwide based on market potential, rather than on local population needs, creating a growing gap between the have countries and have-not countries. Low income countries, on the other hand, control resources (raw materials and labor) that multinationals need and access to local consumer, and they frequently pose barriers to international business operations in an attempt to lessen the development gap. It is important, under this environment, to understand the existing dynamic between countries at different levels of economic and market development and the philosophies underlying those dynamics.

2.2 Different Economic Development Models 不同的经济发展模式

本部分将介绍在世界范围内被广泛接受的两种不同的经济发展模式，即罗斯托提出的现代化发展模式和马克思提出的社会主义发展模式，以及在不同的国家和社会条件下运用和发展的概况。

2.2.1 Perspectives on Economic Development 经济发展前景

Two models of economic development have gained acceptance in the world: a western model, best articulated by Rostow, and the Marxist development model, which still constitutes a dominant development philosophy in some developing countries. It must be noted that the political changes in Eastern Europe and Vietnam have reduced considerably the areas dominated by the Marxist philosophy on economic development.

2.2.1.1 The Rostow Modernization Model

罗斯托现代化发展模式

According to the Rostow modernization model, each stage is a function of productivity, economic exchange, technological improvements, and income. Economic growth requires advancing from one stage to another. The modernization stages are traditional society, transitional society, the drive to maturity, high mass consumption.

(1) Traditional Society

传统社会

Countries in the traditional society are characterized by an economic structure that is dominated by agriculture. Minimal productivity occurs, and only a few exchange transactions take place. Economic change and technological improvements are not sufficient to sustain any growth in per output, which is low.

(2) Transitional Society

转型社会

The transitional society stage is characterized by increased productivity in agriculture, and modern manufacturing begins to emerge. In manufacturing low productivity remains the norm. The preconditions for take-off are the following: society engages insecular education, establishes banks and currency, and has an emerging entrepreneurial class, and the concept of manufacturing merges, with only few sectors developing at first. Overall, there is limited production and limited output. Assuming these preconditions are met, take-off is likely in 10 to 50 years.

During take-off, growth becomes the norm and improvements in production lead to the emergence of leading sectors. Income rises across the board, and a new class of established entrepreneurs emerges.

(3) The Drive to Maturity

走向成熟阶段

In the drive-to-maturity stage, modern technology is fully adopted in all economic activity, and new leading sectors emerge. The economy demonstrates the technological and entrepreneurial skill to produce anything it chooses to. The economy looks beyond the country's border for development.

(4) High Mass Consumption

高消费阶段

In the age of high mass consumption, leading sectors shift toward durable goods. A surge occurs in per capita income and increased allocation to social welfare programs. The masses can afford goods beyond food, clothing, and shelter.

2.2.1.2 Alternative Models of Economic Development
经济发展的其他模式

(1) The Marxist Model
马克思主义模式

The Rostow model of economic development is, in fact, a Western perspective of development. Alternative models exist in spite of the global triumph of the market system and the confirmation of a Rostow-type model in countries that have previously adopted alternative philosophies. One example is the Marxist model, a competing alternative for developing nations seeking to avoid domination by advanced market capitalist economies. It endorses a collective orientation, one adopted by the more traditional developing countries, and competes with market oriented capitalism, fueling anti-colonial and anti-imperialist sentiments. Socialist ideas of sharing wealth; leveling inequality; eliminating homelessness; and providing basic needs such as health care, food, education, and shelter to all citizens appeal to many in the poor, developing countries that were long suppressed and exploited by colonial and imperialist powers. At the heart of this philosophy are issues of equitable distribution of national income, improvement in the welfare of the masses, and economic justice.

The Marxist model and its dialectic materialism theories approach economic development philosophy similarly to the Rostow model in the first stage. The subsequent stages are depicted as a class struggle ending in revolution, which is need for advancement to the next stage. Advancement is a function of the control of means of production, production outcomes, resource allocation, and the development of a mindset devoid of materialist needs.

(2) The Primitive Society
原始社会

Countries in the primitive society stage are similar to those in traditional society. There is joint, tribal ownership of the means of production, which are minimal, primitive, and centered on agricultural tasks, for the use of all the members of the commune within the tribe. Much of the agriculture is slash-and-burn, with the tribes moving in the quest for new territory. All tribal members in this egalitarian society work for the common welfare of the tribe.

(3) The Slavery-Based Society
奴隶社会

The slavery-based society emerges as a result of tribes taking over other tribes and enslaving their population. Slaves are now property of the conquering tribe. Under Roman, Mesopotamian, and Egyptian rule, slaves toiled in agriculture and built infrastructures, such as access roads and irrigation systems. Tribal territory ownership is established as a first step toward establishing private property. Trading agricultural goods and tools between tribes becomes common.

(4) Feudalism

封建社会

Under the feudal society known as feudalism, feudal lords own armies, land, and the dwellers of the land. Land is primarily in the hands of the feudal family, production is still primarily agricultural. Guilds emerge as a production unit, manufacturing goods and training future manufacturers under apprenticeships. Trading is common and widespread, and exchange is now primarily based on gold as currency.

(5) The Capitalist Society

资本主义社会

The capitalist society is represented by two stages. The first stage is characterized by an emerging bourgeoisie(developed from the guild class) as a ruling class alongside the aristocracy(the former feudal family). The bourgeoisie creates lucrative means of production, and it achieves high productivity at the expense of exploited workers. Production shifts gradually from the agrarian sector to the industrial sector. The second stage of capitalism is multinational imperialism. Imperialist capitalism is characterized by a capital that loses its national identity by crossing borders; in fact, the export of capital in international trade is a central mechanism of imperialism. The international firm is a double parasite exploiting its own working class, as well as workers in less-developed countries. Multinational firms represent the modality for national domination of developing countries and for the domination and subjugation of workers and peasants worldwide. The creation of international monopolies (monopolistic capitalism) represents the most advanced stage of capitalist dominance.

(6) The Socialist Society

社会主义社会

The socialist society is also composed of two stages. The first, transitional stage, leads to the gradual disappearance of private property, which is replaced by collective, state property. Countries in this stage typically are formally known as in People's Republic of China. China's ideological elite argues that this stage can take, potentially, hundreds of years, In the case of China, it will take at least 100 years.

Socialism in its more advanced stage takes the form of the multilaterally developed socialist society. Socialist Republics, as countries in this stage are referred to, are characterized by state ownership of all the means of production.

The state also controls the modes of production, allocating resources to industry, agriculture, education, and health care on the basis of societal needs.

(7) The Communist Society

共产主义社会

No country has ever claimed to have reached the communist stage. Under Communism Party and under state ownership, all means of production and private property are under state ownership and /or cooperative ownership. The state is in charge of allocation of resources to sectors as needed and to individuals (goods and services) according to their needs. Communism develops "the new man" who views work as a need and who will work according to his ability. There is no need for private property, and there is no materialism in society.

In the early stages of communism, Lenin argued that foreign capital is important in the development process as a source of advanced technology; his solution was a leasing system whereby foreign firms would participate in particular projects and regions in communist countries for a limited amount of time. In practice, this concept was soon countered by the implications of the Cold War and by Stalin' theory of two parallel markets (capitalist and socialist), which stressed internal integration among socialist countries for mutual economic development; according to this theory, capitalist markets were inherently weak, and socialist countries needed to isolate themselves from the capitalist world. The Rostow and Marxist models are comparable, up to a point.

2.3 Levels of Economic Development 经济发展水平

本部分将从历史上的所谓"三个世界"的划分，联合国以收入水平划分，以及世界银行的标准，逐一介绍关于不同国家的经济发展水平定义，以及新兴市场的发展历程。

2.3.1 Classifications of Counties 国家的分类

There are many competing classifications of countries from an economic development. Historically, the informal and frequently used classification in the West has referred to highly industrialized, developed countries as the First World, to socialist countries as the Second World, and to developing countries as the Third World. Of this classification, only the term "Third World" has been used widely. A

United Nations classification contrasts LLDCS (Least-Developed and the Lowest Income Countries) and LDCs(Less-Developed Countries and Lower-Income Countries) to developed countries. Yet other classifications exist. For example, the term NIC(Newly Industrialized Country) is used to describe the economies of China Taiwan, Singapore, South Korea, and China Hong Kong (known in the 1980s and 1990s as the Asian Tigers), whereas countries such as Brazil, Argentina, Chile, Peru, and the transitional economies of Central and Eastern Europe are described as emerging markets. For the purpose of this textbook, we will refer to three categories of countries, based on the classification used by the World Bank.

(1) High-income countries
高收入国家

These are highly industrialized countries with well-developed industrial and service sectors. In this category fall newly industrialized countries, as well as countries that have had a developed status for many years. Although these countries present great potential because they have consumers with the highest per capita income, they also present challenges to international firms because their markets are in the maturity stage, consumers have established preferences, and competition is intense. The World Bank refers to the countries in this category as high-income countries, with a GNI per capita of U.S. $ 10,726 or more.

(2) Middle-income countries
中等收入国家

Countries with emerging markets are both developing rapidly and have great potential. They are countries in Latin America, such as Argentina, Brazil, Uruguay, Paraguay, Chile, Peru, and Bolivia, to name a few; countries in Asia, such as China, with its immense market, and India, with its substantial middle class; and the transition economies of Central and Eastern Europe, which are rapidly privatizing state-owned industries and adopting market reforms. Important in this category are big emerging markets (BEAMS), which present the greatest potential for international trade and expansion. The World Bank refers to the countries in this category as middle-income countries, with a GNI per capita of U.S. $ 875 to U.S. $ 10, 725. The middle-income country category is further divided into two income groups, as follows:

① Upper middle-income countries
中高收入国家

These countries have rapidly developing economics, and especially in urban areas, they have an infrastructure that is on Par with that of developed countries. Among them are countries in Latin America, such as Argentina, Chile, and

Mexico. In this category are the transition economies of Central and Eastern Europe, new European Union member countries that have rapidly privatized state-owned industries and adopted market reforms, such as the Czech Republic; also in this category are Estonia, Hungary, Latvia, Lithuania, Poland, and the Russian Federation. According to the World Bank, countries considered upper middle income countries have a GNI per capita of U.S. $ 3,466 to U.S. $ 10,725.

② Lower middle-income countries

中低收入国家

This is a diverse group of countries that includes China, much of North Africa and the Middle East, and many of the former Soviet Socialist Republics, such as Armenia, Azerbaijan, Belarus, Georgia, Kazakhstan, Moldova, Turkmenistan, and the Ukraine. According to the World Bank, countries in this category have a GNI per capita of U.S. $ 875 to U.S. $ 3,465.

(3) Low-income countries

低收入国家

Countries in this category are primarily agrarian, have low per capita income levels, and are located in different regions in Asia and in sub-Saharan Africa. Low-income countries are often neglected or underserved by large multinationals and consequently present great potential as niche markets. Even the countries with the lowest per capita income have a stratum of society that can afford global products. Furthermore, because they are primary recipients of international development aid, they present important opportunities for firms operating in the areas of infrastructure development and industrial sector development and for related consultancies. The World Bank refers to the countries in this category as low income countries, with a GNI per capita of less than U.S. $ 875. It is important to note that these markets are gross underserved by the international community and that consumer needs—even the most base ones—in these markets are barely met by local administration.

2.3.2 The Importance of Emerging Markets 新兴市场的重要性

Counties with emerging markets present great potential to international firms. Their attractiveness lies primarily in their rate of economic growth up to 7 percent per year, in the past 20 years, compared with about 2 percent for Western Europe and North America. The following countries have been identified as emerging markets by The Economist in its regular reports on emerging markets:

(1) In Asia: China, India, Indonesia, Malaysia, the Philippines, Singapore,

South Korea, Thailand

(2) In Africa and the Middle East: Israel, South Africa

(3) In Europe: The Czech Republic, Poland, Russia, Turkey

(4) In Latin America: Argentina, Brazil, Chile, Mexico, Venezuela

Other countries are likely prospects for the emerging market category on the basis of their economic policies and performance in the past 20 years. Among them are Slovenia, Slovakia, Croatia, Romania, Bulgaria, the Ukraine, Latvia, Estonia, Lithuania and Belarus in Central and Eastern Europe and Colombia, Paraguay Peru, and Uruguay in Latin America. These countries are rapidly privatizing their economics and adopting the economic reforms necessary to create a stable growing economy.

Counties withemerging markets that are expected to have a successful economic future share a number of traits:

(1) High political stability

(2) A sound currency

(3) A low level of inflation

Privatizationpolicies that reduce government deficit, create firsttime share owners who vote for pro-business conservative policies, and diminish the power of trade unions

(1) Policies that facilitate repatriation of dividends and capital

(2) Policies that are in line with international accounting standards

Open disclosure of directors interests Policies that stress regular reporting of earnings and sales figures

(1) A sound and comprehensive system of corporate law

(2) A liquid and well-traded securities market reflecting fair prices

(3) A high savings rate

(4) Strong government support for internationalization

A people characterized by integrity, a strong work ethic, and respect for the law of interest to multinationals are what the United States Department of Commerce refers to as big emerging markets (BEMs). These markets share all the traits of emerging markets and present the most potential because they are large, have large populations, and, consequently, set the pace for the economy in the region. Among these countries are China and India (both with populations exceeding 1 billion), South Korea, Argentina, Brazil, Mexico, South Africa, Poland, and Turkey.

The big emerging markets are developing rapidly and making rapid strides toward industrialization. However, breakneck growth can be problematic, as in the case of India.

Case studies: The Case of India 关于印度

India has an economy with a double-digit growth coupled with an outsourcing industry that serves the world's multinationals. It also has hundreds of millions of consumers who demand class and comfort. However, this rapid development has created an overheated economy with an inflationary spiral. Food prices are quickly climbing so that the poor can barely afford it. Housing prices are rising rapidly, especially in large cities; and factories are running behind in filling orders. Prices in India are rising twice as fast as in China—its rival for foreign investment and outsourcing and considerably faster than in industrialized countries. In the fashionable neighborhoods of South Mumbai, house prices have increased by 60 percent a year in the recent years, and oil-rich investors are bid ding against India's affluent business elite for these properties. A 2,000 square cap concrete floor and flimsy closets in the chi foot apartment with a chic Malabar Hill neighborhood was selling for $1.5 million. The rising prices are rekindling nostalgia for the 1980s, when India was one of the most highly regulated economics.

2.4 The Political Environment of the International Marketing 国际市场营销的政治环境

每一个跨国公司都必须全面了解它们将要进入的国家的政治环境，否则将不得不承担由于政治风险所导致的巨大经济损失。

Case studies The Case of Iran 关于伊朗

Iran 1970s was in the period before the Islamic Revolution and the Iranian government was focused on projects aimed at increasing industrial development. Iranians were generally satisfied with the increased socioeconomic facilities. In 1976, dissatisfied groups engaged in scattered demonstration against the Shah's regime the demonstrations increased in frequency and resulted in the occupation of state-owned, American, and Israeli facilities finally resulting in the Shah's leaving the country. In 1979, the government and the banking industries were paralyzed.

1979—1984, after the 1979 revolution, the new government took hostile action against foreign multinationals, arresting expatriate staff and local staff related to the former regime and confiscating multinational companies, especially those from the United States and Israel. Business in general deteriorated due to the political intervention and the Iran-Iraq War.

In 1985, the Islamic regime consolidated and local businesses gained ground and stability. In 1907—2006, the European Union is Iran's largest trading partner; companies from the United States are banned from doing business with Iran. The U.S. government continues to threaten sanctions against non U.S. companies doing business in Iran.

2007—Present, the International Atomic Energy Agency, the UN's nuclear watchdog, faulted Iran for violating nuclear agreements by intensifying its efforts to create a nuclear-fuel cycle, while diminishing the IAEA's ability to monitor its activities.

The preceding time line demonstrates the volatile nature of alliances in the present world market. The United States enjoyed a close rapport with the deposed. Shah Reza Pahlavi, and U. S. businesses profited under his rule. The Islamic Revolution targeted the Shah's allies in particular: U. S. firms had all their assets confiscated, and their international executives were forced to repatriate. Today, the United States continues to ban the involvement of U. S. firms in Iran and to threaten sanctions on foreign firms with U.S. interests if they engage in operations in the country. Moreover, the relationship between the United States and Iran has reached new levels of conflict as Iran continues building its nuclear capabilities. This section illustrates the political uncertainties involved in international marketing and the legal challenges that firms face in their international operations.

Companies contemplating any international involvement must have anin-depth knowledge of the political environment in the countries where they do business. This is especially important for companies involved in foreign direct investment companies that undertake the greatest level of risk in a foreign market. Whenever there are discussions of political risk, they typically involve the host country—the country where a company engages in business in accordance with the respective country's political and legal restrictions. It should be noted, however, that the international company is also affected by political developments in its home country—the country where the parent company is headquartered. A U. S. based company planning to enter Cuba in the late 1990s, when the Clinton administration appeared to relax anti-Cuba restrictions, had many more prospects than it had thereafter, when subsequent administrations committed to enforcing the embargo.

At the basis, international law lays the concept of sovereignty. Sovereignty is defined as a county's self-determination and independence from external interference in internal affairs and complete authority over all nationals living in the country and beyond its borders (individuals and corporations). All countries in the world are sovereign, and yet all must curtail their sovereignty to coexist in the world of nations and defend their national interests. By permitting international trade and by entering into international agreements, countries limit their sovereignty. When countries perceive that international firms, governments, or organizations have infringed on their right to self-determination, they can invoke national sovereignty and take actions that erect barriers to trade or even jeopardize the presence of international companies within their borders.

Similarly, the stable environment where a business has operated unfettered for decades could suddenly be at the center of a civil war that nobody had foreseen. In the case of Rwanda, in the introductory vignette, many international businesses were forced to leave their inventory and buildings behind when the genocide began. In other examples, a protectionist measure of one government could launch a series of retaliations both by the government and by consumers: When the United States instituted measures against European protectionism by increasing duties on nonessential European exports (cheese, perfume, soap, accessories), it had not expected the retaliations of Europeans against icons of U. S. business, such as McDonald's and Coca-Cola. More recently, the United States have been faulted by Canada, European Union, Australia, Brazil, Argentina, Nicaragua, Uruguay, Guatemala and Thailand for exceeding the agricultural subsidies limit imposed under WTO rules, through direct payments, loan deficiency payments, and other programs for products such as wheat, soybeans, corn, and sugar. With appropriate political maneuvering at the Doha Summit in 2007, however, the United States averted retaliation.

2.4.1 Evaluating on Political Risks 关于政治风险的评估

A company has several resources at its disposal to evaluate country risk: the Department of state, the Department of Commerce, and other governmental and nongovernmental agencies provide data on country political risk that is current and continually updated to reflect new developments in each country around the world. Some examples of useful publications providing periodic information on country risk are:

(1) Business periodicals such as The Economist and The Wall Street Journal, particularly the European and Asian editions;

(2) Commercial sources, such as Country Report, the Economist Intelligence Unit, the World Business Intelligence. For example, they provide

information on political developments, currency, and the regulatory insurance data and trade information, as well as a country risk rating on a scale from 1 to 10, and risk perception and collection experience for the previous 4 months.

2.4.1.1 Political Risk Signals

政治风险的信号

A number of country risk elements should be monitored on a regular basis to keep track of developments that might ultimately affect the international company. These elements are illustrated in Table 2-1.

Table 2-1 Country Risk Score

Rank/Country	Risk Score (Max=100)	Political Risk (Max=25)	Economic Performance (Max=25)
1 Luxembourg	99.65	25.00	25.00
2 Norway	98.44	24.83	23.95
3 Switzerland	98.03	24.92	23.46
4 Untied States	96.72	24.38	22.34
8 Netherlands	92.80	25.34	18.62
11 United Kingdom	92.23	23.70	18.88
16 Japan	90.14	23.25	19.69
17 Germany	90.12	23.76	16.71
40 Saudi Arabia	68.53	16.12	11.13
41 Hungary	68.50	19.30	9.50
52 China	61.71	17.79	10.68
58 India	56.45	17.03	6.85
62 Russia	54.65	15.15	8.09
91 Pakistan	41.44	11.26	4.98
105 Venezuela	38.06	8.74	5.79
144 Belarus	31.49	6.51	4.57
174 Zimbabwe	21.61	1.71	0.32
175 Burundi	21.54	7.18	0.00
178 Congo	16.51	6.22	2.63
182 Cuba	10.58	3.28	6.32
183 Lrap	4.62	1.48	3.13
184 Afghanistan	4.50	3.56	0.94

Source: Adapted form *Country Risk*, Euromoney, March 2006, P1.

2.4.1.2 Economic Performance

经济运行

A poor economic performance and forecast are likely to lead to greater levels of unrest in the country. Of particular concern are high inflationary rates and high unemployment rates, both of which could lead to political instability.

General business performance is also important. Commercial payment terms and collection experience indicate the availability of hard currency reserves and access to hard currency. Default on loans is likely to be a threat to companies contemplating entrance into the market. Finally, an increase in regulatory restrictions on investment, capital, or trade flows should be closely monitored.

2.4.2 Nationalism

关于民族主义

The expression of fierce nationalist sentiment, or nationalism, in a country where the company is operating could constitute a cause for concern to the international company. The expression of nationalist feelings, such as pride in a country's history and accomplishments, is common in most counties.

Nationalist sentiment may signal attempts at separation from or isolation of a particular segment of society, which could lead to political instability in the country; this is the case of the Tamil separatist movement in Sri Lanka, which has led to economic chaos in the country. Particularly problematic for international business are expressions of antiforeigner sentiment and anti-foreign business bias. In the United States in the 1980s, the "buy American" slogans echoing especially in the automobile and textile industries presented great concern to European and Asian business and private investors. Of special concern to international marketing managers is consumer ethnocentrism, the belief that buying foreign goods will put local companies out of business and is, consequently, morally wrong. Countries where such beliefs predominate are more likely to erect barriers to international trade.

Thailand experienced a military coup in September 2006, resulting in new rules in foreign investment that frightened foreign investors. The military-appointed cabinet initiated more stringent laws of foreign ownership, requiring investors to sell holdings that exceed 50 percent ownership in companies based in Thailand and to give up voting rights in excess of 50 percent. U.S. firms are protected from this rule by a treaty with Thailand that dates back to the Vietnam War, but European and Japanese companies were seriously affected. The Foreign Business Act bans foreigners from owning majority shares in Thai businesses ranging from the media, rice farming, production of Buddha images, legal services, and construction.

2.4.3 Political Risks and Risk Management
政治风险及其管控

Nationalism and claims to national sovereignty can lead to protectionist measures on the part of the host country government, whereas political instability can lead to the failure of the economy. All can harm the operations of the company in the respective country, from hurting its sales and overall prospects in the market to completely losing company assets.

"Risks Related to Government Economic Policy", "Risks Related to Labor and Action Groups" and "Risks Related to Terrorism" are examples of risks a company can experience in international markets.

2.4.3.1 Risks Related to Government Trade Policies
与政府对外贸易政策有关的风险

The host country government can erect trade barriers, imposing tariffs and nontariff barriers on international business, such as exchange-rate controls, voluntary export restraints and other types of quotas, and export/import license requirements. The company could also find itself falling victim to a trade war, in which the host country and home country reciprocally restrict the flow of goods. Or the company's home country government can impose embargoes and sanctions on the host country, which could force the company to exit the market.

2.4.3.2 Risks Related to Government Economic Policy
与政府经济政策有关的风险

Local government can use taxes as a means to control foreign investment. During downturns in the local economy, governments find that taxing foreign companies provides a source of valuable revenue. Under more extreme conditions, especially if accompanied by a radical change in the political leadership, change can lead to the (mainly involuntary) transfer of the firm's assets to local (national) ownership. Companies face the following types of risks: confiscation, expropriation, nationalization and domestication.

(1) Confiscation

没收财产

Confiscation refers to the seizing of company assets and investors' assets without any compensation. In the 1940s and 1950s, most private companies operating in Centraland Eastern Europe had their assets confiscated. More recently, all U. S. firms operating in Iran were confiscated when Shah Reza Pahlavi was dethroned. As a result of the confiscation of U. S. multinationals' assets in Iran after the Islamic Revolution United States imposed an embargo on trade with Iran.

(2) Expropriation

强力征用

Expropriation involves some reimbursement for company assets, usually not at their market value. When Fidel Castro ascended to power in Cuba the assets of U. S. multinationals and U. S. citizens were seized. The Castro government offered payment that was deemed inappropriate, and as a result, the United States imposed an embargo on trade with Cuba that is currently still in effect.

(3) Nationalization

收归国有

Nationalization involves a takeover by the local government with the aim of creating a government run industry. International law regards nationalization as legitimate as Nationalization long as it is in the public interest and it offers fair compensation to the international company and to its investors. In 1997, the Korean government decided to nationalize the automobile Kia Motors by converting the state-run Korea Development Bank's debt into an equity stake in the company. In the aftermath of the Asian crisis, governments began nationalizing ailing banks across the region: In Indonesia, the government controls nearly all the country's biggest banks and has taken over around 75 percent of all bank assets; whereas in Japan, as a result of nationalization, the government, instead of markets, now plays a larger role in determining the flow of capital.

As mentioned earlier, Thailand now requires European and Japanese foreign investors to sell holdings such that they would ultimately own less than 50 percent of the company: the Foreign Business Act bans foreigners from owning majority shares in Thai businesses. In other examples, Venezuela' s former president Hugo Chavez nationalized companies in the telecommunications and electricity industries and attempted to gain more control over natural gas projects. His goal was to change Venezuela into a socialist state with strong state oversight.

(4) Domestication

本土化

Domestication occurs when the local government requires a gradual transfer of ownership and management to locals. This transfer is usually completed over time, through consecutive government decrees aimed at reducing the presence of multinationals in nonessential local sectors(such as the consumer goods sector).

Companies can protect themselves against political instability by understanding the structure of the governments, the political parties, and the ideologies of the ruling party, as well as the competing ideologies of the opposition. As a first step, companies must make every attempt to be exemplary corporate citizens in every country where they operate. A solid reputation for product quality and community involvement can create a general environment that is favorable toward a company's local operations.

A company also can minimize its risk by partnering with local companies, creating local expertise in product manufacturing and management, and using local suppliers. McDonald's, for example, frequently stresses the use of local ingredients in all its offerings. Similarly, companies that produce products deemed essential for local development, such as industrial products, high-technology products, or pharmaceutical products, are less vulnerable to changes in government policies than companies that manufacture goods that are considered nonessential, such as consumer goods.

Companies can obtain insurance coverage against nationalization from private insurance sources. For example, companies such as global risk advisors insure against confiscation, expropriation, and nationalization, in addition to providing insurance against war risk, localized or sub-national conflicts kidnapping, ransom, extortion, property terrorism and currency inconvertibility.

2.4.3.3 Risks Related to Labor and Action Groups
与劳工组织与行动团体相关的风险

In many countries, labor unions are very powerful and can readily influence national policies. For example, layoffs by foreign companies can bring about negative feelings that are likely to affect these companies in the long term. Boycotts initiated by action groups can also negatively affect the companies. Esso (Exxon) was the victim of a "Boycott Esso" campaign aimed at the United State's environmental policies. These actions are not usually sanctioned by the national government, but they are, nevertheless, legal.

Companies have some control over the actions of labor and action groups. Although they cannot control market demand and derived demand for labor, companies can provide severance packages that are fair, as well as invest in the services of job placement businesses in an effort to seek placement for the employees who have been terminated. To avoid negative public sentiment, companies must be politically neutral and keep a distance from local politics. Too close an association with a regime could elicit a negative attitude toward the company and its products. It is important for a firm to be perceived as a good citizen of the country where it operates because a company that has created opportunities for locals and that continues to see their interests.

2.4.3.4 Risks Related to Terrorism
恐怖主义导致的风险

International terrorist attacks against multinational interests gained worldwide attention with the September 11, 2001, attack on the World Trade Center in New York City. In the years preceding this attack, terrorist attacks steadily increased in frequency. Organizations or businesses with a U.S. connection alone were hit 206 times in 2000, up from 169 in 1999; internationally, private-sector facilities were attacked 384 times, up from 276 in 1999, whereas only 17 government facilities and 13 military facilities were similarly hit around the globe. Terrorism was most lethal in Asia in the year 2000, with 281 of the 405 international victims perishing there. Africa had the second highest total, with 73 dead. In 2003, the number of people killed by terrorism was 625 (with 725 killed the preceding year); and 208 terror incidents took place, resulting in the injury of 3,646 people.

Companies have some control, however, in reducing their likelihood of becoming victims of terrorism by training employees in terrorism avoidance, such as briefing personnel on what to expect when entering high-risk areas and offering training for eluding roadblocks and avoiding hazardous encounters. Companies can also purchase insurance against terrorist acts from private insurance companies. For example, Cigna International's International Specialty Products & Services offers insurance products that cover kidnapping, detention (kidnapping without asking for ransom), hijacking, evacuation, business interruption and extra expenses, product recall expenses, and expenses arising from child abduction (such as hiring private investigators or posting rewards for information).

2.5 The International Legal Environment
国际法律环境

本部分将介绍对国际市场营销产生影响的法律环境，并分别讲述世界上不同的主要法律体系，司法管辖权，知识产权保护法，反垄断法和反行贿法。

International marketing is affected by three types of laws:

(1) International laws

国际法

It refers to a body of rules and regulations that countries agree to abide by. International law addresses agreements among countries with regard to trade, protection of property, and other issues in the political and economic sphere. International law agreements, although not enforceable, can be appropriately addressed by international law bodies.

(2) Host-country laws

东道国的法律

These are the laws of the different countries where the company operates. The legal system in the host country could differ substantially from that of the company's home-country.

(3) Home-country laws

母国法律

The laws of the company's home-country. Home-country laws follow the company all over the world. U.S. companies must abide by all three types of law. For example, they must abide by international trade laws and agreements, such as WTO trade regulations; they must abide by host-country laws governing every aspect of the company's operations; and they must abide by home-country laws, such as antitrust regulations and corrupt practices regulations.

2.5.1 Legal Systems 法律体系

Three legal systems are predominant: Common law, Code law, and Islamic law.

(1) Common law

普通法

Common law is based on prior court rulings (legal precedent). It has its roots in English Common Law, on which U.S. law is based. This system of law is shared by many of the countries formerly colonized by Great Britain.

(2) Code law-or civil law

法典法或者公民法

It refers to comprehensive written laws that specify what constitutes legal behavior. Code law has its roots in Roman law. This system of law is shared by most of the countries in the world, including most of Europe, Latin America, China, China Taiwan, Japan, and South Korea.

(3) Islamic law

伊斯兰法

The Islamic law(sharia) is a system of law based on the interpretation of the Koran, Islam's holy book, and on interpretations of the practices and sayings of the prophet Muhammad. Islamic law establishes rules for business practices that can affect firms' operations. For example, it requires the sexes to be separate; in practice, this means that women cannot interact in any environment with men with whom they are not related. It bans the consumption of products such as pork and alcohol, it does not allow banks to offer or charge interest, and it requires Muslims to pray five times a day and to fast in the month of Ramadan.

All these factors have an impact on firms' local operations wherever Islamic law constitutes the basis of the legal system—in North Africa and the Middle East and in Pakistan and Malaysia, among others. For example, business activities must be organized daily around prayer time. During Ramadan, business performance is generally low; in fact, many international businesses rely on the foreign, non-Muslim, workforce to carry out their firms' operations during this month.

2.5.2 Jurisdiction
司法管辖权

With different legal systems worldwide, and with international laws, home-country laws, and host-country laws that govern all aspects of doing business internationally, it is important to establish jurisdiction in international legal disputes. No automatic supranational jurisdiction is assigned to an international court, unless the dispute takes place between companies and/or countries in the European Union; in this case, jurisdiction lies with the European Court of Justice. Legal disputes that arise between governments are usually handled by the International Court of Justice in the Hague, within the United Nations system.

International commercial law is usually handled in the home or host-country of the company, or even in a third country, depending on where there is the place for the jurisdiction for the matter under litigation. Because jurisdiction is often difficult to determine, it is advisable that each contract specifies the venue for handling the dispute and the procedure—a venue that is agreeable to all the parties involved. The contract should also specify whether the dispute settlement process will involve procedures other than litigation, which is often too costly and leads to negative perceptions in the international business community of the companies involved. Such procedures may be as follows:

(1) Mediation
调解

It is a nonbinding procedure that involves an independent third party. The disadvantage of mediation is that any decision of the mediator is nonbinding. The perspective of a neutral third party, however, could provide better insights into how the issue is perceived by the larger business community; moreover, not accepting the terms of mediation could signal to firms outside the conflict that the firm seen as being at fault might not be a reliable future partner.

(2) Arbitration

仲裁

It is a procedure that involves an independent third party; the outcome of arbitration is a binding decision. Agreeing to arbitration does not necessarily mean that the companies found to be at fault will adhere to the decisions; if they do not, however, their reputation in the international business community is likely to suffer. Arbitration is often preferred to litigation. It is a much faster procedure that is likely to cost the company much less than a lawsuit.

2.5.3 Intellectual Property Rights protection
知识产权保护

Violation of intellectual property rights is the most significant threat to the competitiveness of companies involved in international business. Intellectual property is the result of ideas and creativity transformed into products, services, and experiences that are protected for a specified period of time from unauthorized commercialization. Companies from developed countries manufacturing brand name products are the primary victims of intellectual property rights infringement and are leading the fight against violations. Losses attributed to the violation of intellectual property rights are estimated to be $ 60 billion a year, and its primary victims are the most innovative, fastest-growing industries such as software (with estimated annual losses at $ 11.4 billion), pharmaceuticals (with estimated losses at $ billion), and entertainment(with estimated annual losses at $ 8 to $ 10 billion and expected to rise due to Internet piracy).

2.5.3.1 Different Forms of Intellectual Property Protection
知识产权保护的不同形式

Protection of the rights of the inventor or of the firm employing the inventor to use and sell the invention for a specified period of time—this type of intellectual property is known as a patent. In many countries around the world, multinationals are racing to local patent offices to apply for patents to protect and enforce their technology. In Korea, for example, local memory chip and electronics firms are embroiled in patent disputes, fending off lawsuits initiated by multinational firms such as IBM and NEC, and the stakes are high: losers will not only suffer financial setbacks in the form of paying royalties, but will also suffer the stigma of being labeled copycats. This situation will ultimately be rectified by the WTO, which will institute uniformed patent rules thatall members are expected to follow.

Protection of the rights to an original work of art (literature, music, film, design, and other works) allowing the owner the right to reproduce, sell, perform, or film the work—this is known as copyright. National and international associationsare actively fighting copyright infringement. In the United States, such an organization is the International Intellectual Property Alliance, or IIPA. The IIPA was formed in conjunction with the Association of American Publishers. The Business Software Alliance, the Interactive Digital Software association the motion Picture Association of America, the national music publishers association, and the Recording Industry Association of America. In recent years, the IIPA filed petitions with the office of the U.S. Trade Representative to investigate copyright infringement in the CD and CD-ROM markets in Brazil, Costa Rica, Guatemala, Russia, and Uruguay.

Protection of a brand name, mark, symbol, motto, or slogan that identifies a particular manufacturer's brand and distinguishes it from the competitors' brands in the same product category—this is known as trademark. Trademark infringement occurs at many levels, from directly copying the product, as in the case of counterfeit Rolex watches and Gucci and Fendi purse selling for \$ 30 in the streets of New York City, China Hong Kong, and Paris and in many bazaars in developing countries. Brand name counterfeiting involves using the brand name, but not necessarily the product design, as in the case of Oleg Cassini and Christian Dior plain Egyptian cotton t-shirts selling in the streets of Cairo.

Protection of know-how, formulas, and special blends that are not registered, and thus not protected by law—these are shared with licensees, franchisers, or other Partners and are known as trade secrets.

2.5.3.2 Factors Influencing Intellectual Property Rights Violations 知识产权侵犯的影响因素

The degree of intellectual property rights violation is influenced by a number of market factors, such as;

(1) Lack of appropriate legislation, e.g. for software;

(2) Lax enforcement, especially for local firms;

(3) Unavailability of the authentic products, or when available, their high price provides justification for both the violators and the respective governments to allow the practice.

Such violations are also influenced by cultural factors, such as:

(1) Values that perceive imitation as a high form of flattery;

(2) A culture characterized by interpersonal distrust and feelings of not getting a fair deal;

(3) A culture characterized by an emphasis on acquisition of material wealth at the expense of caring for others; in such a culture, the focus of acquisition

is status brands consumed and or displayed publicly, rather than privately;

(4) Beliefs that technology is in the common domain and that use of others intellectual property is appropriated.

Involvement in regional trade agreements and other trade organizations is also sought to diminish the likelihood that a country would tolerate violation of intellectual property rights. In fact, intellectual property rights used to be largely a domestic issue, with individual countries deciding on their own levels of legal protection and enforcement. Today, countries that join the WTO must also sign on to the Trade Related Aspects of Intellectual Property Rights (or TRIPS) agreement, an international agreement that sets out minimum standards for the legal protection of intellectual property.

Multinationals seeking protection under TRIPS around the world still depend each country's patent office to grant those rights and their judicial, customs, and police services to enforce them (in Europe, region-wide patents can be obtained). The TRIPS offers rules describing the protection these systems must provide, include extending intellectual property rights to include computer programs, integrated circuits, plant varieties, and pharmaceuticals, which were unprotected in most developing countries until this agreement. According to TRIPS, patents can be granted for any new technological process or product, and the protection lasts 20 years from the data of application.

In addition to TRIPS and working in conjunction with the WTO, international conventions have been gaining strength. Among these conventions are the Berne Convention for copyrighted works, under the auspices of the world intellectual Property Organization; the Paris convention for the protection of industrial property and the Madrid Arrangement, which established the Bureau for the International Registration of Trademarks.

Helping these organizations and conventions are, in particular, national governments of developed countries, which are protecting their multinationals. In the United States, the Patent and Trademark Office has an annual budget of one billion USD; a staff of more than 3, 000 highly trained scientists, Engineers, and legal experts; more than 600 Judges to preside over patent disputes, and a vast customs service to clamp down on counterfeiting. To protect intellectual property rights in the Internet Age the U. S. Government passed the Digital Millennium Copyright Act.

Developing countries frequently argue that intellectual property protection is yet another arm used to hold them at an economic disadvantage. From their point of view, patents and copyrights impose great cost on consumers in developing countries in recent examples, aids activists and the government in South Africa argued that patents were killing the country's millions of HIV-infected patients who could not afford the drugs, Mexican peasants were enraged that a U.S. company received the exclusive right to market beans in the United States because they have been growing the beans for generations, and the protection restricts their ability to export the beans north of the order. Activists argue that intellectual property protection allows western multinationals to set up monopolies; to drive out local competing brands; to divert research and development away from the needs of developing countries; and to drive up prices while preventing poor people from getting life-saving drugs, interfering with age-old farming practices, and allowing foreign pirates to raid local resources, such as medicinal plants, without getting permission or paying compensation.

Finally, there are examples where companies, even though engaged in trademark litigation continue to cooperate, if it serves their interests. For example, Anheuser-Busch companies and the Czech brewer Budejovicky-Budvar are in litigation over the Budweiser name. The Czech brewer has a long history in Europe, predating Anheuser-Busch' Budweiser. However, even as the two companies continue their international legal fight over the Budweiser trademark, they agreed for Anheuser-Busch to distribute Budweiser's Czechvar Premium Czech Lager, currently sold in 30 states in the United States. Through Anheuser Busch, Budvar thus has access to 600 independent wholesalers.

2.5.4 Home-Country Legislation Affecting Multinational Firms Operating Overseas 母国法律对跨国企业在海外市场运作的影响

2.5.4.1 Antitrust Laws

反垄断法

Antitrust laws of home and host countries are designed to prevent domestic anti-competitive activities, such as the creation of monopolies and cartels. The United States was among the first to impose its antitrust laws on firms in the United States and on U.S. firms operating abroad. Increasingly, governments of other countries are enacting and enforcing antitrust legislation that affects multinationals worldwide. In fast antitrust enforcement in the United States often appears to be more lenient than in other developed countries, for example, the European commission vetoed mergers between competitors after the United States gave these mergers a green light, as in the case of General Electric failed takeover attempt of Honeywell and the MCI WorldCom and Sprint proposed merger.

The United States allows certain types of collusion in the case of small and medium sized firms that might not have the resources to embark on a successfulexport program. The U.S. Congress passed the Export Trading Company Act in the 1980s to encourage firms to join forces in exporting by exempting them from antitrust laws.

2.5.4.2 Corruption Laws

反行贿法

Corruption laws of home and host-countries are designed to prevent multinational corporations from using unethical means to obtain competitive advantage in a particular market. The World Bank surveyed 3, 600 companies in 69 countries and found 40 percent paid bribes, and in the former Soviet Union, it increased to 60 percent. Similarly, the European Bank for Reconstruction and Development (EBRD), which encourages investments in the former Eastern Bloc, has called Eastern Europe's bribe-seeking a deterrent to 46 foreign investment.

The U.S. Foreign Corrupt Practices Act (FCPA) makes it illegal for companies and their representatives to bribe government officials and other politicians or candidates to political office. The Act also prohibits payment to third parties when the company has good reason to assume that part of that payment is being used for bribery purposes. U.S. multinational companies take such laws very seriously, and some even address their commitment to reject bribery and other corruption in their mission statement (Caterpillar does so, for example)—even though forbidding these practices places U.S. firms at a disadvantage. In a number of high-profile cases, investigators found that illegal payments were made by firms operating in Canada, Colombia Cook Islands, the Dominican Republic, Egypt, Germany, Iraq, Israel, Jamaica, Mexico, Niger, Nigeria, and Trinidad and Tobago; these payments ranged from $ 22, 000 to $ 9.9 million and represented percentages of up to 20 percent of the business obtained. Seventeen companies have been charged under the FCPA, with fines ranging from $ 10.000 to $ 21.8 million.

The United States is not alone in the fight against bribery. The Organization for Economic Co-operation and Development (OECD), which consists of 30 primarily developed member countries adopted a Convention on Combating Bribery of Foreign Public Officials in International Business Transaction. Other signatories include nonmember countries Argentina, Brazil, Bulgaria, and Chile. The purpose of the convention is to fight corruption in international business and to help level he competitive field for companies.

2.6 The Natural Environment of International Marketing 国际市场营销的自然环境

本部分将介绍对国际市场营销产生影响的自然环境。一个国家的地理位置决定了跨国公司进入这个国家的最佳路径，地理因素会决定其在整个国际市场的位置，气候和自然资源情况会直接影响如何安排生产。

The natural environment of international marketing addresses the relationship between natural resources worldwide and marketing. A country's geographic location determines how its key markets can be optimally accessed. Its climate determines its production and even its productivity capability. Geography facilitates or impedes relationships with other international markets.

National boundaries determine access to the local market and the movement of goods, access to natural resources, and, overall, the potential for economic development.

2.6.1 Geology and Natural Resources 地理环境和自然资源

A country's access to natural resources determines whether the country can be a viable trade partner in the international market. Its geology determines the natural resources available in the country and its potential for prosperity. For example, oilin North Africa and the Middle East has brought prosperity to countries where the climate is a challenge and whose terrain contains a large desert expanse. Countries in Sub-Saharan Africa that have survived at subsistence level for centuries have found new prosperity from mining gold and diamonds. Botswana and the Central African Republic have attractive markets that are actively courted by multinationals.

A shortage of raw materials is slowly reverberating in most world markets, including the markets of industrialized countries. Prices of oil are steadily increasing, whereas access to oil sources is becoming more and more limited due to geologic and political factors. This shortage is translating to higher prices charged to consumers, which, in the long term, will lead to changes in consumption patterns. In the case of oil, it may mean that Northern Europeans will no longer count on their Southern European and North African vacations, which will, in turn, hurt tourism in Southern Europe and North Africa. Consumers in the United States may have to trade in their gas-guzzling monster trucks and sports utility vehicles for fuel-efficient smaller and hybrid vehicles.

2.6.2 Topography and Access to Markets 地形地貌与进入路径

Topography is important because it determines access to the market and affects distribution decisions. For example, Holland has a flat terrain, allowing for efficient transportation. Holland has also altered its topography to increase access by creating an effective network of man-made canals that cross the country in every direction allowing for easier access to markets.

On the other hand, a mountainous terrain restricts access to markets. The Andes, for example, allow minimal access to local consumers, which can be accomplished only at great company expense. These restrictions are especially difficult to surmount in low-income countries; high and middle-income countries have devised sophisticated access to some of the more remote areas, such as the canyons in Utah, the peaks of the Alps, or across the Brahmaputra mountains.

Tibet was initially reached only by air or by road fromthe rest of mainland China. There is now a railway that facilitates access. Nevertheless, the Brahmaputra mountain chain presents a challenge to the movement of goods and access to the market.

2.6.3 Hydrology and Economic Development 水文条件与经济发展

Hydrology determines access to local markets as well. Ocean access allows for the affordable shipping of goods to the local target market, Rivers and lakes offer access as well as potential for the development of agriculture and manufacturing. Hydroelectric power is essential for local development. In general, economic development is related to hydrology.

2.6.4 Climate 气候

Climate is also an essential determinant of economic development. Arid lands, such as the desert lands of the Sahara and the southwestern United States, are inhabitable only at a very high cost. In other areas, excessive rain and hurricane activity often lead to flooding and the destruction of the local infrastructure. On the other hand, a mild climate year round brings tourists to the Amalfi Coast of Italy, the islands of Hawaii, the beaches of the Caribbean, the shores of Tunisia, and the Sinai.

2.6.5 Population and Human Capital 人口与人力资源

As mentioned earlier, one relevant aspect of the natural environment is the scarcity of natural resources, especially raw materials, in light of today's high population growth. High population growth in spite of limited natural resources has led to famine and precipitated conflict in Ethiopia, Somalia, Rwanda, and Burundi in sub Saharan Africa. In these markets, the overall infrastructure is inadequate and cannot meet the basic needs of the population. The concentration of population in large cities of millions of inhabitants, such as Mexico city and Cairo, has taxed the infrastructure and impeded the optimal functioning of business. Most importantly, today, the world's population exceeds 6 billion and is growing rapidly, especiallyin developing countries.

The World Group 2004 reported the data which illustrates the high annual population growth in low and middle-income countries, compared with that of high-income countries. The population growth rate is highest for the developing countries of South Asia and sub-Saharan Africa.

Population growth determines the types of markets that multinational companies, as well as small and medium enterprises, can target. In the high-income countries, marketers have a more mature market to contend with-markets with a substantial population aged 65 and older. Population growth also has implications with regard to access to goods and services and to the environment.

The implications of population migration for international business are also considerable. Immigration from developing countries to developed countries has often resulted in strong anti-immigrant sentiment and instability of different degrees in counties known for their tolerance and openness to immigration, such as Belgium, Denmark, the Netherlands, France, and Sweden. Immigrants account for about 12 percent of Sweden's population of 9 million and, of those, 450,000 are Muslim. Immigrants in Sweden, as in much of Western Europe, who often live in run-down immigrant neighborhoods, are less likely to learn Swedish, and are more likely to go to all-immigrant schools and remain unemployed and poor. Countries that have, historically, encouraged immigration are now struggling to absorb their large immigrant populations. Most Western European countries have now passed laws restricting immigration.

The new immigrants are not fully aware of their rights or of their obligations to their adoptive country, as such, they end up in an ambiguous situation. The issues that Sweden is grappling with are not unusual. The European mass media regularly address issues related to anti-immigrant sentiment that can, potentially, lead to destabilization. France's 2006 student riots ultimately resulted in anti-immigrant rhetoric from government officials. The mayor of Berlin, on the occasion of the 2006 World Cup, increased security to a high alert and advised all foreign visitors to stay away from neighborhoods in eastern Berlin, to avoid attacks by radical nationalists.

One aspect of migration that has important economic consequences for the country affected is "brain drain", the migration of trained professionals. Historically, this migration has been mostly from developing to developed countries, This migration has created shortages of qualified medical personnel in many countries in Eastern Europe, for example. More recently, open borders in the European Union have created a brain drain phenomenon for countries with high taxation and unemployment. For example, the brain drain from Germany, a country with a rapidly shrinking population, has become an issue of concern to business executives and government leaders. More professionals are leaving today than in the past years. A popular show on German television is Goodbye Deutschland. The show portrays emigrants to South Africa and Spain. About 150,000 emigrate yearly, and only about 50,000 return. The emigrants who leave are doctors, lawyers, and scientists. France has many emigrants leaving for Britain. Adding to the burden of brain drain is the fact that Germany and France are less attractive to people pursuing jobs in medicine, academic research, and engineering. The reasons emigrants give for leaving are high taxes, chronic unemployment, a rigid labor market, a stifling bureaucracy, and the hierarchical structure of some professional environments such as academia and medicine. As a new employee, you have little time to pursue research and are under the thumb of your director.

2.6.6 Environmental Quality 环境质量

Concerns about the effects of the overall population growth and industry on the natural environment have led to the active regulation of business, especially inindustrialized countries. For example, the European Union actively regulates the use of hormones in raising beef and the use of pesticides in agriculture. It continues to raise taxes on gasoline to reduce consumption and encourage the use of public transportation. It charges localities huge sums for refuse and actively encourages recycling at the individual and community level.

Worldwide, there is a concerted effort to reduce air and water pollution, to control the amount and disposal of nuclear waste, to reduce deforestation and land erosion, and to limit fishing and hunting activity to preserve a viable natural habitat. The effort to preserve environmental quality limits infrastructure development in protected areas and charges businesses to take responsibility of consumption by encouraging bottle reuse and recycling, by limiting packaging to its more basic forms, and by producing products that can be consumed with minimal harm to the environment. Outside the United States, for example, Coca-Cola soft drinks and Heineken beer are sold in reusable glass bottles or in recyclable plastic bottles. Ford Motor Company competes in the international market by offering smaller automobiles with low gas consumption. And new, successful industries are emerging aimed at creating alternative energy sources and reducing the cost of electricity consumption. Windmills today populate not just the European landscape; they are increasingly present on the East Coast of the United States.

Vehicular emissions are rising in nearly every European country and across the globe. Greenhouse gases are increasing even in countries where industry pollution is decreasing, due to increased car and truck use, according to the European Environment Agency. And this is happening in spite of the invention of environmentally friendly automobiles: hybrid cars and ethanol buses do not compensate for the effect of the large number of vehicles on the road. High taxes on cars and gasoline, such as those imposed in Denmark-where a Czech-made Skoda automobile costs $ 34.000, compared with $ 18,000 in Italy or Sweden-scare voters away, making even environmentalist politicians reluctant to propose them.

Yet, in spite of these challenges, the European Union remains the world's leader in the fight against climate change. The Kyoto Protocol requires industrial nations to reduce the emission of global warming gasses by an average of 5 percent below 1990 levels by 2012. The EU, on the other hand, committed to reduce greenhouse gas emission by 20 percent from 1990 levels by the year 2020. However, the EU also allows some of Europe's most polluting countries to limit their environmental goals: the former Eastern Bloc countries in the European Union, which rely heavily on cheap coal and oil for their energy needs, are reluctant to move to the more costly environmentally friendly alternative. Consequently, the EU agreed to allow each of the 27 states to set their own targets to meet the renewable energy goals. Effectively, this means that these countries have less stringent targets compared with the other countries in the EU.

Increasingly, environmental pollution is also attributed to developing countries. For example, in many developing countries, cheap diesel generators from China are a preferred mode for providing electricity. They power home appliances, irrigation systems, allowing many in rural villages to grow crops and to connect to the world through television. Demand for energy is increasing in these rural areas, and smoke-spewing diesel generators are bumming all day long, creating pollution in areas that used to have none. In remote and roadless areas in India, Bangladesh, Nepal, as many as half of the households have television sets and pay 40 cents every few days to the owner of the generator supplying the electricity for their bamboo hut. Diesel is cheap, owing to lavish government subsidies, making it difficult to introduce alternative renewable energy technologies. Efforts on the part of local government and international development organizations such as the United Nations Development program to introduce expensive renewable energy have been successful for urban areas; however, the investment is not warranted in remote villages. China is offering a successful alternative: cheap roof-top water heaters that channel water through thin pipes crisscrossing a shiny surface. More than 5, 000 small Chinese companies sell these water heaters to more than 30 million households. Today, China accounts for 60 percent of the market for solar water heaters. One such water heater costs $ 330, and it pays for itself in 2 years.

A study estimates that by 2012, 1.6 million motorcycle owners in developing countries are going to switch to small, inexpensive cars. It is forecasted that demand for vehicles costing less than $ 13, 600 will grow to 18 million vehicles a year by 2012, compared with 14 million today. Renault's Logan, manufactured in Romania, is a hit at less than $ 10, 000: the car is sold in 55 countries, including India, Argentina, and Brazil. Since the Logan was launched in 2004, more than 450, 000 vehicles have been sold. These developments carry with them bleak prospects for the environment, and governments of large emerging markets are attempting to stem the tide. In China, for example, the government imposes a graduated tax on vehicles based on their size: 9 percent for a 2.5-liter engine, compared with 3 percent for engines less than 1.5 liters.

2.7 The Technical Environment
科技环境

全球的科技环境变化非常迅速，新产品的开发日新月异。科技革命，尤其是互联网技术的应用已经彻底改变了跨国公司所处的环境和所实施的国际市场营销的面貌。

The technological environment is changing rapidly new product development is proceeding at breakneck pace, with thousands of patents and trademarks registered worldwide on a daily basis. The technology revolution since the 1980s has radical changed the face of international marketing. Hub-and-spoke networks, warehouse management systems, and electronic data interchange (EDI) systems, which allow intermediaries worldwide to share standardized inventory information, all lower firm's inventory carrying costs, facilitating the flow of products and making it easier to achieve the goal of making the distribution channel more flexible and responsive to customer needs.

The number of Internet users has more than doubled since the year 2000, and now, in 2006, the Internet is available to more than I billion people worldwide; future growth is expected especially from countries with large populations. With only a small proportion of the world population having access to the Internet, there is plenty of room for expansion, and much of this growth will occur, using wire-less applications to access the Internet. Email is still by far the major end-use.

The Internet allows for instant access to new international markets and creates potential for exchange that have never been previously imagined. Multinational corporations, as well as small and medium enterprises, benefit from the long reach of the Internet. The average amount of time each person spends on the Internet is 10 hours a month, visiting an average of 49 different sites, going online an average of 19 times per month. The United States and the Netherlands have the highest penetration of active home users up to 39 percent, compared with the total population. Canada and Australia are next with 34 percent, followed by Great Britain at 30 percent. Table 2 - 2 presents information on Internet usage relative to regional population statistics.

Table 2 - 2 Internet Usage and Population Statistics

World Regions	Population (2006Est.)(%)	Population of World(%)	Internet Usage Latest Data	Population(%)
Middle East and Africa	1 105 295 089	17	52 148 100	13.8
Asia	3 667 774 066	56.4	387 593 457	10.6
Europe	807 289 020	12.4	312 722 892	38.7
North America	331 473 276	5.1	232 057 067	70
Latin America/Caribbean	553 908 632	8.5	88 778 986	16
Oceanial/Australia	33 956 977	0.5	18 430 359	54.3
WORLD TOTAL	6 499 697 060	100	1 091 730 861	16.8

Source: www.internetworldstats.com/stats.htm: Internet Usage & Population Statistics, December 30, 2006

The internet has profoundly changed the lives of individuals, and it has changed the way international business is conducted, too.

Consider these examples:

There are more than 4 million Web sites, with 235,000 new ones being added each month;

There are 200 million email boxes in the United States;

People send more than 7 trillion E-mails each year in the United States;

The average e-mail user receives 31 E-mails per day;

The business-to-business e-commerce in the United States totals $ 1.3 trillion per year; Business will place orders totaling $ 3 trillion per year worldwide via the Internet;

Twenty-five percent of all business-to-business purchases are placed through some type of Internet connection;

Internet retail sales account for almost 2.5 percent of all retail sales.

Numerous companies in the United States have been successful selling to international clients through the Internet. Nevertheless, there are some pitfalls. For example, the company may need to make use of freight forwarders, who handle transportation insurance, and export documentation but also substantially increase the cost to the buyer. Companies must also determine the appropriate payment mechanisms. Countries differ not only with regard to the currency they use for transactions, but also in their methods of payments. For example, Europeans tend to use the Eurocard, which is a debit and, for payments. Also, worldwide, there is a high rate of credit card theft, which increases the risks that sellers might face in the international market. Using the Internet to send Mother's Day flowers from the United States to one's mother-in-law in Holland will become possible. Nevertheless, the online transactions never before thought possible are commonplace due to the advances in the past two decades.

The Chapter's Referential Questions:
本章参考性问题

1. Describing about the Political Risks in international market.
   谈谈国际市场营销中可能遇到的政治风险。
2. List the uncontrollable factors in the global environment that influence an international marketer.
   列举全球市场中国际营销人员可能遭遇的不可控因素。
3. List out the events or trends that have shaped international business beyond today and into the future.
   列举一些会影响现今以及未来国际商务的事件和趋势。

4. Compare conciliation with arbitration in legal environment.
   就法律环境中的协商解决和仲裁解决进行比较。
5. Briefly describe the characteristics of American market and EU market.
   简述美国市场和欧盟市场各自的特点。
6. Briefly describe how Internet has changed the business environment and outlook of multinational companies doing business.
   谈谈互联网技术怎样改变了跨国公司所处的环境和所实施的国际市场营销的面貌。
7. How to evaluate the Political Risks in international environment?
   在国际环境中怎样就政治风险进行评估?
8. How could the natural environment in one country put impacts on international marketing?
   谈谈一个国家的自然环境会如何影响企业的国际市场营销。

微信扫码查看

Chapter 3 Managing the Cultural Differences in International Marketing

国际市场营销中的文化差异管理

Learning Objectives

本章学习目标

1. Identify the elements of culture and examine how they affect marketing practices
   识别文化因素,并且清楚其如何在世界范围内影响营销活动
2. Describe the global consumer culture as it manifests itself around the world
   从全球范围来描述全球化的顾客文化
3. Understand the countermeasure in cross-cultural management
   了解跨文化管理的对策

3.1 The Role of Cultural Forces
文化的力量和作用

针对文化差异对跨国公司实施其国际市场营销战略的困惑，本章将以可口可乐、麦当劳为例，讲述文化的特征、力量及其所产生的影响，以及跨国公司管理文化差异的方法。

A Latin proverb says："Custom rules the law."

The most important factor in determining whether your marketing strategy is a right and proper one or not，is to have a through understanding of the culture in the specific market. Cultures can be painted with very broad strokes or minutely dissected. The more layers that are peeled away， the greater the market segmentation available. It is truly a case in which knowledge is power—marketing power. Because this book deals with multinational business，"culture" will be viewed as the total pattern of human behavior in multinational business situations.

In this Chapter we first discuss the nature of cultural differences and their diverse impact on multinational business. A six dimensional perspective then is developed for becoming sensitive to and thinking about cultural differences. This perspective provides a framework for discussing ways to understand，adapt to and more effectively manage cultural differences that affect the implementation of international marketing plan. Ideally，this process produces synergies by creatively building on the strengths of each of the cultures involved in a situation.

3.1.1 The case of McDonald's
麦当劳的案例

McDonald's golden Arches finally have arrived in India. But if you eat a Big Mac，it may taste not as good as you wished. In coming to this Hindu nation，where cows are sacredand most people don't eat beef. McDonald's changed accordingly the Big Mac for an Indian stand-in. The Maharaja Mac of local style contains two all-mutton patties，special sauce，lettuce，cheese，pickle and onions. All are on a sesame-seed bun.

Although McDonald's restaurants adapt menus to local tastes，serving pork burgers in Thailand,for example. The outlet that opened in New Delhi yesterday is the first to shun beef outright. The purveyor of billions and billions of burgers(all-beef) world-wide hope to serve India's vegetarians with such offerings as Vegetable McNuggets and Vegetable McBurgers.

McDonald's used a common framework, the golden arches and their name, adapted to local tastes and customs. An approach has been called a "GLOCAL" approach. Using such a global-local balanced approach has enabled McDonald's and other firms to blend more easily into a culture and avoid the backlash which can follow from imposing a totally "American" approach, an approach which can assault a local culture and create resentment.

In October 1996, McDonald's announced a further step in its rapid global expansion to offset growth problems in a maturing U.S. market. It was opening its first restaurant in Lima, Peru the 96th country in which the fast-food giant did business and 24th country in the Latin America-Caribbean region. McDonald's said that it expected to be in 100 countries by the end of 1997. By now, the company operated nearly 650 outlets in Latin America and the Caribbean. Worldwide McDonald's did, has nearly 20,000 fast-food restaurants.

Using common framework, as McDonald's did, is to bridge cultural gaps and reconcile cultural diversity when formulating enterprise-wide, business unit and marketing and production/operations strategies and plans, and when doing businesses in different foreign countries.

3.1.2 Definition of the Culture 文化的定义

Dutch writer, Geert Hofstede referred as: "Culture is Software of the Mind-the social programming that runs the way we think, act and perceive ourselves and others." Culture is not innate, but externally cultivated. A society's culture is far from stagnant; rather, it is forever evolving and reinventing itself.

3.2 Resolving the Multinational Paradoxes with Common Frameworks 解决跨国困惑的通用方法

文化的元素包括，人们所共同享有的价值观、信仰、态度、期盼和行为准则。也有这样的解释："文化是一个社会及其个体所拥有的知识、信仰、艺术、道德观、习俗以及其他任何能力和习惯的总称。"

Paradoxes seemed to be contradictions. For example, there is a seeming contradiction in the McDonald's situation when what many perceive as a "beef" fast food chain tries to enter India where cultural attitudes toward beef are unfavorable. The contradiction, however, is only in the perception. By preconceiving the situation, for example, by perceiving McDonald's as a clean, reliable deliverer of fast food services to the masses, represented by its Golden Arches—the contradiction disappears. Indians are interested in common worldwide ideas such as clean, reliable, fast food service they can count on, like people everywhere in the world. There is no reason that McDonald's has to be limited to "beef" products.

Coca-Cola ran into similar problems, as countries had different soft drink taste preferences. For example, traditional Asian drinks often outsell Coke there, so Coke introduced 30 new drinks based on local tastes in Japan alone—to sell through its vending machines and distribution systems.

The solution here was to focus on global aspects of one's products and services and then adapt to local differences within that common global framework. McDonald's and Coca-Cola's experiences illustrates this approach by rethinking (that is, re-conceiving) the idea or concept what a company is and is not.

There are often no universal solutions, just situational ones. For example, Dell Computer's performance in Europeby 1993 was dismal; it used retail sales channels—the commonly accepted way of selling in Europe. In an effort to increase sales, it defied the accepted guidelines that say success formulas often do not transfer across cultural borders and began selling direct in France and Germany, the selling method the firm used in the U.S.. The result is that Dell's sales there rose five times faster than European PC sales as a whole in 1996 and it doubled its market share.

Culture refers to shared values, beliefs, attitudes, expectations, and norms found within countries, regions, social groups, industries, corporations and even departments and work groups within a business firm. AS someone said that the culture is "that complex whole which includes knowledge, belief, art, morals, customs, and any other capabilities and habits acquired by man as a member of society". Culture is a distinctive way of life of a group of people—its complete design for living; it is "the behavioral norms that a group of people, at a certain time and place, have agreed upon to survive and coexist. Culture is acquired. Rather than inheriting culture at birth, an individual learns a set or rules and behavior patterns. For every society, these norms and behavioral responses develop into different cultural patterns that are passed down through the generations, with continual embellishment and adaptation.

For many individuals, cultural conditioning is like a mirage—they are unaware of nine tenths of it. The subtle process of inculcating culture over time through example, and reward and punishment, is generally much more powerful than direct instruction, and individuals tend to unwittingly adopt cultural norms. This process of learning a cultural pattern, called acculturation, conditions individuals so that a large portion of their behavior fit the requirements of their culture and is determined below the level of conscious thought. The depth and length of the acculturation process explains in part why it is so difficult to break cultural patterns.

Many dimensions of culture can be identified. A manager's first experience of a new culture is often though exposure to the less esoteric, more concrete factors that form a culture. This is the explicit culture level. Explicit culture is the observable reality of language and communication styles, time and apace orientation, work habits and practices, all forms of interpersonal and social relationships, food and eating habits, dress and appearance, fashions, art, public buildings, houses, monuments, agriculture, shrines, and markets.

Explicit culture can change over time. For example, in Argentine, where the production and consumption of beef is an important factor in the economy, people are becoming more health conscious. As a result, Argentines, along with Parisians and Americans, are altering their eating habits and eating less beef, Attitudes towards capitalism and towards women in the workforce are also moving closer to Western norms. And worldwide there seemed in 1996 to be a growing feeling that traditions making bribery an acceptable part of doing business were changing.

As for smoking, even in Paris, a long-termsmokers haven, there are more anti-smoking lawsuits and declining cigarette sales.

In London's financial district, the traditional British merchant bankers have been gradually by more aggressive European and American style bankers. Corporate cultures in Japan are also changing, as total devotion, consensus thinking, and jobs for life are being replaced by new models of successful corporate employees, people who are more entrepreneurial and more concerned with personal development, a model much closer to the Western model. While these changes are evident, significant external cultural differences persist. For example, Ford, Chrysler, and General Motors still need to manufacture right-hand drive cars for sale in Australia, Japan, New Zealand and Great Britain.

Explicit cultural differences are often symbols of a deeper level of culture involving norms and values, beliefs and attitudes, and mental processes. Norms are a group's collective sense of what is right or wrong. Norms can develop on a formal level are written laws or on an inform level as social control. Norms are sometimes referred to as character traits in educational programs. Values, on the other hand, defining good and bad are therefore closely related to the beliefs and attitudes shared by the group. In order to understand basic differences in values, beliefs and attitudes, and in the mental processes that reflect them, the history of groups and their struggles for survival need to be examined labeled Implicit Culture factors, these are basic assumptions in bedded in a culture.

Cultural differences can be deeply imbedded and significantly affect society. For example, the deep and pervasive differences in Czechoslovakia led to the country's division into two sections, the Czech Republic and Slovakia, after the breakup of the USSR in 1991. This occurred in spite of the country's small size and the fact that it created sever political and economic hardships for the new Slovak nation.

The extensive fighting among Russians in Chechen and among the Serbs, Croats, and Muslims in the Bosnia/Yugoslavia/Croatia area of the Balkans arose in part from deeply imbedded cultural differences. In 1995 in Canada, such differences led the province of Quebec to vote by only a narrow margin (50.6 to 49.4 percent) to remain part of Canada and not secede to form a new nation. Many wondered whether the bitter election campaign wad a harbinger of the eventual disintegration of a unified Canadian nation.

The Japanese culture provides another example. Developed over hundreds of year's isolation from the rest of the word, the Japanese culture had evolved in the twentieth century into a very closed society, suspicious of the rest of the word. These deep cultural biases have been cited as a major cause of the Japanese aggression during World War Ⅱ: "Hiroshima was simply the end of a ferocious clash of cultures, fueled by intense hatreds and a history of humiliation." Such biases may also have prompted the subsequent Japanese economic aggressiveness. Even today, considerable distrust, and even hatred, persists among some sectors of the Chinese, United States and Japanese populations, a basic cultural barrier that must be taken in account in business and political dealings among the countries: the Chinese culture has been influenced significantly by Confucian philosophy, an understanding of which is useful when doing business in China. For example, China's long tradition of family-based business draws in many ways on Confucian philosophy. The international impact of this tightly controlled family-based approach has been enormous. For instance, in Malaysia in the early 1990s, the Chinese comprised only 28 percent of the population yet controlled over 50 percent of the wealth. The Chinese have a long tradition of international trade, extending back thousands of years to its ancient "Silk Road" which served as a trading link westward to Europe. This cultural tradition encourages international exchanges and suggests that China is primed to greatly expand and eventually become a major force in international trade.

Cultural differences can have a major impact on multinational management.

Failing to recognize and effectively manage then accounts for many of blunders committed everyday by thousands of international executives around the word.

The Strange Customs All Over the World

In this world, on account of different nations and countries, different geographical position and different culture, there are different customs.

Cambodia

Maidens have to learn to smoke before they are married. In their parents eyes, smoking can make their children experience and appreciate all kinds of taste in daily life such as difficulties, happiness. Especially strong smoke can make people have a clear mind.

When girls walking in the forests, because of smoke, they will never lost their way.

If girls can not smoke, they will be considered as ugly women, Even this action is regarded as immorality.

Therefore, although they feel that how terrible the smoking is, Maidens have to make up their mind to learn smoking.

Togo

The people of Togo think, death means that the dead person' soul went back to Gods and ancestors. As a consequence, when People die, they should celebrate instead of feeling sad.

Along with the music and drumbeat, the relatives of the dead began to try their best to dance and sing without any sad look to express their attachment and admire that the dead can go back to Gods and ancestors. Later, they light the candles, continue to dance and sing until days come.

When there are people feeling tired, they can sit at another position, have a rest, drink and eat at random. When they feel relaxed, they will go on it. But the drumbeat does not stop.

As usual, in the funeral, the drummer should be immediate family members of the dead, but, people always invite professional band to replace them.

Because professional band has high quality, elegant danceand natured voice, foreigners will mistake their funeral for performance.

Burma

In Burma, there exists a nationality, the women must wear this sort of copper circle and not pick it up. This action will have bad influence in their bones' growth. The origin of this custom:

(1) These women hope that they themselves look like a kind of Dragon which has very long neck. Because this kind of animal is regarded as everything's father and has significant status.

(2) This action is in order to frighten those hungry tigers in the forests.

(3) Those women' husbands let their wives to wear it on purpose so as to protest their wives from enemy.

(4) This action is the remaining of partriarchy. Because men just need to take off one of copper circles, they can kill their wives easily.

3.3 Managing Cultural Biases and Mental Sets 对于文化偏见和思维定式的管理

文化差异问题已经成为一个跨国性困惑，并影响着企业的国际市场营销活动。而如何理解与控制自己的文化偏见和思维定式是解决这个困惑的前提。

One useful way to become sensitive to, understand and acquire a facility to manage cultural differences is first to understand one's own cultural and personal biases, as well mental sets. Since the U.S. has more multinational companies than any other countries, the North American stereotype model is used as a reference point in the following discussion. The same concept would work as well using any (Preferably the reader's own) national cultural as the reference point. It is simply a conceptual perspective that is useful for discussion purposes. It is not to be taken literally as a recommendation to "think American" in multinational multicultural interpersonal interaction situations.

Not all North Americans, nor all the people of any other nationalities, are like the people described in the following examples. Before going on, therefore, it is useful to review the following general guidelines:

While it is useful to explore generalities and their implications, individuals do not always conform to general cultural stereotypes—not all Japanese, for example, are "typical" Japanese may vary by age, sex and other demographic categories. For instance, young women in all countries now share many common values, as was demonstrated in the August 1995 United Nations Conference on Women in Beijing, which has led to significant differences in Japan between the values of younger and older groups of women.

Differences are not always culturally based. Some arise from individual person alit differences and some from personal, institutional, or business factors. This is true in any country. In addition, any given action may be stimulated by a variety of cultural biases that reinforce each other, not just one bias.

Do not assume that because something works in one cultural, it will work in another. Sometimes there is communality across cultural boundaries, as in the common frameworks described earlier in this book and the increasing trends towards more global products, services, and communications. This is especially true among younger generations in all countries. However, differences will always exist, even among teenagers in different countries who share many common values.

Understand yourself and your own culture first, so that you may be more aware of your own biases or mental set and have a benchmark against which to study others.

Study cultural diversity within your own country, since such a study yields clues to cultural differences and how to handle diversity. The United States, for example, is known as the melting pot of the world since it had such a wide range of cultures within its borders.

The following discussion focuses on continuums, that is, on sets of two extremes between which there can be many varied gradations; try to avoid thinking in terms of extreme black-and-white stereotypes.

Ultimately, it is best to learn as much as you canabout cultural and personal sensitivities specific to the situation you are dealing with, in much the same way you would in any situation involving other human beings.

The same words often have different connotations in different cultures: for example, the French sense of "individualistic" is very different from a North American's sense of "individualism" and both are different from a Latin American's understanding of the word.

3.4 The Six Perspectives on Managing Cultural Differences 管理文化差异的六大原则

根据文化差异对企业国际市场营销活动所产生的影响，本部分将就跨国企业制订战略管理时所采用的方法和理念，介绍管理文化差异的六大原则。

The wide range of cultural differences that impact multinational strategic management dictates formulating an overall conceptual framework to help in organizing, understanding, and dealing with multinational strategic management situations. The discussion in this section describes one such conceptual framework. This working guideline has proved useful to many managers in helping them become sensitive to cultural differences—a critical first step in adapting to and managing cultural differences.

Six critical aspects of cultural diversity can be identified as convenient reference points or perspectives for business managers:

(1) The role of personal relationships: business or people first?

(2) Focus on the individual or on the group?

(3) Status: is everyone crated equal?

(4) Language/information flow factors.

(5) The question of priorities: what is the value of time?

(6) Other Factors：corporate，institution，business individual.

It is important to remember that the above categories are for discussion and understanding purposes only. In practice，actions and motivation do not always fall into such clearly defined categories. People of other countries and cultures may judge North Americans against such reference points，however，so it can be useful to have general cultural categories as reference points during interpersonal interactions situations.

For example，many French people think Northern Americans are naïve，shallow，uninteresting and unaware. Managers in the United States at times cite such typical French traits as arrogance，self-congratulation，stubbornness and unwillingness to compromise. Both views are most often exaggerated and wrong，since each person can differ from any typical preconceived national personality profile，depending on their personality，age and upbringing.

Often it is useful to view differences as opportunities. For example，the Japanese are noted for their concern for cleanliness. This has inspired such products as automated teller machines that iron and sanitize the dispensed bills，germ-free pens and pencils whose barrels are impregnated with an antiseptic chemical to kill bacteria，as well as antibacterial stationery，origami paper，bicycle handles，and even maracas and tambourines. When managed creatively，such differences can also lead to synergies that create new and better solutions.

3.5 The Role of Personal Relationships 人际关系的作用

人际关系在不同的国度里发挥着不同的作用。与欧美国家相比，亚洲国家（尤其中国）的人际关系显得更为重要。

The social context and human aspects of a situation are given different emphasis in different cultures. They are，for example，very important to Asians，who tend to develop personal relationships with the parties involved before getting to the specifics of a negotiation. This explains in part why family relationships are so often important to doing business in China. Americans are likely to want to get to the point more quickly and their relying on superficial bias is reflected in such phrases as "I don't have to like someone I do business with." Like most cultural biases，this statement is true and the bias can be useful in cultures like that in the U.S.. It can，however，create problems in other cultures.

Focusing on developing personal relationships is not uncommon among salespeople anywhere in the world when getting to know their customer; the way it is done in different countries, however, can differ. For example, in Egypt it takes much more time to develop a relationship that leads to a sale than it might in North American.

Two aspects of this cultural trait can affect managing cultural differences: the importance of developing personal relationships and the way people form relationships in the culture you are dealing with. For example, a multinational company with a subsidiary in Mexico, a culture in which personal relationships are important, might think very carefully about whom they send to replace a male sales manager from the U. S. in Mexico City who had long term personal relationships with Mexican customers. If one chooses a let's-get-down-to-business female from New England, it might create problems, given the minimum, one needs to carefully plan a transition period which is managed in a very personal way by both the new and former sales managers.

One business implication this varying emphasis on personal relationships is that a more complex task or negotiation may require more time in order to build a human relationship context when dealing with cultures that place more emphasis on personal relationships. It would also mean that interpersonal communication media subjects, whereas face-to-face meetings would be more effective for complex cross-cultural undertakings.

The notion of a personal relationship in the U. S. can be quite different from the view of other, more "relationship-oriented" cultures. For Americans, relationships are often casual and do not require deep commitments, especially in business situations Americans often do not seem to have the time nor inclination to pursue the one-on-one learning about each other that is necessary to form deep friendships. In their breezy style, they are informal and friendly, and often have difficulty cultivating friends in business situations involving cultures with opposite traditions, where deep, long-lasting relationship are required.

For example, a Chinese firm wishing to purchase paper making machinery negotiated with two suppliers, one French and one American. The American firm had superior technology yet lost the contract. During the negotiations, the American business negotiation style was seen as confusing, time-consuming and not getting to the point. The American firm lost the deal due to insensitivity to the importance of personal relationships in the Chinese culture. This and numerous similar incidents make the point that during intercultural exchanges one should communicate mutual respect, be nonjudgmental, realize that perceptions are personal, show personal empathy, and tolerate ambiguity.

The way in which business relationships are formed in different cultures varies. Americans often build relationships with breezy hospitality, cheeriness, informality, a playful disrespect for status and position, and an expectation that everyone will find this charming and friendly. It is friendliness—not necessarily friendship. Europeans, on the other hand, are less open, especially in England, where respect for differences and status is particularly important. In this European cultural context, the casual, informal American approach appears shallow, superficial, and insensitive.

The French especially enjoy highlighting differences as a way to define their individualistic character and to ascertain another person's true character, an approach that may seem unfriendly to people from other cultures. They are often perplexed by. Americans search for similarities as a way of establishing a relationship. To the French, such an approach lacks the depth that develops from getting to know the distinctive character of another person. The French traits combine a kind of personal individualism and a natural suspicion of anyone they do not know. This individualism seems to generate a resistance to adapting to anyone's needs and has led to the reputation the French have for rudeness. This is especially true of salespeople in Paris, who are known for their surliness and for not smiling or being accommodating.

Cultural variations also exist in regard to the display of emotions. During business negotiations, for example, at the upper management level among individuals just getting to know each other, the range of emotional expression considered acceptable is greater for Americans than for the British, and greater still for Latin Americans. In contrast, for Japanese and most Asians the display of emotions is more restricted than for the British. In other settings such as social events, of course, these relationships change.

At one cultural extreme there can be a tendency to keep relations harmonious by not talking directly about problems, as in Asians and some Latin American cultures. Confrontation isavoided in cultures where human relationships are highly valued. In contrast, in other cultures, for example in the U.S., there can tend to be a desire to confront problems quickly and directly, in spite of the fact that such an approach might embarrass someone personally and publicly.

Since the history of pioneer America instilled in its citizens the belief that hard work and persistence can make things happen, Americans are likely to insist on specific information that will enable them to plan. For example, an Arab negotiating with an American was puzzled by the insistence on specific information about future delivery dates and available quantities. He had hoped that building a relationship would have developed enough trust to make such detailed information unnecessary.

After discussing the matter and explaining the need, the solution in this instance was for the Arab to understand the American's need and to take the time to supply more information, even though he felt that being asked for that informationwas unnecessary and showed a lack of trust. Such a solution is common in these situations: first understand the cultural difference and its basis, and then take the steps necessary to accommodate a sensitive human situation.

Before proceeding overseas to negotiate, it is important to understand that the purpose of a negotiation may vary by culture. Often, the primary purpose is not to accomplish a task and arrive at a deal, as in the U. S. Negotiations, in other cultures, may be a process of getting to know the other parties and establishing a long-term personal relationship that will serve as the basis of many future deals. This is one reason why so little often seems to be accomplished during early stages of negotiations in China, Japan, and South America and why negotiations there seem to take so long.

This does not mean that an uncomplicated deal cannot be written or that simple matters cannot be handled quickly among cultures. Nor dose it mean that personal relationships are the only factor. It simply means that building relationships is a significant means of doing business over a long period of time among and across cultures.

3.6 Focus on the Individual or on the Group 基于个人主义,还是集体主义

崇尚个人主义的文化通常鼓励彰显个人,而崇尚集体主义的文化则不喜欢有人出风头,这同样体现在东西方文化之中。

Succeeding in managing cultural differences does not depend on becoming or acting like the nationality being dealt with. Success generally simply requires adapting or bending to some degree.

Relative to other cultures, Americans as a whole are very extreme in the value they place on individualism. U. S. History and its educational system support an individualistic culture. For example, children are taught to be self-reliant and are rewarded for individual achievement. In contrast, in the past young Japanese children might have worked in groups with the pride of achievement and reward being for the collective group output. This accounts in part for why such extensive training is needed in companies as they move towards more reliance on interactive teams.

This trait can cause problems during negotiations. For example, Americans often expect the Japanese to make decisions at the negotiating table. In turn, the Japanese are continually surprised to find individuals on American side advancing their own ideas and opinions and at times contradicting one another. This creates a cultural gap that has to be bridged by one side or the other through initiating a dialogue about the gap and reaching an understanding on how to bridge it. Again, this usually requires more time than Americans originally were prepared to spend on negotiations.

At American expatriate in Malaysia who managed Motorola Penang's Research and Development operation for several years reflected on his experiences there in these words: "When I was transferred to Penang it was a cultural shock. I remember when I tried to publicly reward some people for exceptional effort, how embarrassed they were. Rewards such as free time or free lunch for the team as whole were more appropriate. I didn't realize that teamwork is more important there than standing out as an individual. In the states we fight for recognition."

Another Malaysian manager described what he learned in this way: "Australians are taught to be strong and speak their minds. Italians are more emotional. I had to role-play an American. I cannot act like American. I cannot act like Americans; they are more aggressive and individualistic."

Cultures of the United Kingdom, the Netherlands, France, and the Nordic countries also have strong individualistic tendencies. More collectivist cultures, in addition to the Japanese, include many Asian and Latin American countries. Guatemala is considered the most group-oriented culture, due to its Mayan tribal heritage.

Cultural values are changing, however. For example, in Japan a system of competitive "cram" schools has been developed to train children (two years and older) to compete for positions in better grammar schools, which leads to entrance into better universities and subsequently better jobs at graduation. This is creating a "individualistic and independent thinking" mold.

At time, the origin of the collectivist cultural values is not historical tradition, but ones acquired during communist rule. For example, when doing business in Russia or Central Europe, one often encounters situation such as:

The inability to negotiate individually and make decisions during meeting because approval is needed from higher authorities;

Final arrangements may to be worked out with labor groups which still control many of the decision processes;

Many constituents still have to be paid off with bribes and under-the-table payments, raising serious ethical questions for U.S. executives.

While it is easier to make decisions and take action in an individualistic frame—it takes longer to reach decisions and act in collective contexts—and while Americans are noted for being action oriented, group-oriented cultures can also be action oriented. For example, in Hong Kong, Singapore, Korea, and China, small family-based businesses have been very successful throughout Asia, often growing into major conglomerates, though that may be changing as the family sons and daughters move into controlling positions.

In the United States, one hears the phrase, "The squeaky wheel gets the grease". In collectivist cultures, the opposite may be true: the outspoken individualist may be views as disharmonious and a danger to the group, and so be ostracized. In collectivist, group-centered cultures, harmony is an important goal—harmony with groups and society and harmony with traditions that may have developed over many hundreds of years. This dictates some careful judgment and restraint as to the timing of outspoken criticism and objections during business negotiations. Where appropriate, business people should resist the urge to get down to business and into the task of help establishing bargaining positions prematurely.

Cultures with a high social conscience, such as in China, tend to prefer to work in teams and work for group consensus. At the other extreme there are cultures, such as in North American, that place a high premium on individualism and individualistic reactions, and so tend to believe that "God helps those who help themselves". Such people are more likely to be more individualistic and not always inherently natural team players.

In light of these cultural and historical differences, it is necessary to be contingence oriented. First the situation context should be examined for individual and cultures, as well as the task being dealt with. Some factors to look at and be sensitive have been discussed in this section. Others factors can be relevant as well. Being sensitive to these differences is a major first step in adapting to, and managing, perceived differences. Above all, when in doubt, ask questions gently to find out what situation context is being dealt with.

3.7 About Equality
关于平等

要注意东西方文化另一现象，即亚洲文化重视人的地位和阶层，重男轻女；而欧美文化则注重人与人的平等。

In some cultures, such as those in Asia, northern Europe and South America, great value of social status is placed. For example, this is reflected in seating arrangements and other protocols based on position, for example. At the other extreme, Americans tend to give more importance to competence. The U.S. has to egalitarian culture which believes all men are created equal. Next to Australia, it is probably the world's most informal culture.

In many cultures, formal protocols are important, however. Early in business relationships, people are referred to by their formal titles Mr. and Mrs., not by first namesas in the U.S.. Business cards are treated seriously, from the titles printed on them (corporate rank, title, and educational degrees) to the way they are exchanged (start with the highest-ranking person) and stored. Gift giving practices also vary by culture. Gifts are common in Asia, usually in relation to some specific service, such as giving a talk. Business people should be aware that customs in regard to dinner invitations and appropriate host or hostess gifts vary widely, as do the timing and length of meals. You can expect to be invited to a business associates home in Australia, though rarely in China or Japan. If you are invited to a home in France, bring flowers, but never roses. Dinners are much later, close to 11 p.m. in Spain; look for three-hour lunches in Buenos Aires. It is important to learn these protocols as quickly as possible.

Embracing egalitarianism leads to a willingness to speak frankly as an equal to anyone, a very direct approach. U.S. business people tend to speak on matter what the rank of the listener. Protocols based on status or custom dictate a somewhat different approach, however. In cultures where rank and position are considered more important—such as Mexico, Italy, and even France—such directness can appear vulgar, harsh, and impersonal. Many other cultural values dictate ambiguity and indirectness in order to maintain harmony, respect status, elaborate points within larger contexts, and save face. The status values also dictate that it is prudent to praise contributions to increase a listener's status before offering any criticism—a good idea in any culture.

The desire to avoid diminishing another's status in public leads to considerable confusion. In Asia especially, people have difficulty saying "no" directly. Instead, they may equivocate, saying, "We must study the question further," or "We will try to solve the problem or overcome the difficulty". However, in Asia "yes" means only "I heard you"; it is not to be taken as an affirmative reply. In its extreme, at many stores when you are dissatisfied or want something changed, clerks may say "no problem". What they mean is there is no problem for them, but a big problem for you, as you discover later when you find nothing has been done.

North Americans have always had trouble dealing with bureaucracies. They prefer to seek out the person making the decision to get a direct answer as quickly as possible. This is not possible in many cultures. Hierarchies for their own sake are common in many cultures, where they are often based on history and past practice. They require time to work through, and are often manipulated, as in Japan, to exploit or win concessions. They are also the source of much crime and bribery. They can be especially troublesome when trying to introduce change in business, such as empowering workers to make decision. For example, Moroccan teams can have trouble with empowerment because they are used to a hierarchical religious, social, and political environment.

North Americans are often at a loss to explain why contracts are ignored so often broken or renegotiated in Asian, Latin American and Central European countries. An egalitarian system is built on the assumption that laws and standards (ethical and moral) permit all people to be treated equally. Other countries are more pragmatic and judge each new event based on the existing circumstances. In China, for example, the later seems to be true.

American contracts tend to be long because the parties try to anticipate and cover all contingencies. Forthe Chinese, a contract is the beginning of the negotiation, not the end, since they may depend on the trust and relationship with their Western partner to help resolve difficulties that arise. This is why it helps a great deal to work though family ties when doing business in China.

While women are viewed as equal to men in many cultures, such as in Scandinavia, many other cultures do not believe in such equality. In very masculine-oriented countries, such as Japan, women may have trouble in negotiating and interacting with business people. The same may also be true in some of the Arab states. These attitudes are changing, of course, but change is coming very slowly. In Russia, women entrepreneurs are becoming more numerous and Yemen is giving more political power to women under pressure from women activists there.

The direct approach is also a problem during employee's performance evaluations. While desirable in egalitarian cultures such as in the U. S. being honest, frank, and open—or working with objective standards fairly developed during management by objectives programs—is not as effective in non-egalitarian societies. First, such behavior is often perceived as a threat to the status of the person being evaluated and usually violates associated cultural values related to avoiding unpleasant subjects and confrontations. Second, working with a person to set work objectives, just like asking for their opinions about work practices, violates hierarchical allocations of power, since in many collectivist cultures bosses are supposed to have the answers. Cultural differences also affect performances-reward systems: individual rewards for performance are out of place in societies where the group or collective is the primary driving force.

3.8 Language and Information Exchange 语言与信息交流

在国际市场营销活动中,最显而易见的文化差异就是语言问题。尽管英语是通用的第一语言,但作为跨国企业的领导人,除了母语之外还应掌握第二语言。

The most immediate and obvious cultural difference is language. Obviously, in multinational company management the more languages one speaks the better opportunity one could take. In practice, except in rare instances, this is almost impossible for most of us. Since English is the generally accepted language of business, most international managers shall have to use the second language, not their primary one.

This can cause problems. People may be a little uncertain, self-conscious, and hesitant when using a second language. They may have difficulty finding the right word. One should be sensitive to this and try to make the speaker feel comfortable. If you come from an English speaking country remember that the person who learned your language is making an enormous effort to bridge a cultural gap. Appreciate it—saves you the year it might have taken to learn their language. Also, remember that others often think that people from English speaking countries are arrogant since they expect others to speak English. Often, this resentment has to be overcome in business dealings.

Even when English is used, there can be misunderstandings and problems. For example, the word "right" can mean "opposite of left", "correct." Colloquialisms, such as "Run that by me again", instead of "please repeat that", are easy to misconstrue. Avoid jargon and idioms. For example, "that idea seems out of left field" only makes sense in a culture that enjoys baseball. And jokes rarely travel well across cultural borders.

Interpretations of body language can also vary among cultures. Cultural differences can account for misunderstandings about personal space that arises during conversations. For example, people from the more socially oriented cultures tend to stand very close while talking, while others including Americans prefer to keep a little more space between speakers during a conversation. Eye contact also has different meanings in different cultures; not looking directly at someone might be interpreted in India as a sign of respect, whereas intensely looking someone in the eye is thought a way to show personal interest in someone in other cultures.

As another example, an American businessman whose hand be suddenly taken by a Thai associate, or who is embraced by a Latin business partner, might attribute a sexual meaning where there is none. In turn a Thai or Latin associate, meeting resistance to these nonverbal gestures, might attribute a coldness or indifference to the American where none is intended.

The way information is conveyed also varies by culture. For example, a typical Western trait, especially in Germany and the United States, is to talk about "getting straight to the point". In other cultures, both the speed and path of information flow can vary. Getting to the "point" may first involve "getting to know each other" which can take much more time. Also, more than one point (including family affairs), not just a point, may be discussed along the information flow path as a getting to know each other.

3.9 The Value of time
时间观念

不同的文化环境导致了人们具有不同的时间观念。欧美国家的人通常具有线性的时区时间观念,而亚洲国家(尤其中国)的人的时间观念呈环形扩散状。

Northern Europeans (strongly) and Americans (moderately) tend to favor treating events in an "orderly" fashion, on at a time. This is a monochromic time perspective. Monochromic time is linear. Things are done separately one after another. Time is compartmentalized, organized, and controlled. It is commodity that has value because of its scarcity and its usefulness in defining the context in which activity occurs.

Polychromic time, on the other hand, is more circular. It is endless; there is plenty of it has no beginning or end. Most important, many things can happen at once. This cultural perspective is prevalent in Arab countries, Central and Southern

Asia, and Latin American countries such as Mexico. For example, at conferences there one might find many topics, involving family and business, being discussed at once—because it is part of the "getting to know each other" ritual and there is less pressure to stick to an agenda.

Monochromic cultures tend to focus on the present or immediate future and to believe that an individual can future outcomes Polychromic cultures tend to be more futuristic and fatalistic-reflected in the phrase "whatever will be will be". This can lead to an attitude that tomorrow cannot be controlled, so why not make the best of today. Time factors, therefore, affect our approach to dealing with people from other culture. For instance, will in a specific situation at hand decisions be made and action taken quickly, or will many meetings be needed just to get to know each other? Can the task be discussed directly or will it be necessary to socialize, avoid confrontations, and talk about peripheral context issues first? Will the meetings proceed in a linear fashion, moving step towards a conclusion or will a less task-focused, discursive discussion take place? Managing cultural differences requires preplanning along these contingency lines. The specific situation requirements, not theoretical universal formulas, dictate how cultural differences are managed.

Such flexibility should not surprise any American who is familiar with the rural versus big-city lifestyles in the U.S. Managers in Now York City work on tight time schedules, hurrying from one meeting or task to another. In contrast, managers living in smaller towns might be less controlled by tight time schedules and more accustomed to dealing with people they have gotten to know personally over the years. This can include shopkeepers, relatives, mail carriers, and even the refrigerator repair staff. Managers who can imagine, or have experienced, such different settings are aware that managing styles change in different environments. The same is true among national cultures.

When conducting training or other business in France, for example, times should be adjusted for lunch and breaks. For the French, lunch can be a two-hour or longer event and time must be allocated to accommodate such habits. For the French, as for many business people around the world, lunch is not just a time to eat. It is also a time to conduct interpersonal business, carry out internal politicking, and clarify possible misunderstandings.

Even in societies that favor tight schedules, decisions may be made at a much slower pace. Other cultural traditions may intervene—traditions related to long histories that create the feeling that near-term future is not very important and that other considerations such as society, respect for other group members, and the like are more important and therefore must be given equal time. This same cultural perspective regarding time is also to be expected in Sao Paulo or Mexico City.

Deadlines are also the victims of cross—cultural differences. For example, whenever a culture emphasizes other agendas, deadlines can give way to them. While the French value efficiency, they also have great respect for quality. When problems arise, they may disregard the deadline in order to meet quality standards.

The action taken in these situations is often dictated by common sense: pay attention to complimenting others for what they do well (quality, for instance), take time to socialize with othersbefore a meeting data, and above all keep asking what is needed on both sides to help make each meeting work.

Cultural perspectives about time also affect training programs. Schedules have to be adjusted to allow for discussions of related contexts, contexts which may not initially seem to a Westerner to be relevant to the task objectives. Times also must be allocated for interpersonal sessions where individuals are given the opportunity to get to know each other. While this sort of thing occurs at sessions in the United Stares, the amount of time allowed for breaks and for meals (longer lunches, for example), way be different.

Another adjustment across cultures involves the difficulty of setting agendas and of "sticking to the subject" across cultures. Polychromatic cultures have different agendas that allow for simultaneous discussion of related topics—at least those felt to be related from their cultural perspective. Such discussions—which might include family matters, related social and group matters, or the need for information someone who is accustomed to the narrowly focused tasks/decisions, tight time schedules and point-by-point agendas.

Monochromic cultures emphasize linear time and are concerned with causality. Communication and argument arebased on the need for logical, step-by-step activities. Polychromatic cultures look for equilibrium. The emphasis on simultaneous activity, communications, and argument is based on a need for balance. It is important to accept these differences and use them as a working premise when managing cultural difference.

3.10 Institution, Business, and Individual 机构、项目与个人

在国际市场营销活动中，在机构、项目和个体之间，不能过分关注文化差异而忽略了个体行为。应该明白，影响一个人行为的不仅仅只有文化，还有其他的很多因素。

It is important not to become absorbed in cultural differences as to lose sight of the fact that individual actions are influenced by many factors, not just cultural ones.

An individual's personality may influence action. All of us have had to deal at meetings with people who were just contentious by nature, a character trait that may have been stimulated and conditioned by the individual's culture but which may not be totally caused or explained by cultural influences. In other words, action may not have a single cause.

Institutional policies may stimulate and condition behavior. In Russia and other more controlled economies, approval policies may require different executive levels to approve the terms of a contract. The delays in these instances are neither necessarily related to cultural perception of time nor to a reluctance to talk directly about controversial subjects. They are related to institutional policies. Corporate cultures may also be the source of behavior.

In another negotiating situation, country's high inflation rate, over 100 percent per month, prevented making long-term commitments. Cultural factors created a reluctance to talk about the problems immediately and directly, but the root cause was an economic/business condition.

Often, more than one cultural or other factor generates and explains behavior. People do not always act based on one motive nor can their behavior always be traced to one cultural stimulus—anywhere in the world. The six-perspective framework developed in this chapter is, therefore, useful for discussion, understanding, and recall purposes only. Such segmentation does not necessarily replicate reality, in practice, events can actually unfold in a more integrated way.

3.11 Managing Cultural Differences, Situation by Situation 管理文化差异要具体情况具体对待

在实施国际市场营销战略中,文化差异问题会非常复杂而棘手。不要期待有“放之四海而皆准”的好方法去应对文化差异,而需要有具体情况具体对待的理念。

As multinational management business experiences show, reconciling and managing differences generally seems to involve five kinds of approaches: modifying one's own behavior and adapting to a situation; taking steps to change the situation environment; abandoning the situation or project; exploiting the differences wherever possible; or using any combination of the first four.

3.11.1 Being Sensitive to Accept and Adapt Differences 对待文化差异要敏感,更要接纳和适应

Thousands of examples exist of companies modifying products, reconfiguring manufacturing facilities, adapting advertising, and making other moves to accommodate local country situation requirements.

Amultinational or market-by-market approach is often required by local circumstances. Accommodating local tastes was, for example, necessary in the McDonald's situation in India and other Asian countries described at the outset of this chapter.

Many of thecultural differences that need to be recognized and adapted to have been discussed—including simple things like protocols at conferences for seating arrangements, the way to address individuals, the order in which they are to be addressed, the time to discuss personal matters and the time to discuss business matters, what to wear on different occasions, where to go for entertainment, and what to serve for meals. Knowing and adapting to customs and habits is useful in many business and personal dealings. Many books guide business managers and business in adapting to, surviving, and prospering in local cultures. While adapting to local customers is at times effective, it is not always the best approach. Other approaches are discussed in the following paragraphs.

3.11.2 Modifying the Impact of Cultural Differences 善于转化文化差异所导致的影响

With the growing sophistication of international business managers, a small but noticeable trend toward increasingly sophisticated manipulation of the expectations arising from this growing awareness of cultural differences has emerged. For example, a Japanese negotiator might be aware that sophisticated American know negotiations in Japan can take longer because of the culture need to get to know each other. This can be exploited, for example, by using this cultural rationale simply to down American negotiators and create time-scheduling problems and the need for hasty last minute decisions.

As another example, the phrase "This is the custom (or way we do it) here in our country" may surface during legal negotiations anywhere in the world. Fortunately, those experienced in legal negotiations in the U. S. know that this phrase often used during negotiations there as well. When used by lawyers during many business negotiations for someone else to pay additional expenses not previously agreed upon. It is essentially a negotiating ploy used to con someone into paying for something, such as a property transfer fee, that she does not have to pay for. An obvious way to handle such a situation is to keep one's temper and point out that each negotiation is a separate event and each item is open to negotiation; past practices are irrelevant. The same can be done in negotiations overseas.

Another commonly encountered exploited scenario involves depending on a relationship of trust to avoid difficult decisions. For example, during a negotiation someone may try to avoid committing to deadlines by saying, "You can trust me" just to find an excuse to avoid making a normal business commitment. It is not always necessary to yield or adapt in this or other situations, just because there is a possibility that the phrase is culturally based. Professionalism, not retaliation, is often more appropriate when you sense that someone appears to be trying to exploit you, since they may simply be testing limits.

Ignoring or circumventing alleged and real local differences and customs has proved useful in many areas. Many readers are familiar with the picture of President George Bush becoming ill in Asia presumably from excessive toasting. In contrast, in over 100 business dinner banquets the authors attended in Asia and Central Europe, no one ever served high-alcohol-content liquor or smoked. This occurred simply because the hosts were informed that someone in reasons wine was the only alcohol desired. It was indicated that we realized the impoliteness of refusing to toast with hard liquor and wanted to avoid being impolite, but that if we were served liquor the drinking. If any guests smoked, the person who was allergic to smoke would have to leave the room since her eyes would begin to water and she would begin coughing.

These requests created no problems. Courtesy to guests and guest hospitality are strongly in the Chinese and Central European cultures, as it is in almost every country/culture, and so made compliance with our requests normal and acceptable. In addition, some cultures such as the Muslims do not allow the drinking of any alcohol, so it is not a new concept in many countries with diverse cultures. Sophisticated executives and managers in China and other countries apparently are used to accommodating justifiable requests based on cultural differences providing they are timely and politely introduced.

The impact of differences is diminishing, as more multinational companies mount mass global marketing programs of products ranging from Frito-Lay potato chips (it was found that it was unnecessary to adapt them to local tastes) to Gillette razors to Coca-Cola. Rapidly expanding mass media, especially satellite television, is also helping reduce the impact of differences, for example, as 24-hour shopping channels are started and major distributors make billion dollar purchases of overseas films and TV programs (or domestic versions of them) that are becoming popular world wide.

3.11.3 Exploiting the Potential Value 发掘潜在价值

For example, Aflaco Inc. (American Family Corporation) of Columbus, Georgia, a leading supplier of cancer insurance, was able to use a niche strategy in Japan because of cultural differences andpersistence. In the United States there is very little interest in separate insurance policies for individual sicknesses, which accounted for the low sales of cancer insurance policies. In Japan, however, where cancer is recognized as a serious concern and existing Japanese insurance policies paid minimal cancer benefits, the market and culture were favorable for separate cancer insurance policies. It took the company four years to meet and accommodate all the local legal and regulatory requirements needed to get a license to sell insurance in Japan. However, once licensed, the company received the favorable treatment generally afforded Japanese firms but denied to most foreign competitors. In 1991, 75 percent of Aflaco's \$ 3.5 billion in revenues came from Japan.

3.12 Synergistically Managing Cultural Differences 将差异转化为合力

跨国企业由来自不同国家、不同文化背景的人构成。然而,正是因为有差异才能构成强大的团队,差异产生力量。重要的是,要将差异转化为合力。

Almost every business management situation anywhere in the world has differences among participating parties thatmust be reconciled. Taking the time to establish personal relationships in order to reconcile these differences has to be balanced with time limitations and situation requirements. At one extreme, General Electric took almost four years to introduce changes into its workforce in its Hungarian light bulb plant, as it gradually introduced its corporate-wide programs in which workers formed teams and became receptive to American participate management styles and production efficiency methods.

Most often it isnecessary to accommodate order to deal with them, however. Rather, it is necessary to recognize and adapt to others' customs in the same way you might reasonably expect them in some ways to adapt to and accommodate yours. A mutual give-and-take process will help create a balance.

At the same time, in a rapidly changing and increasingly sophisticated global business environment, overemphasizing differences can often create barriers to building cultural bridges and create a negative, counterproductive atmosphere. It can also at times leave one vulnerable to exploitation. Personal experience and a growing body of research literature show that, too much can often be made of differences too early in business and business education situations. The unique requirements of each specific situation being dealt with must be studied.

Multinational companies' strategic management involves reconciling and balancing disparate factors in many different ways. Earlier chapters focused on balancing global and local factors, with rapid information transfer, when both planning and doing at the operational and enterprise-wide management lever to meet present and longer-term future needs. This chapter focused on another area—balancing the cultural factors encountered during interpersonal interaction. An example would be balancing an American's desire to stick to task sequence agendas during a meeting with another person's culture-based to desire to randomly discuss problem topics that might help develop deeper personal relationships and provide information on broader contexts.

Going beyond balancing and accommodating different cultures, it is possible to synergistically the best of different cultures and come up with creative solutions. This was reportedly the case in Hungary after the purchase of what eventually grew to be a controlling interest in Matav RT. Hungary's state telephone company, by American Corp. of the U. S. and Germany's Deutsche Telekom AG. After initial cultural clashes over multiple operating details, Elek Staub, the newly hired Hungarian manager, skillfully eased tensions first with off-site leadership training sessions called "Vision and Value Training". He then tapped executive strengths by dividing up responsibilities according to corporate culture and experience. The American executive at Matav was put in charge of marketing and the Deutsche Telekom executive in charge of administration and personnel, with Mr. Staub, representing the Hungarian State alliance partners, as the link to Hungary and the government. According the executives, "everyone in the Troika has an equal voice and equal say", and all are able to come up with better decisions and actions than when working alone. They still have cultural clashes, but they now have in place enabling leadership, as well as an enabling organization structure, processes and culture, that enable synergistically going beyond just reconciling differences to creating innovative solutions.

3.13 Conclusion 结语

The universally successful approach to balancing cultural factors seems to be to respect all cultures while adapting in interpersonal interactions to some degree, but not always, and focusing on developing personal relationships and getting the job done as quickly as possible within this framework. This includes asserting oneself where necessary, being your own person, and avoiding confrontations. The secret is not so much what is done, as how it is done. The skills come largely from personal experience and from studying the experiences of others.

Personal experience can come from many sources. It can come from your associations with other culture. For example, like many countries, the United States is a diverse melting pot which provides many opportunities for this. In addition, most Americans are at most third—or fourth—generation foreigners. In a sense, then, traveling and interacting overseas can be a king of coming home, going back to other countries of origin—whether in Europe, Asia, South American, or Africa. It is possible for many of us to examine the foreigner within ourselves and our families as a start in developing a cross-cultural perspective. In that way it will be not so much a chore in accommodating differences as a journey in enjoying and taking advantage of the richness of diversity and discovering the rich rewards arising from integrating global and local thinking and action. Our country and ourselves can, in this sense, be viewed as a microcosm of how this can be and is being done.

The Chapter's Referential Questions: 本章参考性问题

1. Discuss the definition and concept "culture" and the different ways it can impact on international marketing.
   谈谈关于"文化"的定义和概念,以及文化对于国际市场营销活动所产生的影响。
2. Describe some of the problems involved in balancing global and local approaches in international marketing.
   叙述在实施国际市场营销中平衡全球化思维和当地化运作过程中会面临的问题,并举例说明。
3. What are common frameworks in managing the cultural differences?
   在管理文化差异方面,有哪些可以应用的通用型方法?
4. Identify some general guidelines for understanding and managing cultural

differences.

叙述在理解和管理文化差异方面的普遍原则。

5. Discuss the role of personal relationships in different cultures and the ways in which these varying roles can affect business dealings in different countries cultures. Give specific examples.

举例说明人际关系在不同文化中的作用，以及人际关系在不同文化背景下商业运作所起的作用。

6. How to synergistically managing the cultural differences in international marketing?

在国际市场营销实践中，如何将差异转化为合力？

7. Why is that the English is the generally accepted language of business, but most international managers shall have to use the second language, not their primary one?

为什么英语是通用的第一语言，但作为跨国企业的领导人除了母语之外还应掌握第二语言？

8. Being a student majoring International Marketing, do you have your own Cultural Biases and Mental Sets and how to manage them?

作为一名学习国际市场营销专业的学生，你有自己的文化偏见和思维定式吗？如何管理你的文化偏见和思维定式？

微信扫码查看

Chapter 4 Global Market Segmentation

全球市场细分

Learning Objectives

本章学习目标

1. Understand the meaning of the international market segmentation
   了解国际市场细分的意义
2. Identify the necessary conditions for effective international market segmentation
   识别有效的国际市场细分的必要条件
3. How to use market segmentation strategies in global markets
   在全球市场如何运用市场细分策略

The concept of market segmentation has triggered the imagination of many international marketers during the last decade. It is a strategy which enables the company to maximize the results of a given marketing effort by exploiting clearly identified strength in relation to a submarket which is either inadequately satisfied by other manufacturers or where the company is particularly well placed to do an effective job.

4.1 The Meaning of International Market Segmentation 国际市场细分的意义

国际市场细分是指企业按照一定的细分标准,把整个国际市场细分为若干个需求不同的子市场,其中任何一个子市场中的消费者多具有相同或相似的需求特征,企业可以在这些子市场中选择一个或多个作为其国际目标市场。

Every marketer recognizes that it is most possible to satisfy the specific needs and requirements of every consumer. It is necessary to deal with groups of consumers or clusters of individuals who manifest similarities in consumption habits, social behavior, and economic characteristics or in some other distinguishable criterion. The extreme logical choices for the marketer are either to focus the attention on a wisely selected subgroup or submarket or to aim to differentiate the marketing programmer so as to satisfy the largest number of heterogeneous members of the total market.

Market segmentation can be defined as the strategy whereby the company partitions the market into submarkets (segments) likely to manifest similar responses to marketing inputs; the aim is to maximize the penetration of such segments rather than spread the effort thinly over the total market.

Market aggregation where the company treats the total market as one undifferentiated mass and whilst acknowledging that many social, cultural and economic differences are inexistence, chooses to ignore such differences and standardize the marketing effort.

It is the objective of the first part of this Chapter to discuss market segmentation in general terms. The second part will explore how this concept can be usefully applied to international marketing activities.

4.1.1 Alternative Base for Segmenting Markets 市场细分的选择基础

Few areas of planning have evoked as much scope for creative thinking as the exploration of methods of market segmentation. The marketer who is able to identify anovel way for segmenting markets for his product or service may often escape the strong and harmful competition. Indeed segmentation can be an extremely effective way of rejuvenating declining products or giving them a new lease of life. Furthermore, it may enable a relatively small company to hold its own in an industry in which it has to compete against giant companies.

There are many conventional ways for segmenting markets. The aim here is to concentrate on those bases of segmentation which have international relevance and applicability.

4.1.2 Socioeconomic and Demographic Factors 社会经济与人口因素

Age, sex, family size, income, occupation, family life cycle, race, religion, socialclass, etc. are all such variable factors.

The system for segmenting markets has to encapsulate a number of socioeconomic parameters into one package. Thus when we talk about segments, we should now that members of each segment possess certain income, occupation and social status characteristics. It enables the average marketer to divide the market into categories which are well understood and well monitored. Thus we can easily establish not only who consumes what but also who reads a specific magazine, who is the audience for a certain TV programmer—and all this in accordance with a classification which is standard amongst all marketers and their supportive service.

The international marketers are less fortunate—they don't have access to such a system on a global scale. They may find various types of segmentation systems in a number of countries but unfortunately they seldom lend themselves to comparability analysis. Furthermore in many countries no formal segmentation system exists. The only way for the marketers is to develop their own broken down of each market, measure the size of each segment and analyses the opportunities.

To take an example: a car manufacturer (France based) has identified that his main product, Model X, is popular among consumers who satisfy the following description; age group—35 ~ 49; family size—2 or 3 children occupation—professional, executive and business; income—least 15,000 francs per month; social class—middle/lower-upper. Research has indicated that 68 percent of the buyers over a period have fallen into the segment described. This is very useful in so far as the company now knows which socioeconomic group it should try to satisfy and in which direction its marketing strategy should be concentrated. The fact 32 per cent of the buyers do not fall into the same segment is not very important. It is the greatest happiness of the greatest number "that should matter". This is the underlying principle of the segmentation approach. The company will now advertise its product in media which are used by the target group described. The price will be geared to the segment's expectations. The distribution system will be selected in accordance with the buying habits and social behavior of the submarket thus identified. However, so far all this has been done in relation to one domestic market. Can the company's marketing personnelextend this micro-approach to word markets? Ideally the answer must be yes; but this must depend on the availability of data about each market in which the company wants to sell its products. If one in able to identify a socioeconomic grouping in each country, which is identical in most respects to the one that has been selected in France, where life could be relatively easy—a standardized approach would be applied all round. If, on the other hand, it transpires that the variables change too drastically strategy. This is one of the major decision areas of international marketing and no effort should be spared in ensuring that the correct input is assembled. Decisions taken with inadequate information may prove costly and certain circumstances a source of serious problems.

Similarly the Volkswagen cars during its heyday sued to satisfy distinct segments: in some countries it was the main family car bought by middle class, reasonably high-earning, medium size families. In other countries it served as the second family car bought for the wife's use. These represented two different segments and as such called for different marketing approaches. It would have been ideal for VW if they could have identified a standard segment throughout the world. In their case it was not possible. In certain situations this is possible and it is the job of the marketer to spot these rare opportunities.

4.1.3 Cultural Groupings
文化群体

This method for segmenting markets is particularly important in international marketing. Cultural influences are to a great extent determinant of the way the consumer behaves and the kind of consumption pattern which they develop. Cultural factors determine the kind of food that people eat, the type of homes they aspire to have, the style of design they favor and so on, Fashion is thus linked to culture and so are general attitudes.

Cultural attitudes, for instance, will determine whether a sewing machine in the household is a status symbol, a do-it-yourself type tool or a "necessity". Similarly, in some countries the role of the mother in the home is such that she represents the ultimate authority when important issues are involved such as the purchase of expensive items. Another example is the cultural difference in relation to the treatment of children.

Grouping markets in accordance with their cultural differentiation can be very helpful to the international marketer. It may in certain circumstances be more useful than dividing markets in accordance with political or geographical borders. To take a simple example: in cultural term the French part of Switzerland has probably more in common with France than with the German speaking part of Switzerland. In terms of market segmentation one is fully justified to cluster the French speaking part of Switzerland with France. This may be totally unworkable on political grounds or in monetary/fiscal terms but it is certainly logical on a cultural basis. Most international marketers accept political borders much too readily in their marketing planning. In fact there are many situations where much borders are quite meaningless in terms of marketing logic and potential synergy. The fact that a market is shown on a political map as a separate entity does not automatically make it into a separate marketing entity. This would apply to Monaco and France. This point gains significant proportions where one deals with large blocs of markets which from a distance look homogeneous but in cultural terms are extremely varied. One often tends to bulk all the Latin American countries as one geographic submarket because a glance at the map indicates that they all belong to the same subcontinent. A partitioning on cultural basis may yield a different segmentation decision by paying attention to the Spanish and Portuguese backgrounds of countries like the Argentine and Brazil. Similarly the former Soviet Bloc seems a logical geographic/political segment for the international marketer. In cultural terms Czech and Slovak probably have more in common with Austria than with Bulgaria. Many companies opt for the political segmentation approach and probably not always for a rational reason. The fact that marketing tin the former Soviet Bloc calls for a different kind of negotiating skill than in free economies in not always a good reason for suggesting that the man responsible for selling to Bulgaria or Rumania should therefore be responsible for selling tin Germany or in Czechoslovakia.

4.1.4 Geographic Factors 地理因素

Most marketers recognize geographic variations within their market. On the domestic marketing scene one encounters companies who distinguish in their marketing strategy between city customers and rural customers. Other companies may distinguish between various parts of the country and choose to devote more time and effort to those customers who happen to be located within easy access to the company's main office and installations. In fact companies that organize their selling activity on a geographic basis have tacitly segmented the marker by this variable.

It is easy to see that in international marketing the segmentation concept is similar except that it assumes a very much larger dimension. A company that has decided to concentrate its marketing effort in Europe alone has in fact selected to satisfy one large segment in the overall context of the global scene. The world, in other words, can be partitioned into conveniently divisible segments provided on can identify similarities among the various submarkets. Those similarities may be cultural or linguistic or expressed in standard of living terms. By taking this approach one actually endeavors to identify segments based on more than one dimension. The segmentation by a geographic, or any other variable, in compunction with some other dimension can be illustrated very simply in diagrammatic form Figure 4 - 1.

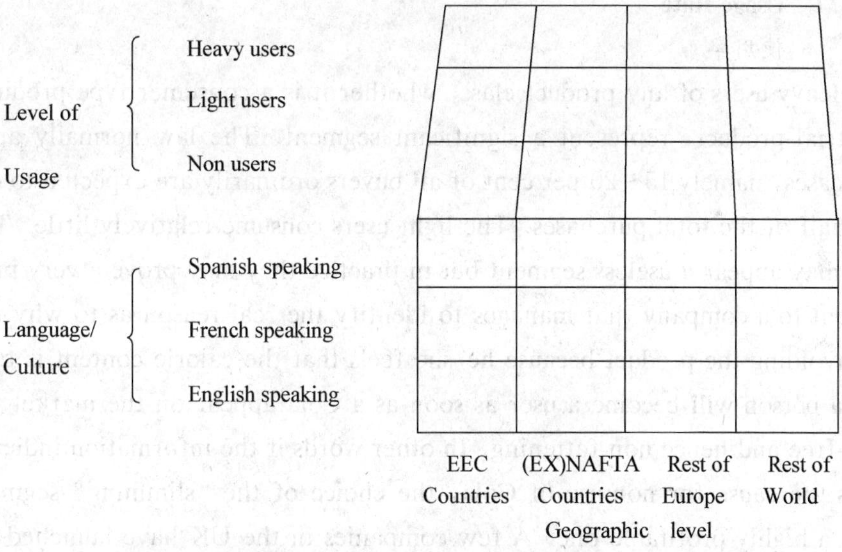

Figure 4 - 1 Segmentation by Geography, Language, Culture and Usage

In this illustration, which is highly simplified, the world market is segmented by geography, by language (and culture) and by usage rate. Altogether in this illustration there are $4 \times 3 \times 3 = 36$ segments. Each segment represents a possible opportunity area and has to be appraised and measured with the view of assessing whether it offers a worthwhile submarket area for commercial exploitation. Other parameters can be chosen or added thus increasing the number of permutations. Where the number of dimensions exceeds three is not possible to illustrate the various combinations in a graphical form. It is still possible, however, to list them in a non-pictorial way. By using this approach to segmentation it is possible not only to identify a profitable geographic segment but also combine it with another dimension of significance to the company's marketing strategy. One may finish in this illustration with a certain part of the world which is specifically, say, French speaking and where the population tend to be high users of the company's product. This may represent a small portion of the world but in commercial terms may mean the best use of the company's resources and strengths as identified by the planning process.

4.1.5 Consumer Behavioral Patterns
消费者行为结构

Under this heading a large number of variables can be considered assuitable bases for segmenting markets. It must be emphasized that no attempt is being made here to list all the available alternatives; the aim is purely to list a number of useful ways in which markets and consumers can be segmented.

4.1.5.1 Usage Rate
使用率

Heavy users of any product class, whether it is a consumer type product or an industrial product, represent a significant segment. The law normally applies to most cases, namely 15～20 per cent of all buyers ordinarily are expected to consume over half of the total purchases. The light users consume relatively little. The non-users may appear a useless segment but in practice they may prove a very profitable segment to a company that manages to identify the real reason as to why the non-user avoiding the product because he/she feels that the calorie content is too high. Such a person will become a user as soon as a Cola appear on the market which is sugar-free and hence non-fattening. In other words if the information indicates that this is the cause for non-use of Cola, the choice of the "slimming" segment may prove a highly profitable one. A few companies in the UK have launched a whole series of dietetic foods such as sugar-free biscuits and chocolate. This is an interesting way to segment the market especially for companies that wish to escape from the rigors of competition which prevail in the branded biscuit and chocolate business.

Figure 4 - 2 illustrates the relative importance of the non-user, light user and heavy user segments in the U. S. in relation to a number of product categories purchased by American households. The details show the significance of the heavy user segment. These details only relate to consumption pattern in the USA. Similar analysis in other markets may show important differences especially in relation to the non-user group. Such data must be carefully studied and understood because they may yield useful ideas as to the marketing strategy that the company should adopt in its international operations.

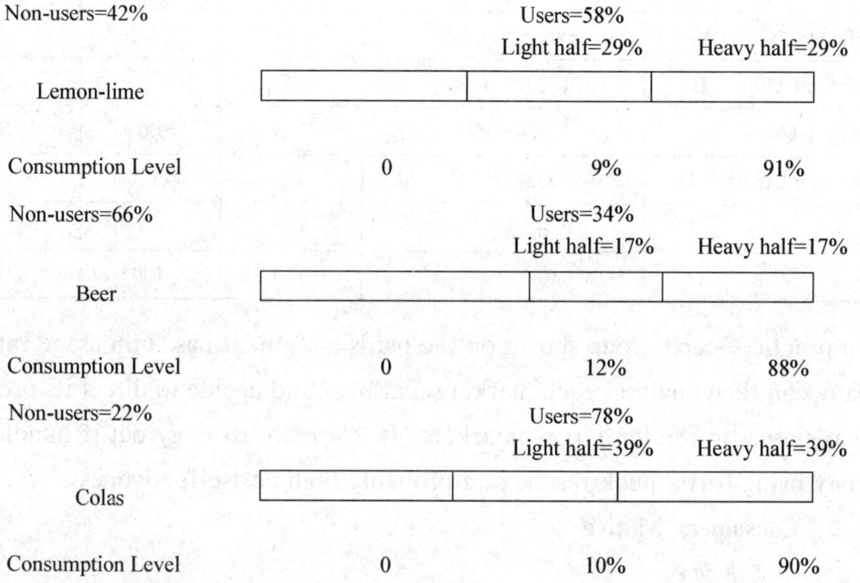

Figure 4 - 2 Usage Pattern of A few Products in USA

The marketing profile analysis can provide a lot of the information that the marketer will require in this connection. If the marketing manager of a wallpaper manufacturing company discovers that 95 percent of the consumers in Turkey do not use wallpaper he/she must try to understand the underlying reasons may be such a high non-user pattern before he decides to abandon Turkey. The reasons may be such that a good marketing effort could overcome them to the supplier's great benefit. If, on the other hand, the main reason is the lack of purchasing power coupled with the disastrous housing shortage, no marketing skill could overcome such a constraint.

In the case of industrial products data about past purchases are a useful indication of the customers' buying habits to buy in the future. The usage rate is an important basis upon which to segment one's marketing program. In industrial marketing, a company's dependence on a small number of customers can be even more critical than in the case of consumer products, in so far as the market is usually narrower, in the sense that a far smaller number of customers exist in the marketplace. It is therefore possible for a company to list its customers in a "usage" ranking as illustrated in Table 4 - 1.

Table 4-1 Segregation by Usage Ranking

Group	Annual consumption in units	Number of customers	% of Total customers	% of Total no. units sold
Heavy Users—A	exceeding 2000	8	5	38
Medium Users—B	1,000~1,999	22	13	28
Light Users—C	100~999	102	60	30
Occasional Users—D	Under 100	38	22	4
		—	—	—
		170	100	100

In practice, each group shown on the list is a segment based on usage rate. The company can then analyses each market separately and decide to direct its product to the heavy users in the ten largest markets. It is a risky strategy but if handled with care may bring forth quick results and probably high cost-effectiveness.

4.1.5.2 Consumers' Motive

消费者动机

A market can be segregated by the motives that propel the customers to the buying act. A host of motives operate in a person's buying decision process. These motives differ between one buyer and another, between one nation and another and between one culture and another. It's impossible to extrapolate motives from one market to another without an in-depth study.

Motives are extremely important in understanding the marketing ecology of different markets and hence in determining the segments available for the most profitable exploitation. We saw earlier that sewing machines are purchased in different parts of the world for either satisfaction of physiological need as a motive, or as a hobby satisfaction motives, or as a status symbol, a purely emotive reason.

In a study of the watch market the researcher was able to divide the market quantitatively on the basis of the following motivational options:

(1) Approximately 23 percent of the buyers bought for lowest price.

(2) Another 46 percent bought for durability and general product quality.

(3) And 31 percent bought watches as symbol of some important occasion.

With such eat a watch company can decide which segment is the most profitable within its specific physical and marketing resources. Rolex have opted for the "leaders of the world" segment. It is not clear as to what Rolex mean by this expression but presumably this segment includes those who project characteristics of leadership, as well as those who fancy themselves as leaders-in other words the status seekers. Once such a segment has been selected as the company's main target group every ingredient of marketing mix is influenced by such a decision. The price will reflect the prestigious nature of the product; the prom, and we will appear in suitable media and the message will also reflect the "snobbish" favorite of the product; distribution will take place through equally "high class" channels.

In contrast Timex have undoubtedly close a different segment for their marketing objectives—the cost conscious, rational consumers who buy a watch as a device for time—keeping purposes only.

4.1.5.3 The Adoption Process

接受过程

The "adoption process" can offer a highly creative basis for segmenting markets. People respond at a difference to the stimulus of new products or concepts. Behaviorally a number of individual buyers tend to respond favorable to any kind of innovation—as soon as they perceive a new product they desire it. These are the kind of people who would purchase a digital watch the minute it is launched. At the other extreme one encounters the so-called "laggards". These are the kind of individuals who resist change and in marketing terms they only respond to a product when it has been on the market for a long time, sometimes when the product has in fact reached the end of its life cycle.

Between these two extremes one finds other adoption characteristics of varying intensity. Five adoption segments normally exist and can be summarized in Table 4-2.

Table 4-2 Adoption Categories and Segregation

Possibilites Adoption Category	Percentage (%)	Typical Characteristics
Innovations	2.5	Venturesome; prepared to experiment; higher social; status; higher income group; urban
Early Adopters	13.5	Same as the "innovators" but less venturesome
Early majority	34	Display less leadership than previous two; avoid risk; rural rather than urban types; active in community life
Late Majority	34	Conservative; imitators; extra cautious; dislike change; older; lower income group; less prestigious occupations; more oriented to local contacts
Laggards	16	"Isolate"; stubbornly resist change; unimaginative

The significant of this type of segmentation can be of considerable interactional value. An example from the pharmaceutical industry can illustrate the point. Doctors can be easily divided into the five adoption categories listed above. A well-known company in the pharmaceutical business decided of examine the prescribing habits of the doctors that can be categorized more easily into four segmentation groups:

(1) Innovators. These are doctors who normally prescribe a pharmaceutical product as soon as it first appears on the market.

(2) Early Adopters. These are doctors who wait for a while before they venture to try the new drug. They want to read the results of clinical test before prescribing.

(3) Late Adopters. This segment is slow to adopt modern drugs and reluctant to change from existing prescribing habits. They adopt a new product under some social and professional pressure.

(4) Laggards. These are the extra cautious, professionally isolated doctors who stubbornly resist change. Their adoption of a drug may occur so late that the product may already have been replaced by another.

For the purpose of the study the company in question has divided the four categories into equal—size groups of 25 percent each. A comprehensive study was, conducted into the prescribing habits of doctors in a given simple and the impact of time on the volume of sales ascribed to each category monitored. The outcome of the study was most valuable. It showed that the top two segments namely the innovators and the early adopters(50 percent of the total sample) accounted for 92 percent of the company's sales. In other words the company, its products and general image appealed to the more modern-minded, more sophisticated and probably more venturesome doctors. These were segments which the company decided to develop and mountain in its domestic market, and following a similar study in the main foreign markets, adopted as target groups in its international marketing effort. In other words company geared all its marketing effort, including its are R & D, towards meeting the special requirements and expectations of the innovators and the early adopters among the world's doctors. The fact that in some countries the innovators are more conservative than in others didn't matter in the company's overall plan.

4.1.6 Other Bases for Segmentation 细分的其他因素

As stated earlier, with creativity one can consider a large number of novel segmentation possibilities. For examples:

(1) Segmentation by attitudes, taste or predispositions

(2) Personality traits

(3) Channels, patronage or store location(Where do people buy?)

(4) Sensitivity to pricing or advertising policies

(5) Original equipment or own label merchandise

4.2 Conditions for Making Segmentation 市场细分的条件

企业在计划和实施市场细分时需要考虑以下条件:

(1) 市场的规模,要保持该市场的可衡量性,以及企业的覆盖能力

(2) 可赢利性

(3) 可进入性

It is normally suggested that before one can determine whether a segmentation strategy is worthwhile one must fulfill three fundamental conditions.

4.2.1 The Size of Each Segment 市场规模

Under consideration the size of each segment must be measurable. The market must make sure that sufficient data is available about the segment in question or, alternatively, that an appropriate measurement methodology exists. To select a segmentation policy in circumstances which make measurement impossible or too costly may defeat the whole purpose of such a strategy, the optimization of resources.

In international marketing this condition is of paramount importance in so far as there is little point selecting a specific segmentation policy if the measurability of the segments under consideration is problematic. A manufacturer of drills tried to market his products to the "do-it-yourself" segment in world markets. He knew the size of this segment in European markets but found it impossible to measure the size of this segment in most countries outside Europe. Measurement of the cement would have cost a fortune—far in excess of the eventual hoped for rewards.

4.2.2 Yielding Adequate Returns 可盈利性

As a corollary of everything that was saidhitherto the signal and to selected must be such that if you can yield adequate returns. In other words must be substantial enough to be profitable. This is simply a basic question of common sense. The trouble is that marketers that have been bitten by the segmentation bug, often tend to indulge in excessive segmentation; this in turn may mean that segments selected, although creative to the extreme, are too small to earn an adequate return on the effort involved.

4.2.3 The Segment Must Be Accessible 可进入性

Finally the marketer must make sure that a segment chosen can be reached in an effective manner; it must be accessible. The institutional bodies that facilitate the marketing process must be in existence. Channels of distribution must exist in the marketplace; promotional media must be available; the type of selling that one would propose to use must be acceptable. It would be senseless to select a segment which calls for an efficient retail distribution where such a system just does not exist. Similarly, the marketer who chooses a segment that depends entirely on television advertising medium is not available or not likely to become available for some time.

4.3 Applying Market Segmentation to Global Market 对全球市场进行细分

对巨大的国际市场进行细分,除了市场的规模、可赢利性和可进入性之外,企业还必须考虑该细分市场的差异性,并制订相应的差异化营销战略。

In a domestic context most marketing men recognize that the choice of a marketing strategy depends to a great extent on whether a decision to segment has been taken. Broadly speaking three marketing strategies are available to the domestic marketer: undifferentiated marketing, differentiated marketing, and concentrated marketing.

In the case of undifferentiated marketing the company places on the market one product and seeks to draw as many consumers as possible with one uniformed and standardized marketing mix. It ignores the existence of specific segments with special needs and demands. In the case of differentiated marketing the company modifies the product and the supportive mix ingredients to appeal to a number of submarkets. Through such a differentiation the company hopes to satisfy a larger number of segments and their specific needs and desires. In the third situation concentrated marketing, the company isolates one or more segments for special treatment and concentrates the total effort on these limited submarkets.

These three strategies apply with equal relevance to world markets. The only thing which is different is the dimension of the total market and each segment. At one end of the spectrum one encounters the company that decides sales to derive most of its sales from the domestic markets and tends to regard sales abroad as grist to the mill only. Such a company adopts an undifferentiated or standardized approach. It realizes full well that through differentiation it could achieve a greater penetration of its markets, but it opts for the more cost-effective strategy viz. standardization.

At the other extreme one meets the company that chooses to satisfy as many consumers in world markets as possible. This is achieved through a differentiated marketing strategy. The company has identified a host of needs and it has embarked on the gargantuan and costly task of attempting to gear the product, the promotion activity, the distribution policy, the price and the selling effort to each country or each sub-market. This often leads to a gradual decentralization of effort so as to bring the marketing activity closer to the market place. Sooner or later each sub-market becomes a self-contained marketing entity. This is why one often associates differentiation in international marketing with decentralization.

It is normally true to say that differentiated marketing, whether it is applied within a domestic market or is extended to world markets, tends to be sales orientated rather than profit orientated. If Coca-Cola. Decided to adjust all the ingredients of the marketing mix to every sub-market, it would soon find itself producing scores of flavors in dozens of different bottles or packs. The advertising effort would differ enormously from country to country; the pricing policy would be in a state of anarchy and distribution strategy would be a logistical maze. On the other band Coca-Cola would probably sell more but at what extra cost? In fact, the product cease to be Coca-Cola; it would become a host of differentiated products-each market would have a specially. Designed, flavored and bottled beverage produced and marketed by a company belonging to or associated with Coca-Cola.

The third strategy open to international marketer, as mentioned earlier, is concentrated marketing. The first two strategies, differentiated and undifferentiated, imply that the marketer goes after the whole market. Whilst the undifferentiated strategy aims at maximum sales with one single mix, the differentiated strategy is based on the acceptance of changes in the product and the mix to satisfy different requirements. The concentrated marketing approach is based on a decision to achieve a maximum penetration of one or more segments to the exclusion of the rest of the market. Instead of spreading itself thinly may parts of the world, it decides to concentrate its forces on a few clearly-defined areas. The company tries to reach a strong position in those countries or sub-markets—which its strengths and competences have been clearly identified. It seeks to satisfy the local consumers of such selected markets with a limited cluster of highly standardized products and marketing mixes.

This brings us to one of the sky decision areas of international marketing. How far should one differentiate in international markets? Every international marketer who has ever experienced the agonies of differentiation on a global scale would no doubt admit that standardization of marketing strategies is his deeply felt, albeit elusive, ambition. This does not mean that standardization is the best strategy in all circumstances. There are situations where standardization, with or without concentrated marketing, could mean a complete failure. The concept that the international marketer must appreciate is that before selecting a strategy it is necessary to gauge which approach is likely to help the company to achieve its over all objectives. Obviously standardization coupled with concentrated marketing is attractive in effectiveness terms but if it fails to attain corporate objectives it must be avoided. In other words one cannot be doctrinaire in this respect and state categorically that one strategy is to be preferred over another.

The first ingredient required in choosing the right strategy is information quantified data about one's international markets. Inadequate knowledge of international markets usually leads to the abdication of marketing decisions to local management and this in turn means that the opportunity to standardize the marketing mix has been lost. Decentralization has its place in international marketing and in certain situations it is highly desirable but it must not occur through an omission to plan the company's strategies or by accident.

It was suggested with some emphasis that the essential "input" that the international marketer requires is comprehensive knowledge of the various markets in which the company hopes to operate. The marketing profile analysis which we discussed atsome length earlier is an excellent starting point. It must be assembled with great care and with systematic thoroughness. It is a tedious process but should yield rich rewards. Each profile analysis represents, together with its supportive schedules, a "thumbnail" sketch of each market. With such information it is possible to determine which markets lend themselves to a single, standardized approach and which do not. Alternatively, it should be possible to separate the many markets into a small cluster of territories capable of being handled in a homogeneous way, thus reducing the marketing mixes to a manageable number. By the end of such an exercise one should find oneself in the position of selecting one of two strategies. In the first place develop a concentrated strategy in relation to a "hand-picked" cluster of markets and devote all one's energy and resources towards the full exploitation of this cluster of markets. In the second place one can adopt a limited differentiation policy with a small but manageable number of "mixes"—each mix applied to a clearly defined cluster of markets, countries or regions.

The concepts of undifferentiated marketing differentiated marketing and concentrated marketing are illustrated in relation to world markets. It will be readily noticed that concentrated marketing can easily drift into a differentiated strategy if allowed to develop into an excessive number of packages.

The essence of concentrated marketing is the deliberate limitation of the marketing effort to what one considers the most profitable segment in world markets. The minute one broadens the number of segments, one inevitably tends to embark on a differentiation policy. In other words differentiation commences as soon as the company decides to accommodate the special needs of its various markets. Further more, a company may adopt a concentrated approach in one part of the world and differentiate lavishly in another part. In this book the term concentrated marketing is applied to situations where the company has a small number of marketing assemblages in relation to rationally-linked clusters of markets.

The idea behind is that with adequate information one should be able to "pair" markets that manifest similarities in their vital characteristics. Whilst onerecognizes that complete pairing is not likely to occur where foreign markets are concerned, one is prepared to accept the minor differences. Thus, for instance, Norway and Denmark are different countries. In marketing terms there is a strong case for underlying the approach to both these markets. Finland has a language and a culture which differ from the other Scandinavian cultures. Nonetheless it has enough in common with the others to justify a clustering approach when applying a concentrated marketing strategy.

The clustering approach described here presupposes that every company has one single market which can be treated as the basic "bench mark" territory. The bench mark is selected either because itrepresents the company's strongest marketing center or because it is intended to turn it into the focal point for international marketing. In other words there is no point in selecting a bench mark which does not represent a marketing opportunity in its own right. Thus if, for tax reasons, the company's headquarters are located at Liechtenstein, choosing that small country as a bench mark would be quite absurd. Similarly, there would be little point in choosing a large country like China as a bench mark in so far as in marketing terms it is yet a desert in the sense that it is neither measurable, nor fully accessible and probably in purchasing power terms not yet substantial.

The aim of the clustering method is to identify, in a somewhat qualitative way, how far other markets come close to the bench mark. The top row in Figure 4 - 3 shows once again the various elements of the mix; the left column lists the countries selected for observation. Each element of mix has a scale and in relation to each country, ranging from 0 to 9. Different scales can of course be chosen if so desired as long as they provide sufficient scope for highlighting variations. "0" on our scale implies that there is no scope for standardization in relation to the bench mark territory and the appropriate element of the mix. "9" means that standardization is perfectly feasible, probably even desirable. In between these two extremes one can insert an X at the point which seems to the international analyst most appropriate after having studied carefully the implications contained in the various marketing profile analyses. Inevitably subjective judgment creeps into this methodology. This subjectivity is at least based on a through knowledge and understanding of the facts. Ideally this method should be tackled by a group of people who are close to the marketing function; this should reduce subjectivity. An average of the various opinions expressed on the grid will be tantamount to the outcome of a "jury of informed opinion" methodology.

By its very nature the bench mark will be shown as "9" all round. Other markets are compared to the bench mark and an X inserted at a point on the scale which reflects the opinion of the analyst or the committee. The 6 - 9 illustrates the matrix completed in respect of the listed countries. One can discern at a glance those markets which enjoy some marketing similarity with the bench mark in relation to a specific product. At this point the international marketer must take an important decision that is an acceptable variation from the bench mark beyond which differentiation is inevitable. If one decides that "7" is the limit of tolerable difference for standardization to be justified one can now cluster all those markets that represent this, or a higher, level of similarity.

The 4 - 3 shows that in relation to a specific product (a domestic appliance) all the ingredients of the mix have been marked "7" or over in Germany, the Netherlands, Belgium and Switzerland. In these four markets it is now logical to

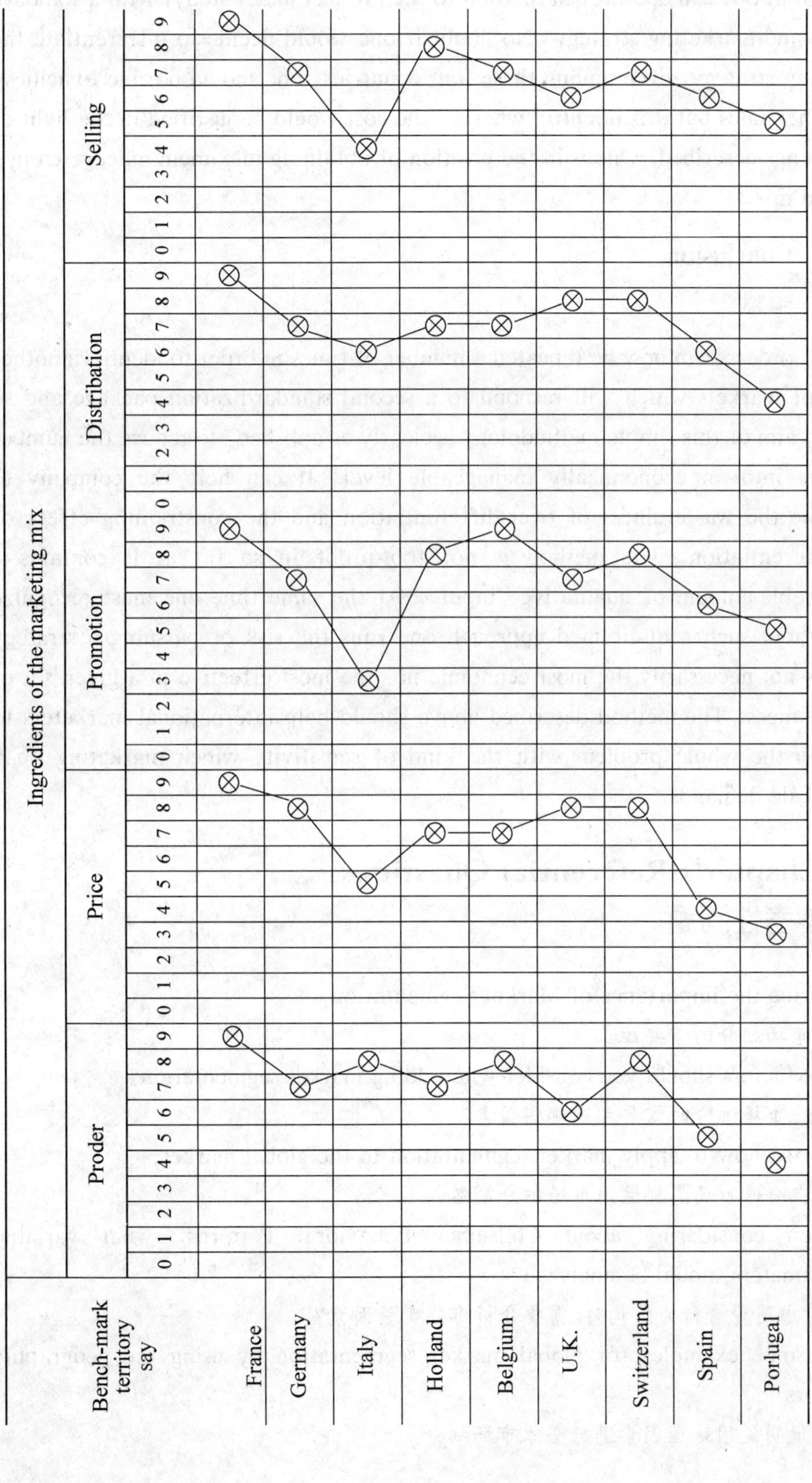

0=standardisation impossible;9=standardisation desirable.

Figure 4 – 3 Analysing Clustering Possibilities

assume that one can operate, in relation to the product under study, with a standard product and marketing strategy. No doubt if one would decide to differentiate the marketing strategy, even among these four countries, one should be able to achieve still higher sales but it is doubtful whether the cost would be justified in the light of the findings described. One is in the position of obtaining maximum mileage from a standard mix.

4.4.7 Conclusion 结语

The process can now be repeated a number of times in order to identify another cluster of markets which will respond to a second standardization package and so on. The aim of this simple methodology is clearly established: to reduce the number of mixes into an economically manageable level. It can help the company to overcome the wastefulness of over-differentiation and the constraining effect of non-differentiation. The method is not fool-proof in so far as it contains a considerable amount of qualitative "input". At the same time one must recognize that without such a disciplined approach one runs the risk of pursuing a strategy which is not necessarily the most economic nor the most effective in a given set of circumstances. The method described above should help international marketers to approach the whole problem with the kind of sensitivity which marketing on a global scale demands.

The Chapter's Referential Questions: 本章参考性问题

1. Describe the importance of Market Segmentation.
   谈谈市场细分的重要性。
2. What factors should you consider when doing market segmentation?
   在实施市场细分时需要考虑哪些因素?
3. Describe how to apply market segmentation to the global market.
   叙述在全球市场怎样运用市场细分策略。
4. When considering about Consumer Behavioral Patterns, what variable parameters should be analyzed?
   在考虑消费者行为结构时,需要分析哪些变量因素?
5. List some examples for global market segmentation by using the geographic factors.
   举例说明使用地理因素进行全球市场细分。

6. For China's High Speed Railway System entering overseas market, what types of market segmentation and positioning method should be adopted?
我国高铁打入国际市场,应该采取哪种细分模式和定位战略?
7. What is the STP strategy in international marketing theory?
什么是国际市场营销理论的 STP 策略?
8. What is the definition of the Global Market Segmentation?
全球市场细分的定义是什么?

Chapter 5 International Market Research

国际市场调研

Learning Objectives

本章学习目标

1. Methods of international marketing research
   国际市场营销调研的方法
2. Concept of international marketing research decision support system
   国际营销调研决策支持系统的概念
3. How to make sales forecasts
   如何进行销售预测

International marketing managers operating in unfamiliar environments need to have a thorough understanding of their target market if their marketing efforts are to be successful. Numerous marketing plans fail due to an incomplete understanding of the market. Companies selling consumer products are especially prone to experiencing difficulties in foreign markets. Many such examples exist: European and U.S. multinationals have entered many low and medium-income markets with large and expensive bottles of cleaning products and tubes of toothpaste, only to find that consumers will not purchase them, in spite of the fact that they prefer Western brands. As soon as those products were packaged in cheap, small sachets, consumers started purchasing large volumes. As we have seen in earlier Chapters, sales of Coke packaged in 200 ml recyclable bottles took off instantly in India. Unlike in the U. S., where 24 packs of any drink fly off the shelves, internationally, products sell better when they come in smaller packages. In fact, smaller-sized products do better in general, as the following example illustrates.

Case Studies: Living in an Apartment in Western Europe 西欧人的居住方式

It is not unusual for a European family of four to live in a one-bedroom apartment. That apartment can very well be on the fourth floor (according to U.S. floorcounting european on the third floor, counting the "European" way) in a five-story building with no elevator. Try to sell this family a package of 12 giant Bounty-brand rolls of paper towels, and they will ignore your product and go on to the next aisle. Sell them just one giant Bounty roll and they will think twice. Do they really need paper for cleaning and drying when they can use and reuse their kitchen towel? Environmentally conscious Western Europeans will think twice before they create more waste because waste is expensive and difficult to unload.

Let us assume that our Western European shoppers are at least open to the idea of using Bounty for a limited number of jobs. Where will they store this giant Bounty? Kitchens are tiny, so hanging a roll above the sink will impede access to the sink, and counter-tops, in principle, have to be free to allow for any food preparation.

Western European apartments are not unique. In Japan, many apartments are small, with just 500 square feet and paper-thin walls. Storage space is limited and products are best sold in small quantities. In Japan, as in Europe, products for the consumer market should be smaller in size. Procter & Gamble did not take into consideration woman's needs for a thinner diaper due to high frequency of changes and limited Storage space, and their market share was quickly eroded by a local competitor that provided thinner diapers that were in line with market demands.

Companies must conduct research in their local markets to understand consumers, their needs and wants, and consumption patterns. This chapter defines marketing research and examines its broad scope across all components of the marketing mix (product, place, price, and promotion). The chapter addresses the international marketing research process and the complexities of the process in an international setting.

5.1 The Need for International Market Research 国际市场调研的需求

《孙子·谋政》:知彼知己者,百战不殆。只有通过科学的市场调研,才能做到熟悉海外目标市场。由于国际市场调研非常复杂,营销人员可能会遇到与本国国情大不相同的问题和困难。

Marketing managers need to constantly monitor the different forces affecting their international operations. Marketing information, which should constitute a basis for all executive action, must be taken into consideration to improve the chances of success in a complex global environment. Such information, although amply available in highly developed, industrialized nations, needs to be carefully evaluated and viewed in light of the purpose for which it was collected. In developing countries, relevant data may not be available at all, and if available, it is often questionable in terms of both quality and integrity. For example, production and sales data reported may be tainted by pressures of governments on factories to exceed unrealistic plans or production quotas.

International marketing research is especially complex. International managers are likely to encounter not only the obstacles they have learned to master when conducting research in their own countries, but also obstacles laden with the specifics of the international market where they are conducting the research, specifics that may differ substantially from those of their national market. Consider, for instance, a male marketing researcher working for a hair care firm interested in launching its lines in the beauty salons of the Middle East. In the United States, it is perfectly appropriate for this individual to assess interest in the company's product line by collecting data in beauty salons. In most countries in the Middle East, however, Woman's Beauty Parlors cater exclusively to women (Man's Barber Shops cater exclusively to men), and the presence of males in this environment would constitute a breach of Islamic law, which forbids males from seeing a woman's hair if they are not closely related.

Another aspect of the difficulty of engaging in research internationally is readily observable in Eastern Europe, where consumers remain suspicious of attempts by foreigners and locals to investigate local markets and related consumer behavior. Consumers are simple not accustomed to responding to opinion polls and regard such attempts as an intrusion or as suspect. And, since the transition to a market economy, prospective respondents are also likely to promptly demand payment for any time and effort demanded by the investigation.

These and many other environmental factors encountered in international marketing research complicate the task of marketing researchers, who should have not only an expertise in the most advanced techniques of scientific inquiry, but also a profound understanding of the markets under investigation.

5.2 Defining the International Marketing Research 国际市场调研的定义

国际市场调研是指系统地设计、搜集、记录、分析、整合和报告与本企业国际化运营中的特定营销决策有关的数据和信息。

We define international marketing research as follows:

International marketing research is the systematic design, collection, recording, analysis, interpretation, and reporting of information pertinent to a particular marketing decision facing a company operating internationally.

This definition of international marketing research contains a caveat also present in the general definition of marketing research: an acquired understanding of the market environment. In an international setting, the environment is particularly complex, and it displays obvious and important subtle differences in culture, religion, customs and business practices, and general market characteristics from the environment of the company's home country.

5.3 The Scope of International Marketing Research 国际市场调研的范围

国际市场调研同本土市场调研相比具有更大、更广范的领域,营销人员需要用专业的方法获取额外的数据和信息,并进行分析和处理,提供给管理者制订国际营销战略。

International marketing research has a broader scope than domestic research: managers need additional information to compensate for lack of familiarity with the foreign environment. This section describes some general research categories.

5.3.1 On Industry, Market Characteristics, and Market Trends 关于行业发展、市场属性和市场趋势的调研

Studies of industry, market characteristics, and market trends, often in the form of acquisition, diversification, and market-share analyses are conducted regularly by marketing research suppliers and shared with subscribers. Export research is yet another type of research in this category; it is prompted by the shortening of the product life cycle and the intensity of international competition, as well as by the rapid technological change that increases the need to segment markets more frequently. The research techniques range from formal methods, such as focus groups and concept testing, to more informal approaches.

Table 5 - 1 Types of International Marketing Research

Research of Industry, Market Characteristics, and Market Trends
Buyer behavior Research
Product Research
Distribution Research
Promotion Research
Pricing Research

5.3.2 Buyer Behavior Research 关于购买行为

Examining brand preferences and brand attitudes falls into the category of buyer behavior research. To the uninformed, Chinais an emerging market that cannot afford many luxuries. However, buyer behavior research found that the Chinese luxury market is growing, and this market is demanding. Researchers at General Motors (GM) know that well. The following is Eastern European and Chinese cosmetics consumer segments.

Russians want to impress at any price; Russian women focus primarily on outward appearance and strive to make a bold personal statement. They spend heavily on cosmetics: many twenty-something professionals spend \$ 300 a month on cosmetics and even students manage to spend \$ 150 in spite of little or no income. In fact, Russia spends 1.3 percent of GDP on cosmetics and toiletries double what Western Europeans spend. Russian women have high awareness of and receptivity to Western brands. Russian women desire opulence and are drawn to audacious retail environments. In line with these research findings, brands such as Olay are marketed as prestige brands, rather than products for the mass market strategy used in Western Europe and the United States.

In comparison, Polish women are more concerned with products that make a difference from the inside out. They desire Western cosmetics which are heavily advertised, but they are also price conscious and have high ethnocentric purchase tendencies; consequently, much of their cosmetics expenditure goes to domestic brands. They expect retailers to be knowledgeable about the cosmetics they sell.

Chinese cosmetics segments, on the other hand, are receptive to different strategies. They prefer less color and simple graphics and typography. White is the preferred color for all skin products because it projects luminescence and clarity of skin. Black is acceptable as well, as an indicator of quality and brand status. Consumers enjoy going through skin care regimens and rituals, unlike Western women, who have less patience for rituals. They also respond better to prestige messages than Western consumers.

Case Studies: Cadillac in China 凯迪拉克在中国

General Motors conducted extensive buyer behavior research in China to find that luxury consumers responded well to special treatment. Its Chinese dealerships greet visitors with cigars and Napa Valley wines on black-marble bars, VIP rooms with leather sofas, and movie shots of the brand. GM has done well with Buick and Chevrolet, and now it is ready for a sales offensive that will ensure that Cadillac will succeed in this market. Cadillac is expensive because the Chinese government adds a 25 percent import tax. Models sold in China are 4 inches longer than the U. S. model, which is in deference to Chinese customers who tend to have chauffeurs.

Buyer behavior research found that luxury automobile brands are the fastest growing segment in the Chinese market and that consumers desire luxury-brand automobiles and related accessories.

Consumers in China tend to go for established luxury brands, such as Rolls Royce, BMW, Audi, and, very likely, Cadillac. In fact, in most Asian countries, uncertainty is strongly avoided, resulting in high brand consciousness, brand loyalty, greater insistence on quality, and consumers' active reliance on reference groups and opinion leaders. People tend to shop in groups, and they are slower to accept new products. Whereas consumers worldwide are concerned about monetary, functional, physical, psychological, and social risks, Asians tend to be more sensitive to social risk than Westerners.

Brand awareness research and purchase behavior studies are often conducted by companies to assess their position in the market. Hilton hotels, in an attempt to change the way customers perceive them, engaged in a worldwide study of brand awareness of the Hilton brands, including its limited service offerings.

Case Studies: Hilton Hotels 希尔顿酒店

Hilton Hotels Corp. aims to create a truly global company and expand the Hilton brand in Asia, Europe, and the Middle East. In China and India, it is partnering with companies to convert underutilized office buildings and retail space into limited-service, home-away-from-home type hotels, such as the Hilton Garden Inn, Hampton Inn, and Double Tree hotel. In China, it stood ready to meet the lodging needs of the 2008 Olympics. In Europe, it is also focusing on the limited-service sector, where comparable, lower-service hotels are nonexistent.

Hilton studied consumer hotel perceptions worldwide and brand awareness of its own Hilton brand. In Europe, it found that, except for resorts, consumers perceive them as expensive and snooty, with hired doormen to keep out riff-ruff. Accordingly, many Europeans are unaccustomed to staying in hotels in the first place. Based on the studies, Hilton believes that limited-service hotels could do the most to create brand loyalty among travelers. The company is working to change consumer awareness of the broader Hilton brand, and to position their limited-service offerings as an extension of the home, without an imposing exterior and without the grand entrance.

Other useful studies that belong to this category are consumer segmentation studies, which are conducted to identify market segments. Such studies are also used to identify profiles of heavy product consumers and occasions for consumption. Cosmetics companies, for example, have conducted research looking at emerging market cosmetics consumers in Eastern Europe and China. The segments behave differently when it comes to Cosmetics, as the following examples illustrate, and cosmetics companies need to devise marketing strategies accordingly.

5.3.3 Product Research 产品调研

Concept development and testing studies are usually performed in developed countries by the firms' research and development departments. When going international, firms usually already have a successful product to bring to the marketplace, nevertheless, it is still important that they evaluate the product/service they offer and the related marketing mix in light of the different regional and local target markets. And, although the initial concept development and testing studies are performed in high-income countries, increasingly, they are bring performed in important emerging target markets, such as China.

Brand name generation and testing is used not only in the consumer goods industry, where its importance is obvious, but also in companies that have traditionally marketed their products regionally, such as agricultural goods companies. These companies need to test brand names when they market their products internationally. The annals of marketing are replete with examples illustrating the importance of testing a brand name in different countries.

Product testing identifies the extent to which the product conforms to local tastes. For example, PepsiCo Foods International decided to undertake extensive product testing in China before introducing its Cheetos snack food brand. The outcome of the rest was not favorable: Respondents indicated that they did not like the cheesy taste of the snack. As a result, PepsiCo's local joint-venture, Guangzhou Frito-Lay, decided to get rid of the cheese and replace it with cream and steak flavors. Sales increased dramatically.

Other types of studies that would be appropriate are competitive product studies, which are helpful in determining the overall product strategy for the product, the price that the market will bear for the respective product category, the promotion that is appropriate in light of the competition, and so on.

As for product packaging design studies, firms need to take into consideration consumer's reaction to the package, the extent to which the package adequately communicates information to the consumer, and the distribution implications of the packaging decisions. For instance, in many emerging markets, packaging distinguishes between local products and international products. In the Czech Republic, Poland, and Romania, many local dairy products are available in recyclable glass jars, have no brand name (just the product name, such as yogurt, kefir, etc.), and may contain only the dairy's address information. International products, on the other hand, come in colorful, sophisticated, disposable packaging. To the local consumers, however, simple packaging represents freshness and a lack of additives, after researching this phenomenon, Tesco Extra, the U. K. hypermarket, is selling its Tesco brand packaged in the same no-frills packaging.

The choice of package color is another important dimension that necessitates researching. One color could have different meanings in different countries: green signifies abundance in North Africa and the Middle East, disease in the Amazon region, and healthful contents in North America and Western Europe. In Western Europe, bio (organic-type) foods are most often presented in green packaging.

In another example, Primus, a Belgian beer manufactured under license in Rwanda, is sold in 1-liter bottles, rather than in the 33 cl bottles that most other Western beers use in this market. In researching the Rwandan market, Primus found that the Rwandan consumer typically drinks beer at night, sharing with family and friends. Research also showed that beer is usually purchased and transported on foot for distances of 1 or 2 Kilometers. Consequently, the bottles are typically sold in crates of 12 fitted such that they could be easily transported on one's head, allowing the individual to also carry other goods.

Test marketing is another important research procedure belonging to the product research category. Procter & Gamble test marketed Swiffer, a disposable mop, in Cedar Rapids, Iowa, and Sens, France, among other international markets. The company hoped to craft an international new-product success with the goal of evaluating whether a consistent brand image could be achieved in a number of major markets. This research was the first step in the company's strategy to introduce the product worldwide in 18 months, rather than in the traditional 4 to 5 years.

5.3.4 Distribution Research 分销渠道调研

The distribution function is particularly important in international marketing, where special attention should be given to import /export regulations and practices, and where companies are well advised to engage in comprehensive analyses. For example, import /export analyses aid companies in identifying the logistics companies most capable of handling the paperwork and getting products through customs in a timely and cost-effective manner. Federal and state governments in the United States are often instrumental in helping with this type of research.

Researching individual exporter and importer expertise and the firm's local influence are crucial to the success of the firm in a particular market. In one example, a private shipper from the U. S. firm attempted to export older, high-quality Louis XV armchairs from Romania to the United States. In the process, the firm obtained the appropriate documentation from the State Patrimonium Commission, attesting to the fact that these armchairs were not antiques or important local historical artifacts. However, the large local export company (a vestige of the former communist firm called ROMTRANS) encountered obstacles involving the local customs office that prevented it from exporting the armchairs. Only after contacting a different and much smaller firm, owned by a well-connected former government official, was it possible to export the armchairs. This same influential firm arranged for the chairs to be shipped via the Romanian airlines directly to New York at a fraction of the cost of the shipment quote from the initial top shipping firm, by ship. Had the U.S. shipper researched the local import/export service providers, it would have found that influence is crucial in facilitating shipments.

Trade with Turkmenistan serves as an example of the importance of researching specific requirements imposed on importers by the local government. The government of Turkmenistan tightly monitors all foreign trade through the State Commodity and Raw Materials Exchange. All import and export contracts must be registered with the exchange at a 0.3 percent commission. According to foreign companies, connections with someone holding a seat on the exchange facilitate regulation.

Consider another example. Kazakhstan is a small but growing market for U.S. consumer goods. Distributing products in this large and sparsely populated country is a challenge. Geography and the inexperience of local wholesale distributors require exporters of consumer products to pay close attention to developing and maintaining a distributor network in this region—a task that is not easy to implement. Most of the population is located in two areas: the southeast, around Almaty, and the north and northeast, the republic's industrial and mining centers. Some existing infrastructure already supports distribution. An extensive railway network carries products within Kazakhstan, to other newly independent states (NIS), and to Europe. On the other hand, poor roads and bad telecommunications, when combined with geography, make it virtually impossible to rely on just one regionally based distributor. Smaller foreign companies may wish to start with a small, regionally located distributor and gradually build a countrywide network from there. Larger firms may consider a larger up-front investment to establish their own infrastructure in Kazakhstan.

Another important type of study is that of channel performance and coverage studies, which may reveal either that channels need to be further developed at significant expense to the company, or that, in certain markets, particular channels dominate much of the activity in a particular area. In Japan, channel performance research reveals that the dominant firms who can offer the most effcient and broad distribution for the firms that can afford their high fees are large trading companies, such as Mitsui and Mitsubishi. This research also finds that distribution in Japan is multilayered, with many distributors involved at each level. Much channel performance and coverage research has been conducted to data by U. S. multinationals in Asia to devise ways in which to adjust U. S. distribution practices to better fit with local market practices.

Finally, plant/warehouse location studies are important, as are evaluations of the transport infrastructure (roads, shipping, and warehousing infrastructure). In countries with an underdeveloped infrastructure or a mountainous terrain, warehousing is available only in the main cities or just in the capital city. Consequently, distribution to a more remote location is complicated, and firms may elect to avoid it altogether. Research in this regard is important. For example, in the case of Ecuador, transportation between the capital city, Quito, and its second largest city, Cuenca, is facilitated by the well-developed highway system between the two cities, both of which are at a high altitude. Moving products from one location to another should not present problems because the transportation infrastructure is adequate and warehousing facilities exist in both cities. If, however, a firm is to transport goods to Guayaquill from the capital city, it is likely to encounter difficulties because the transportation infrastructure between these two locations is complicated by the terrain. Guayaquill is easily accessible by sea—the route taken by most imported goods and services aimed at the islands' tourist market. Goods from Quito are more likely to be transported by air than by truck.

5.3.5 Promotion Research
促销调研

Promotion research is crucial for companies doing business internationally. By doing such research, the firm evaluates the extent to which it effectively communicates with the market, it ensures that certain promotional strategies are appropriate for that particular market, and, finally, it evaluates the extent to which the local media are appropriate for developing the intented message.

First, in terms of studies of premiums, coupons, and deals, it is important to identify the practices in each country where the specific promotion will run. When an agency has developed an idea to run in a number of countries, it first needs to check on the legality of premiums and coupons across those markets, As European Union(EU) countries are relaxing their limits on consumer promotions to align their retail policies with those of the EU, IKEA decided to introduce a loyalty program. It conducted a full year of testing of an innovative family-loyalty promotion, testing the family club card in the United Kingdom. It offered cardholders a 25 percent discount on selected "family" products in the store—for example, bicycle helmets, luggage, silverware, and bathroom accessories. The goal for the card was to also create a useful vehicle for direct marketing. After the year-long test of the card, the company decided to launch the promotion across Europe.

Some examples of family card promotions are 9 euros for a lamp table that normally costs 25 euros, a 24-piece silverware set for 1.49 euros, and 11euros for two children's tennis rackets. IKEA even has a magazine publication called IKEA Family Live, which is supposed to cost 1.75 Euros but is actually available for free, promoting the family card and living with IKEA products. The magazine carries advertising from Hilton Hotels for family deals and other travel-related advertising.

It is important to determine whether consumers are likely to respond to promotions as expected, In the recent past, it was a challenge to engage in promotional activities in Eastern Europe because consumers were not accustomed to entering competitions and sending off coupons. However, these consumers are becoming gradually more receptive to promotional strategies. In the EU, consumers are keen on in-store promotions, going shopping in droves to take part in competitions for free product giveaways and the like. In Latin America, research conducted by ACNielsen in Argentina, Brazil, Chile, Colombia, and Mexico found that the diverse consumers had diverse reactions to consumer promotions, but that, in general, promotions clouded price perception accuracy for consumers, acting as a driving force for the increase in the bargain-hunting segments.

Advertising effectiveness research is often conducted to examine the effectiveness and appropriateness of advertisements aimed at individual markets. Frequently, ads that are initially developed for home-country markets and tested there are later used abroad; such ads are frequently dubbed and do not fit with the culture of the local environments where they are broadcast. Tailoring the ads to the local market will always pay off, but it is more expensive.

Advertising must appeal to the target customer to be considered effective. In one example, Switzerland's tourism authority launched an advertising campaign aimed at soccer widows (women temporarily abandoned by their husband spectators). The ads showed beefy, waxed men in various states of undress performing uniquely Swiss tasks, forking hay at the farm, sawing logs, milking cows. In the ad, Switzerland invites women to visit because Swiss men would pay more attention to them. What the ad created was, in fact, a homegrown version of the Village People, and it ended up attracting more gay men as a result. The ad was effective in promoting tourism to Switzerland, but not in the way the tourism authority had intended.

Media research also is important. In particular, it is important to determine the appropriate media outlets for advertising the company's products. In many countries, television advertising is broadcast only in between programs, rather than at 10-minute intervals as in the United States, and consumers often use the advertising time to take a break from television. In many developing countries, the primary television channel is government owned and often will not broadcast advertising for consumer products and they might advertise programming and city events, but they might not offer commercial advertising opportunities.

Researchers do not always have access to information regarding programming audiences. They can find out who are the formal cable subscribers or satellite dish users, but not necessarily all the viewers. In Germany, for example, many purchase a digital box to append to the television set (for about \$ 30) and are able to receive numerous subscription programs. Thus, even though satellite dishes dominate the apartment landscape, research cannot possibly identify the millions of users of digital boxes and understand their viewing behavior.

Finally, studies pertaining to personal selling activities, such as sales force compensation, quota, and territory studies, are crucial in helping to determine the appropriate strategies for different markets. Even the highly industrialized countries witha translation of a well-trained sales force have deficits with regard to sales force compensation. For example, sales research in the electronic component supply industry shows great dissatisfaction with sales operations among salespeople in Europe, as seen in the following discussion.

Case Studies: Sales Commissions in Europe
欧洲的销售佣金

Many electronic component suppliers are encountering disappointing results from their sales operations in Europe. First, there has been a mass exodus of production to China. Second, many are still using the same geographic orientation and sales commission structures they had in place in the late 1990s, which have added to their costs and eroded the motivation of their salespeople. European component suppliers need to develop a worldwide structure and a more logical and consistent approach to determining and awarding sales commissions. Otherwise, Europe will be squandering its last chance to remain a major player in high-tech industry.

For example, design centers, where purchasing decisionsoften start, tend to be far from manufacturing centers, where parts orders are scheduled and shipments are received. Thus, it is difficult to determine which sales team should receive a commission and how much it should earn. To deal with this problem, the companies split the commission among different regions based on complex and arbitrary methods. As a result, sales staff motivation suffers.

5.3.6 Pricing Research Internationally 国际市场价格调研

Pricing research is much more problematic than when it is performed locally, in a developed country. In addition to studies projecting demand, such as international market potential studies, sales potential studies, sales forecasts, cost analyses, profit analyses studies, price elasticity studies, and competitive pricing analyses, which are typical of most pricing research studies conducted by U.S. firms. In the United States, the firms also must look at issues regarding countertrade and currency issues, inflation rates, and a national tradition of bargaining for every translation, all of which have implications for pricing decisions. At the retail level, pricing decisions could make or break a product. In countries where salespeople typically keep the change, it is important to price the product a few pennies/centimes below the amount that can be paid using larger currency denominations. For example, for a product costing $ 10.00, pricing it at $ 9.50 will give the salesperson a $ 50 "tip" because customers would not demand change an important consideration, especially in markets where salespeople have a considerable latitude as to which product they make available to the consumer.

In industrial marketing, research in cost analysis would reveal that high product certification cost could significantly contribute to the price of a product and ultimately adversely affect its marketability. This is the case in Russia, where the lack of transparency connected with certifying products confronts both foreign and domestic companies. Although such companies are awaiting political solutions to these problems, marketers should be aware and plan ahead for certification. Often, the process may be cumbersome. Generally, there is some choice among the certification centers inside and outside Russia that are accredited to certify a given type of product or equipment. In some cases, however, the product itself may fall into several categories, and two certificates may be required.

5.4 The International Marketing Research Process 国际市场调研的步骤和方法

在国际市场,营销人员会遭遇太多的问题,因此从事国际市场调研必须学习并掌握一整套科学的步骤和方法,如根据特定的问题设定调研目标、制订调研计划、确定信息来源、搜集和处理信息等。

Researchers attempting to obtain accurate and reliable information regarding a problem experienced in the firm's international operations are likely to encounter a number of difficulties, such as translation and cross-cultural comparison complications, which do not, as a rule, affect firms engaging only in domestic research. These difficulties will be addressed for each step in the subsections titled "International Constraints".

5.4.1 Defining the Research Problem and Research Objectives 明确调研的问题和目的

The first step in the international marketing research process requires the international marketing manager and marketing researcher defining the research problem and jointly agreeing on the research objectives. The complexity of the environment of international operations does not afford marketing researchers the opportunity to have a clear idea of the specifics that the research study should examine. Instead, they may need to engage in exploratory research of the problem to define the relevant dimensions of the problem investigated. Exploratory investigations may help to further define the problem, suggest hypotheses, or even actually identify additional problems that need to be investigated, Descriptive research, on the other hand, portrays a situation-for instance, how frequently shoppers in Cairo shop for food items; whether they prefer to shop for meat products in state stores, which are cheaper but offer inferior-quality products, or in private stores, which are more expensive but offer a higher quality and assortment of meat products, Finally, causal research examines cause-and-effect relationships, such as the extent to which Sony's offer of financial incentives to electronics salespeople in Ahmadabad, India, is likely to increase sales of the Sony brand.

Managers must note that a fine line should be maintained between identifying the problem too broadly—"What are French consumers' entertainment needs?", or too narrowly—"Will enough French consumers pay an additional 4 euros to gain access to a specific American movie channel to make an investment in such a business worthwhile?" Better questions are: "What should be the price of this service in order to draw sufficient subscribers?" and "What is the interest of French audiences in the movies carried by this channel?" "To what extent would the recently rekindled anti-American feelings affect subscriptions?"

At this point, the researcher, in conjunction with the marketing manager, sets specific research objectives identifying:

(1) What is the interest of French audiences in the types of movies offered by the American movie channel?

(2) How many subscribers will the company have if the subscription costs 4 euros? 3 euros? 2 euros?

(3) Will the channel gain customers in spite of the anti-American cultural-dominance feelings in France?

5.4.2 Developing the Research Plan 制订调研计划

The research plan is a blueprint for the study, indicating all the decisions to be made with regard to information sources; research methods; data collection instruments; sampling procedures; data collection methods; data analysis; and, based on these decisions, the projected costs of the research.

5.4.3 Deciding on Information Sources 确定信息来源

After the international manager and researcher define the problem and set the objectives, the researcher must determine the extent to which available information may shed further light on the problem at hand. The researcher starts by identifying useful information pertaining to the issue that has been collected either by the company itself (internal) or by some other firm or agency (external) secondary data. The secondary data may, if needed, help the researcher more clearly define the problem and set better objectives. It also helps the researcher pinpoint the type of information that needs to be gathered for the goals articulated in section 5.4.1, "Defining the Research Problem and Research Objectives"; the data collected to address the problem at hand is known as primary data.

5.4.3.1 Functional Differentiation 关于产品功能差异

Products themselves may be used for different purposes in different country environments. Whereas, in many countries, jewelry is used to advertise status and style and to reflect concern with appearance, in countries such as India and Pakistan, jewelry is used as a way to accumulate wealth. In other examples, refrigerators might be used in the United States to chill soft drinks, whereas, in much of the world, soft drinks are consumed at room temperature or with just one ice cube. In the United States, ice is consumed in large quantities, so the refrigerators have ice makers. However, in much of the rest of the world, ice is consumed in small amounts, and ice trays are common. Compartments that are filled with water and frozen. Then, the ice is squeezed out, as needed.

In another example, coffee, in southeastern Europe and the Middle East, is the quintessential drink for socializing. It is ground finely, boiled with water in a special container called the Ibrik, and then poured into cups carefully, reserving the foam, which is added at the end. Close friends socializing over a cup of coffee might, when finished turn the cup over to read each other's fortune in the grounds. In France, making coffee, and many cigarettes later, they may still continue to socialize. In Austria and Germany, coffee is also a tradition called the kaffeehaus tradition. Smoky, elegant coffee houses pride themselves on the coffee and cakes they serve. The instant coffee popular in Britain would not work in these markets. In Asia, tea replaces coffee, and the tea ceremony is central to many cultures there. With all these traditions, it is an impressive feat that Starbucks has done so well worldwide.

Problems also are encountered when companies assume that, if individuals have a certain purchasing power, the market is ripe for time-saving devices that appeal to Western consumers. Standard of living is not necessarily an indicator of such needs, however, particularly in countries where a wide gap exists between the haves and the havents. In many middle-class and upper-class families worldwide, household work is done by hired workers, and there is little likelihood that much thought would be given to facilitating their work. Servants themselves perceive time-saving device is a threat to their job security.

In fact, the immense popularity of Western luxury goods among high-income earners and teenagers in Asia is not necessarily proof that they have joined the rest of the world's Western consumers. They may try some goods, but for different reasons, Brand name goods such as Louis Vuitton bags may be bought more for "face" reasons and the importance of the regard of others than from an individual preference for the product. Remy Martin cognac and Lafitte red wine may not be consumed because consumers really prefer it over local liquor or beer but because of peer pressure. Strong market position can therefore be built on foundations different from those in the West and require different marketing activities—in other words, an approach especially geared toward globalization but more efficient in terms of creating value for the consumers, and, as a result, earning higher returns. In yet another example, consumers shop differently worldwide. In China and the United States clearly shopping has different meanings in each of the two cultures.

5.4.3.2 Secondary Data

二手数据

Researchers first must determine whether information is available, and if so, how much. Doing so may aid in gaining insights into the problem at hand. Secondary data are defined as data collected for a problem other than the problem at hand.

Secondary data are typically examined first, and they offer the advantage of low cost and ready availability in many of the more-developed countries. Secondary data can be categorized as internal, collected by the company to address a different problem, or collected by the company to address the same problem but in a different country, or external, collected by an entity not affiliated with the company.

5.4.3.3 A Comparison between Shoppers in China and the U.S.
关于中美两国超市购物者行为的比较

ACNiclen's annual reports on Chinese shoppers' habits suggest that foreign retailers have focused on the wrong things, assuming that consumers want a one-stop shopping experience when, in fact, they do not. Mass retailers such as Carrefour SA and Wal-Mart Stores, Inc, have built hundreds of look-alike sprawling stores offering food, appliances, and housewares but met with declining sales per store and little consumer loyalty. What went wrong? These retailers built these stores around the Western one-stop, infrequent shopping concept. But Chinese consumers prefer to go daily to open-air markets selling fresh product, meat, and dry goods. In fact, these markets account for more than 80 percent of food expenditures.

Yet, when Chinese consumers do go to supermarkets, they spend more than 1 hour there, expect the experience to be relaxing and entertaining and spend relatively little money, compared with consumers in Europe and the United States. Indeed, U.S. consumers expect some entertainment, hence the success of creative supermarket retailers such as Stew Leonard's and the fun product sampling experiences provided by many retailers. However, in the process of enjoying their shopping experience, U.S. consumers spend substantially more compared with their Chinese counterparts.

In other differences, U.S. supermarket consumers shop in bulk at supermarkets once a week, loading the family automobile with large packages of food, freezing meat and vegetables for later consumption, or purchasing these products frozen, in contrast, Chinese consumers place little value on convenience. Overall, Chinese households spend 72 percent on fresh food, 9 percent on frozen food, 9 percent on convenience food and canned food, and the rest (10 percent) on basic necessity food, items such as packaged rice, edible oil, sauces, and chicken stock. The fresh food products most often purchased by consumers in China are the following, oranges, apples, and bananas; choisum (Chinese cabbage), lettuce, and bean curd; pork, pork soup bone, and pork spare ribs; and mandarin fish, golden thread, and big head fish.

5.4.3.4 Secondary Data Sources

二手数据来源

Researchers must check established sources of information on countries, regions, markets, competitors, and consumers. As a first step, researchers can conduct online searches using search products such as Dialog, Lexis-Nexis, and others, as well as Google, Yahoo, and other similar search engines or portals. They provide sufficient country background information, information on the people, language, customs, lifestyles, government, economy, and other important facts useful for a summary country analysis (see www.culturegrams.com).

As a second step, researchers can access various publications and national and international marketing associations.

Research suppliers such as ACNielsen and others offer subscribers extensive information on different markets. Overall, secondary data collected by different research suppliers is quite useful. In the past, U.S. research suppliers dominated the market; nowadays, there are more and more international players. The leading firms in all areas of market research are ranked in Table 5-2.

Researchers searching secondary data internationally are likely to encounter a number of constraints, which are addressed in the next section.

Table 5-2 The Top 10 Market Research Organizations

Rank	Organization	Parent Country	Research-Full Time Employees	Global Research Revenue (U.S. $ millions)
1.	VNU NV	Netherlands	37,884	3,537.90
2.	Taylor Nelson Sofres plc	U.K.	13,580	1,802.7
3.	IMS Health Inc	U.S.	6,900	1,754.8
4.	GfK AG	Germany	7,515	1,311.3
5.	The Kantar Group	U.K.	6,600	1,237.2
6.	Ipsos Group SA	France	6,100	964.6
7.	Information Resources Inc	U.S.	3,604	624
8.	Synovate	U.K.	5,559	602.9
9.	Westat Inc	U.S.	1,835	420.4
10.	Arbitron Inc	U.S.	1,057	310

Source: From *Top 25 Global Research Organizations*, Marketing News, August 15, 2006

5.4.3.5 International Constraints

国际限制性因素

In many international markets, information sources may be limited and inaccurate. Although information accuracy is usually closely linked to the level of country development, the data collected may have shortcomings attribute to factors other than development, such as translation, correspondence, and so forth.

(1) Data inavailability

信息不便性

In many markets, the detailed data readily available in developed countries may not exist in numerous regions in developing countries, where, for example, population censuses are frequently collected based on estimates made by village elders. If, for instance, demographic information—reliable and readily available in developed countries—is deemed important to the project but it not available for the local market to be researched, the researcher may have to collect this type of data. Also, data on income and sales from tax returns can be inaccurate in countries where this information is not declared. Finally, state-run research organizations are often reluctant to disclose the details of the data collection method and process used; no information may be available on response rates, questionnaire development, and the nature of the sample.

Errors also may be unintentional, attributed to lack of education or mere carelessness. Regardless, unless the researcher is convinced of the research firm performing the study, it is best that the secondary data be regarded with skepticism.

Overall, the accuracy of government-published secondary data is questionable. Published statistics contain high margins of error, beyond the tolerance range of reliability. In addition, published data may be fragmented or aggregated in inconsistent formats by different research organizations; researchers may pull the data for estimation, but, in most instances, they are likely to view the data skepticism.

Some reliable sources of data are the World Bank, the United Nations Development Program, and the Organization of Economic Cooperation and Development. Finally, even countries whose research reporting has been questionable for decades are revamping their data collection and reporting systems. For example, the Chinese government started to improve its marketing research infrastructure in the 1980s, introducing criteria for high-quality statistical service: accuracy, timeliness, relevance, diversity, and richness. Overall, the State Statistics Bureau has expanded its role from data collection and compilation to a role similar to that of a business consultant.

Regardless of the source, secondary data must be carefully scrutinized and interpreted. Researchers may construct a checklist to determine the extent to which the data is usable. This list may contain items such as:

① Who collected the data and for what purpose? Was this actual research, or was it used to support a decision already taken (i.e. is it pseudo-research)?

② When was the data collected? What were the governmental country-conditions then?

③ What stakes did the firm managers have in the study?

④ What states did the research shave in the study?

⑤ Who else may have a stake in the findings of the study (government entities business)?

⑥ What methods were used?

⑦ How consistently were the methods applied?

⑧ Do the findings appear to be consistent with the findings of previous studies or with studies conducted in similar countries?

(2) Lack of primary

缺少一手数据

Primary research is used internationally far less than it should be cost-benefit analyses suggest that spending on research in to remote markets of questionable value is unwise; consequently, the temptation is to use secondary data to serve all research functions.

Often, even the largest firms use a wide variety of quick research techniques and look at data-bases and online information to get their projects off the ground.

Yet many U.S. firms are interested in conducting research in the international markets where they operate. In an interview of 313 executives at major U.S. corporations who were responsible for conducting research and hiring outside research firms, most international marketing research projects involve the collection of primary data, information collected for a specific purpose, to address the problem at band. It requires substantial expertise in both instrument design and administration and, as a consequence, it is expensive and time consuming.

(3) Lack of marketing infrastructure

缺少市场信息专业机构

The costs of collecting primary data in foreign markets are likely to be much higher, given the lack of a marketing infrastructure. Many markets do not have research firms or field-interviewing services; consequently, the sponsoring firm would have to invest in developing sampling frames and training interviewers.

(4) Infrastructure factors

基础设施落后

Research using the telephone as the contact method has changed greatly in the past decade alone. It used to be that, in many countries, the use of telephones limited the data collection to a handful of individuals who had access to a landline. However, today, with cheaps chess to prepaid cell phones, pretty mach anyone can be reached. Because most subscribers do not have to pay for phone calls they receive, telephone interviewing is mush easier than in the past. Random digit dialing is probably the best method to use to ensure a representative sample of the population. Using the telephone book as the sampling frame is problematic because it restricts the sample to landline subscribes, who are likely to differ from the target population.

Using mail surveys is problematic in many international markets where mail is unreliable and slow. Even in India, which has one of the best home delivery mail systems in the entire developing world, mailing surveys to consumers homes or offices has never been a part of the business culture of Indian society; similarly, in Saudi Arabia, which has one of the most efficient mail systems in the world using the most modern technologies, studies cannot be conducted through this venue because the system restricts the use of mail surveys.

In the lowest-income countries, another obstacle to the mail survey approach is the low literacy rate, which eliminates most potential respondents. Here, a telephone or personal interview is the preferred data collection approach.

Finally, the sampling frames needed for data collection (mailing lists, telephone books, or other relevant databases) may not be available. In business-to-business research, sampling frames such as industry-associationdirectories are often used.

Given the many constraints that this type of research imposes on the researcher, experimental research findings are difficult to transfer to other countries where the control factors behave differently. Given the fact that results are not easily generalizable to similar environments, and that this type of research can be costly, experimental research is rarely used in international research.

(5) Language barriers

语言障碍

Instruments developed in one country require translation into the language of the country where they will be administered. Many concepts, however, are likely to lose some of then meaning when translated into another has language. Idioms are particularly problematic, and their literal translation has led to numerous marketing blunders.

In cross-cultural research, all steps should be performed by individuals fluent in both the original language of the questionnaire and in the language of the country where it will be administered. First, a questionnaire is translated from the language in which it was originally written into the language in which it will be administered. There are two possible alternatives to further ensure that the instruments have been translated as intended. One is back translation, whereby the translated questionnaire is again translated into its initial language by a different individual. Another possibility is parallel translation, whereby the questionnaire is translated from its original language by two different individuals and the two versions are compared. The successive translation (by different translators) of the instrument between the original language and the language of administration with the purpose of obtaining an instrument that is closest in meaning to the original questionnaire known as decentering.

5.4.4 Determining Research Approaches 确定调研的路径和方法

When collecting primary data, researchers may use qualitative and quantitative research approaches. Qualitative research methods typically have some of the following characteristics:

(1) Fewer respondents belonging to a no random sample

(2) Open-ended answer format

(3) Non-systematic observation

(4) Researcher involvement as participants

5.4.4.1 Qualitative Research 一般性调研

Qualitative researchhas been particularly useful either as a first step in studying international marketing phenomena. When conducting exploratory research or as one of the methods of exploring the problem at hand in a multiple method approach. Focus group research and observation fit in this category. In certain countries, such as France and Italy, there is a preference for qualitative data as a complement to quantitative data, whereas in others, such as Germany, the United States and Scandinavian countries, quantitative data are deemed as most valuable.

(1) Focus group interviews
小组座谈法

Focus group interviews typically involve 6 to 12 participants recruited to meet some previously decided characteristics for instance, ethnic background, certain age group, social class, tribal allegiance, and use of certain products and a moderator who guides the discussion based on a certain discussion agenda. Often, representative from the sponsor observe the group's deliberations through a one-way mirror or on closed circuit television. A video camera or tape recorder may also be used to record the group's deliberations on a certain topic of interest to the sponsor. The participants are typically given a small financial reward for participating in the study or products such as free beer and food, product samples, and the like.

Depth interviews are one-on-one attempts to discover consumer motivations, feelings, and attitudes toward an issue of concern to the sponsor using a loose and unstructured question guide. They are typically used if the issue under study is a complex behavioral or decision-making consideration or an emotionally laden issue.

Focus groups, consumer panels, and depth interviews are frequently problematic to apply in international settings. In Eastern cultures, responses are likely to be affected by "acquiescence bias" or "good-subject role", whereby consumers agree to please the interviewer. When conducting international research using focus groups, researchers should be aware of the significance of culture in the dialogue because many societies do not condone open exchange and disagreement between individuals. Also, topic such as domestic and consumption habits are considered too private and embarrassing to discuss with strangers. In these environments, researchers would benefit more from using observational approaches.

(2) Observation

观察调研法

One type ofobservation research that is particularly useful in international research is naturalistic inquiry. Naturalistic inquiry requires the use of natural rather than contrived settings because behaviors take substantial meaning from their context. The researcher is the data collection instrument and part of the behavior-verbal and nonverbal. The analysis performed by the researcher is inductive, rather than deductive; that is, unlike in conversation research methods, the researcher does not rely on previous theory in the process of developing hypotheses, but, rather, theories are developed from data. Ethnography—the study of cultures—is largely based on naturalistic inquiry. Both academic researchers and practitioners have used observation to better understand international consumers and consumer motivations. It is often used by researchers who attempted to increase the validity of their studies by acquiring an intimate knowledge of a culture's daily life thorough personal observation.

Other observation methods—such as the study of garbage (garbology); physiological measurement methods, which measure a respondent's non-voluntary responses to stimuli; eye tracking, which is used in packaging research and in advertising; and response latency, which measures the time interval between the question and the response to that question—are used only to a limited extent in international research, usually in developed countries. They are costly because they require sending expensive experts to the research site abroad and obtaining data only on limited, usually no representative samples.

Observation can have a number of shortcomings. Individuals in difficult cultures may react differently if they know that their behavior is being observed. Also, the observer may need to be familiar with all the different languages spoken at the study site.

International technology provides new sources for observation-based information, such as point-of-sale (POS) store scanner data, which can offer outlets high quality, instant, as well as longitudinal, information on the movement of goods. Such resources are amply available in the United States, Canada, and the counties of the European Union. Increasingly, they are available in Asia and in the emerging markets of Latin America. This information is used for tracking, as well as for managerial decision making.

5.4.4.2 Quantitative Research
量化调研

Quantitative Research methods are more structured, involving either descriptive research approaches, such as survey research, or causal research approaches, such as experiments.

(1) Content analysis
内容分析法

Content analysis, an example of descriptive research, is a quantitative analysis that entails counting the number of times pre-selected words, themes, symbols, or pictures appear in a given medium such as printed materials or any medium with verbal or visual content. Content analysis is particularly useful in international marketing research, helping international marketing practitioners understand the complex multicultural environments in which they compete. At the same time, content analysis makes them aware of the subtle qualitative differences—such as taste, traditional, and symbolism—that are especially useful in market segmentation.

One area where content analysis is used extensively is advertising research, in an attempt to discover themes that are more popular in certain countries, for particular product categories. One study examined differences in the portrayal of women in magazines of different countries. Using U.S. and international male and female judges, the study found that, in general, North America and Western

European magazines portrayed women displaying more positive emotions，compared with Latin American，East European，and African magazines. In addition，the woman from Latin America appeared to be older，sexier，and more aggressive than their Western counterparts.

(2) Survey research

问卷式调研

Survey research，another example of descriptive research，typically involves the administration of personal，telephone，mail，or Internet questionnaires. The use of the questionnaires assumes that respondents are both capable and willing to respond to the questions. A cheap survey method involves the use of mail questionnaires; however，this method is fraught with obstacles in many developing countries. And，in most developing countries，there is a high level of illiteracy，which renders impossible the use of mail surveys. Nevertheless，this method is most popular in international marketing research，especially because it can be effectively used in cross-national comparisons.

(3) Experimental research

实验性调研

Experimental Research has the highest validity and reliability of all types of research. This research looks at cause-and-effect relationships，eliminating or controlling other extraneous factors that may be responsible for the results，and eliminating competing explanations for the observed findings. It requires the use of matched groups of subjects who are subjected to different treatments to ascertain whether the observed response differences are statistically significant.

5.4.5 Collecting，Analysing，and Interpreting the Information 信息的收集、分析和理解

In the final stage of the marketing research process，the researcher or research team is ready to collect the primary data. This expensive undertaking can be eventful. Researchers are frequently faced with respondents who have never had any experience participating in surveys. Nonresponse(inability or，more frequently，refused to participate in the study) can be a particularly serious problem，as previously seen. Even lateral processes that do not involve data collection，such as briefing the field force(training the interviewers) and evaluating the fieldwork quality，can be particularly difficult if the marketing researcher is not a national because communications may be encumbered by language and culture differences. Ideally，local researchers should be in charge of implementing the data collection process because they are aware of the particulars of the environment that may have an impact on the data collection.

Finally, it is important that marketing managers not base all their decisions on the data collected because even proper planning of the data collection effort does not exclude the possibility of shortcomings in the study. For example, after one market research firm indicated that there was a substantial market for a specific product, a Swiss pharmaceutical firm built an 58 million manufacturing firm in Southeast Asia. The researchers, however, overlooked an important aspect of that market. the black market controlled by government officials. The added competition of the black market led to lower earnings for the company.

5.5 Decision Support System for Global Marketing 全球营销的决策支持系统

该系统是一个计算机程序,用于处理所搜集到的海外目标市场的数据和信息。该程序的设计考虑了三个信息源:母国市场、东道国市场和国际市场。

A decision support system defined as "a coordinated collection of data, systems, tools, and techniques, complemented by supporting software and hardware designed for the gathering and interpretation of business and environmental data". In a global environment, the environmental data takes into account home country and host-country developments as well as development in other global markets that may affect operations.

Ideally, a global marketing decision support system should be:

Computerized—Having a computerized support system is not possible in the case of many global markets, including those of developing countries, due to the increase in the capacity of personal computers to perform more complex tasks.

Interactive—Managers can use online instructions to generate reports on the spot, without assistance from a programmer, who now may need to be present in the country of operations only periodically for system updating and training. This, of course, reduces the number of expatriates necessary at the operations site and the overall costs to the company.

Flexible—Managers can assess and integrate data from a variety of sources and manipulate the data in a variety of ways (producing averages and totals, sorting the data, etc.). The system should allow managers to access information about firm operations in similar markets where the firm may be present and competitors' operations in the respective market where such information is available.

Discovery-Oriented—Such systems should produce diagnostics that reveal trends and identity problems.

In a global environment, there are different, country-specific information systems. Integrating the different approaches may lead to operational difficulties; managers must continuously take into consideration such as differences as they interface with the system.

A number of areas lend themselves well to Marketing Decision Support Systems (MDSS). In later Section "Sales Forecasting", we discuss different possible applications for such systems.

5.5.1 Sales Forecasting 销售业绩预测

Different approaches to sales forecasting are discussed in this section. The more complex these techniques are, the more their efficiency can be improved in an MDSS environment. Nevertheless, input obtained from using the simpler methods (sales force composite estimates, jury of executive opinion, and the Delphi method) can be used to cross-validate the estimates given by the more sophisticated forecasting techniques (time series and econometrics models).

5.5.1.1 Sales Force Composite Estimates 根据销售人员报告预估

Forecasts from sales force composite estimates are based on the personal observations and "hunches" of the local sales force. These people are in the closest contact with the international consumer, and they are likely to find out about consumer desires and overall changing market trends. The sales force is likely to be constituted of locals who have a good understanding of the market. They, in turn, report to the manager, who may or may not be an expatriate sent abroad by the home office. Ideally, the individual occupying this position is schooled under both home and host-country systems; if not, it is recommended that this individual should undergo at least some training in host or home-county approaches, respectively, to doing business. This training is important because this individual is typically responsible for interpreting the predictions of the sales force.

5.5.1.2 Jury of Expert Opinion 专家估算

Forecasts from the jury of expert opinion are based on the opinions of different experts about future demand. The experts' opinions are then combined, and an aggregate demand estimation is offered. Because experts could come form both home and host country, as well as countries where other companies, or the company in question, may face similar problems, obtaining a consensus perspective or aggregate forecast may be more difficult to achieve. At the same time, the awareness of the different possible outcomes or individual perspectives may prove invaluable in gaining insight on demand, particularly for a market new to the company.

5.5.1.3 The Delphi Method

德尔菲法

The Delphi Method entails asking a number of experts to estimate market performance, aggregating the results, and sharing this information with the experts. This process is repeated several times until a consensus is reached. Clearly, such an approach would be most cumbersome when dealing with a global company. First, in addition to impositions on executive's time, the company also must incur expenses related to the logistics of bringing together experts from different countries. Second, should the company attempt to use the Delphi method by mailing forecasting surveys, there is always the risk that international mail may impose, in addition to the high likelihood of noncompliance by executives, who may perceive such an exercise as an imposition on their time. Typically, these types of studies are performed at yearly or quarterly meetings of international managers.

The Delphi method has been used in within-country studies to identify the needs for professional training for life insurance sales representative and examine the competencies needed by thosesales representatives in the United States and in China Taiwan. Sales representatives of the same company receive the same training in both the United States and China Taiwan, but the Taiwanese did not exhibit the same high performance levels U.S. counterpart. A study using the Delphi technique revealed that the company needed to offer additional training to the Taiwanese salespeople especially in problem solving, communication, and information technology utilization.

5.5.1.4 Time Series and Econometric Models

时间序列与计量模型

Time series models use data of past performance to predict market demand. Typically, these models give more weight to recent developments. These methods assume that the future will be similar to the past. Econometric models, on the other hand, take into account different deterministic factors that affect market demand-factors that may or may not depend on past performance trends.

An example of an application of econometric models to global marketing is provided by the application of an auto regressive moving average (ARMAX) to predict consumer demand for beer in the Netherlands. The variables used as predictors of the demand for beer were temperature, price, consumer expenditures, and company advertising expenditures. The study concluded that advertising expenditures are not good predictors for beer demand; the authors suspected that the reason is a saturated market where all competitors advertise extensively and where additional advertising efforts may go unnoticed.

Time series and econometric models are dependent on the availability of historical data, data that are mainly available in developed countries but not in developing countries. For these markets, then, it is appropriate to estimate demand by analogy, nothing responses of markets with similar relevant characteristics, levels of economic development, cultural characteristics, and so forth.

5.5.1.5 Analogy Methods

类比法

The analogy method is an estimation method that relies on developments and findings in markets with similar levels of economic development, markets where the product is in the same development stage, or markets with similar cultural characteristics, or it may be based on sales of a related product in the key market of study. For example, to estimate anticipated adoption rate of cell phones in Latvia, it may be appropriate to identify the proportion of new adopters in a more advanced country in widely available, but which shares a similar history and similar geopolitics with Latvia. This is an example of country performance analogy.

To estimate the adoption rate of Internet service in Sri Lanka, it may be appropriate to evaluate the adoption rate of computers in this country. This is an example of product performance analogy.

Typically, in the country performance analogy, adjustments are made based on development level, cultural differences, trade barriers, competition, and so on. In the product performance analogy, adjustments are made for consumer traits such as purchase power, consumer innovation rate, and competitive environment.

5.5.1.6 POS Sales Based Projections

网点POS机销售记录预测

Point-of-sale-based projections are made with the help of store scanners, which are increasingly used by research suppliers, particularly in the United States (ACNielsen and Information Resources, among others), to assess market share and other relevant market dimensions. Weekly or biweekly store audits reveal the movement of goods within the store and from warehouses. Internationally, although scanning technology is widely available, it is mainly used for inventory purposes, rather than for research purposes. For example, British retailer Marks & Spencer uses bar code and wireless local area network (LAN) technology to improve operations in its states. The company installed a Symbol Technologies Spectrum 24 wireless LAN, mobile computers, and bar code laser scanners to increase accuracy and efficiency and to improve customer service at its more than 300 European-based stores. The scanners send data over the LAN, allowing Marks & Spencer to reconfigure POS stations or add and subtract stations based on need. Overall, scan rates are lower in Europe when compared with the United States, but higher than rates elsewhere around the world (with the exception of China); Europe, Great Britain, and France have 100 percent scanning for most food products. Surprisingly, in the United Kingdom, unlike the United States, consumer data collection is dominated by face-to-face interviewing, which still accounts for more than 50 percent of U.K. research, whereas retail data collection is still dominated by the conventional retail audit. The use of scanners at POS and the difference in the level of development in the major store groups make it impossible to construct a nationally representative sample of scanner stores.

The Chapter's Referential Questions:
本章参考性问题

1. Suppose that you have been hired to evaluate the purchase behavior of adolescents in Latvia. What types of research studies could you conduct?
   假设你受雇做一个关于拉托维亚青少年购买行为的调研与评价,你将采用哪种调研方法?
2. What are some of the limitations of secondary data available to international marketing researchers?
   对于国际营销调研人员,在收集二手数据方面存在哪些限制?
3. Describe the challenges that researchers experience when designing and administering questionnaires in countries that are dissimilar from their own.
   谈谈国际营销调研人员在外国市场设计和实施问卷调研时会遇到哪些挑战。
4. Describe the international sales forecasting methods that marketing managers can use to better monitor and more efficiently react to information in the foreign business environment.
   叙述营销经理在应用销售额预测法时,如何能够控制并有效应对海外市场获得的信息。
5. How to apply the method of POS Sales Based Projections?
   如何运用网点 POS 机销售记录进行销售预测?
6. How many methods can be applied for doing Sales Forecasting?
   有哪些方法可以被应用于销售业绩预测?
7. What is the function of market survey for KFC to select and decide its new

locations?

KFC 在开店之前所做的市场调查对其选址有何作用?

8. What is the function of the Decision Support System for Global Marketing?

全球营销决策支持系统的功能和用途是什么?

微信扫码查看

Chapter 6 Entering the Global Market

全球市场进入战略

Learning Objectives

本章学习目标

1. Organization of multinational companies to enter the international market
   跨国公司进入国际市场的组织
2. Problems that may be faced by companies in entering the overseas market
   企业进入国际市场可能面临的诸多问题
3. The choice of modes of multinational companies to enter the international market
   跨国公司进入国际市场的模式选择

A growing number of large companies have transferred geographical andnational boundaries and become truly multinational in nature. For most other domestic companies, the question is no longer. Should we go international? Instead, the questions relate to when, how, and where the companies should enter the international marketplace. The past 30 years have seen the reality of a truly world market unfold. In today's world, the global economy is becoming almost totally integrated. Primary reasons for previously separated, individual markets evolving to a network of interdependent economies include:

(1) The growing influence and economic development of lesser developed countries. In years to come, the real battleground for the two trade powers, the United States and Japan, will take place in the developing world. Containing 80 percent of the world's population and with growth rates nearly double those of industrial nations, these countries have emerged as the "fourth engine in the world economy" following the United States, Europe, China and Japan.

(2) The integration of world financial markets. For example, changes in currency exchange rates between the Chinese RMB and the U. S. Dollar greatly influence issues relating to import and export activities for all countries.

(3) Increased deficiencies in transportation and telecommunication and data communication networks. To illustrate, consider the cases of Eastern Europe, China, and Russia. In these countries, technological advances have allowed the emergence of stock exchanges on which brokers throughout the world can trade.

(4) The opening of new markets. For example, the political and economic reforms in China have the country to the opening of a market that for decades was closed to western countries.

Multinational Companies invest in foreign countries for the same basic reasons they invest in own country. These reasons vary from company to company but all under the categories of achieving offensive or defensive goals. Offensive goals are to:

(1) increase long term growth and profit prospects;

(2) maximize total sales revenue;

(3) take advantage of economies of scale;

(4) improve overall market position.

As many markets reach saturation, such as Japan and Germany, companies of these countries look to foreign markets as outlets for surplus production capacity, sources of new customers, increased profit margins, and improved returns on investment. For example, the ability to expand the number of locations of McDonald's restaurants in the United States is becoming severely limited. Yet, on any given day, only 0.5 percent of the world's population visits McDonald's. This fact illustrates the vast potential markets still open to the company. Indeed, in the recent past, of the 50 most profitable McDonald's outlets, 25 were located in Hong Kong. For PepsiCo, the results are similar, and its restaurant division operates 7,400 Kentucky Fried Chicken and Pizza Hut outlets abroad, deriving over $ 5.6 billion in sales from these foreign locations.

Multinational Companies also are investing in other countries to achieve defensive goals mainly desiring to:

(1) Compete with foreign companies on their turf instead of at their homes;

(2) Have access to technological innovations that are developed in other countries;

(3) Take advantage of significant difference in operating costs between countries;

(4) Taking advantage of competitors' global moves;

(5) Not be locked out of future markets by arriving too late.

In many ways, marketing globally is the same as marketing at home. Regardless of which part of the world the company sells in, the marketing program must still be built around a sound product or service that is properly priced, promoted, and distributed to a carefully analyzed target market. In other words, the marketing manager has the same controllable decision variables in both domestic and non-domestic markets.

Although the development of a marketing program may be the same in either domestic or non-domestic markets, special problems may be involved in the implementation of marketing programs in non-domestic markets. These problems often arise because of the environmental differences that exist among various countries that marketing managers may be unfamiliar with.

In this chapter, marketing in a global context will be examined. Methods of organizing global versus domestic markets, global market research tasks, potential marketing strategies, but mainly the methods of entry strategies into global markets for a multinational company will be discussed.

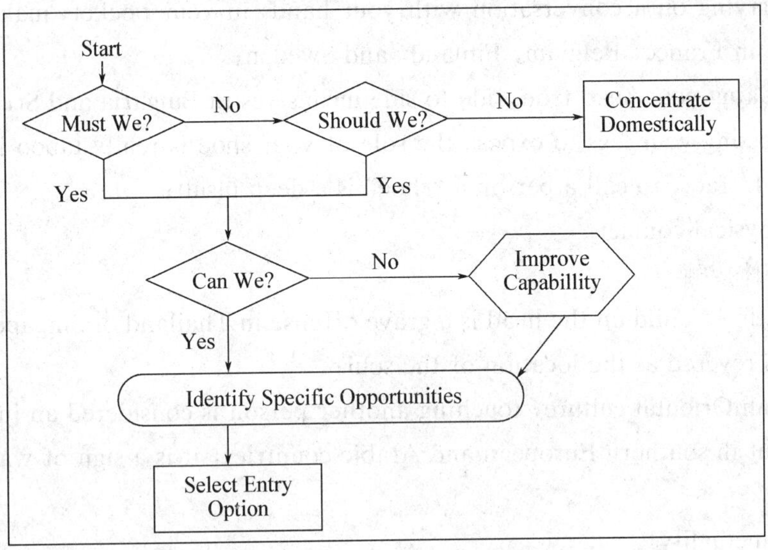

Figure 6 - 1 The Decision Process Involved in Determining Whether to Compete in Global Markets

6.1 Organizing for Global Marketing 全球市场营销的组织

与国内营销相比较，全球营销要面临更多的不定因素和更大的风险。因此，企业需要针对可能遇到的问题，对全球营销进行卓有成效的组织设计与管理，根据所确定的市场采取相应的进入方式。

When compared with the tasks it faces at home, a company attempting to establish a global marketing organization faces a much higher degree of risk and uncertainty. In a foreign market, management is often less familiar with the cultural, political, and economic situation. Many of these problems arise as a result of conditions specific to the foreign country. Managers are also faced with the decisions concerning how to organize the multinational company.

6.1.1 Problems with Entering Foreign Markets 进入外国市场会遇到的问题

While numerous problems could be cited, attention here will focus on those companies most often face when entering foreign markets.

(1) Body language

形体语言

① Standing with your hands on your hips is a gesture of defiance in Indonesia;

② Carrying on a conversation with your hands in your pockets makes a poor impression in France, Belgium, Finland, and Sweden;

③ Shaking your head from side to side means yes in Bulgaria and Sri Lanka;

④ Crossing your legs to expose the sole of your shoe is really taboo in Muslim countries. In fact, to call a person a "shoe" is a deep insult;

(2) Physical contact

身体接触

① Patting a child on the head is a grave offense in Thailand or Singapore, since the head is revered as the location of the soul;

② In an Oriental culture, touching another person is considered an invasion of privacy; but in southern European and Arabic countries, it is a sign of warmth and friendship.

(3) Punctuality

时间观念

① Be on time when invited for dinner in Denmark or in China;

② In Latin countries, your host or business associate wouldn't be surprised if you arrived at the appointed hour.

(4) Eating and cooking

饮食习惯

① It is rude to leave things on your plate when eating in Norway, Malaysia, or Singapore;

② In Egypt, it is rude not to leave something;

③ In Italy and Spain, cooking is done with oil;

④ In Germany and Great Britain, margarine and butter are used.

(5) Other social customs

其他风俗

① In Sweden, nudity and sexual permissiveness are quite all right, but drinking is really frowned on;

② In Spain, there is a very negative attitude toward life insurance. By receiving insurance benefits, a wife feels that she is profiting from her husband's death;

③ In Western European countries, many consumers still are reluctant to buy anything (other than a house) on credit. Even for an automobile, they will pay cash.

6.1.2 Cultural Misunderstanding 文化方面的误解

Differences in the cultural environment of foreign countries may be misunderstanded or not even recognized because of the tendency for marketing managers to use their own cultural values and priorities as a frame of reference. Some of the most common areas of difference lie in the way dissimilar cultures perceive time, thought patterns, personal space, material possessions, family role's and relationship, personal achievement, competitiveness, individuality, social behavior, and other interrelated issues. Another important source of misunderstandings is in the perceptions of managers about the people with whom they are dealing. Feelings of superiority can lead to changed communication mannerisms.

Foreign managers must make the necessary efforts to learn, understand, and adapt to the cultural norms of the local managers and customers they deal with in other parts of the world. Failure to do so will result in missed market opportunities because cultural differences could lead to marketing problems.

On the other hand, companies should not shy away from attempting to enter global markets because conventional wisdom says that products and service will not succeed in some regions purely because of cultural reasons. For example, PepsiCo's Pepsi division entered into a $ 500 million offensive to try to grab a larger share of the $ 6 billion Brazilian soft-drink market. Understanding the dramatic changes that had taken place in Brazil, Pepsi re-positioned itself as the choice of a new Brazil. Advertisements for the Pepsi brand feature young people listing recent changes in Brazil, such as perhaps the devaluation of its currency in 1999. Does this campaign sound familiar? It should since it's a takeoff on the popular "Pepsi, the choice of a new generation" theme utilized in the United States. Actions taken by PepsiCo's Frito-Lay unit serve as another example of a successful adaptation to cultural differences. In China, Frito-Lay recently introduced its popular Cheetos snack food. The twins to this effort lie in the fact that the Chinese are not big consumers of dairy products. In China, cheetos are cheeseless, instead consisting of flavors such as "Savory American Cream" and "Zesty Japanese Steak". As a result of these and other adaptations, it's no wonder that PepsiCo ranks among the leaders in the global food and beverage industry.

6.1.3 Political Uncertainty 政治的不稳定性

Governments are unstable in many countries, and social unrest and even armed conflict must sometimes be reckoned with. Other nations are newly emerging and anxious to seek their independence. These and similar problems can greatly hinder a company seeking to establish its position in foreign markets. For example, companies scaled hack their investment plans in Russia due to the following reasons:

(1) A business environment plagued by mobsters;

(2) Political situation is heavily corrupted;

(3) An economy troubled by runaway inflation and a too soft ruble.

This is not to say investment in Russia is a poor choice. Rather, in situations like this, caution must be utilized and companies must have a keen understanding of the risks involved in undertaking sizable investments.

6.1.4 Import Restriction 进口限制

Tariffs, import quotas, and other types to import restrictions hinder global business. These are usually established to promote self-sufficiency and can be a huge roadblock for the multinational firm. For example, a number of countries, including South Korea, China Taiwan, Thailand, and Japan, have placed import restrictions on a variety of goods produced in America, including telecommunications equipment, rice wood products, automobiles, and produce. In other cases, governments may not impose restrictions that are commonly adhered to in the United States. For example, Chrysler pulled out of a proposed investment deal in China, worth billions of dollars, because the Chinese government refused to protect its right to limit access to technological information.

6.1.5 Exchange Controls and Ownership Restriction 外汇管制和控股权限制

Some nations establish limits on the amount of earned and invested funds that can be withdrawn from it. These exchange controls are usually established by nations that are experiencing balance of payment problems. In addition, many nations have a requirement that local nationals hold the majority ownership of a company operating there. These and other types of currency and ownership regulations are important considerations in the decision to expand into a foreign market. For example, up until 1990, foreign holdings in business ventures in India were limited to a maximum of 40 percent. Once this ban was lifted later on numerous global companies such as Sony, Whirlpool, JVC, Panasonic, Kellogg's, Levi Strauss, Pizza Hut, and Domino's rushed to invest in this markets.

6.1.6 Economic Conditions 经济情况

As note earlier, nations' economies are becoming increasingly intertwined, and business cycles tend to follow similar patterns. However, there are differences, mainly due to political upheaval or social changes, and these may be significant. In determining whether to invest, marketers need to perform in-depth analyses of a country's stage of economic development, the buying power of its populace, and the strength of its currency. For example, when the North American Free Trade Agreement (NAFTA) was signed, many American companies rushed to invest in Mexico, building production facilities and retail outlets. These companies assumed that the signing of the agreement would stabilize Mexico's economy. In the long term, these investments may pay off. However, many companies lost millions of dollars there due to the devaluation of the peso. Indeed, the crash of the peso cause the retailer giant Wal-Mart to scale back a $ 1 billion investment project to open stores throughout Mexico.

6.2 Organizing the Multinational Company 组建跨国公司

组建跨国公司基本有两种形式：一种是联合若干国内企业组建，从事跨国经营，针对不同的目标市场实施差异化营销战略，各个国家的子公司的经营相对独立；另外一种是国际组合，整合所有资源，实施一体化无国界营销和经营战略，各个海外市场的子公司彼此依赖，协同作战。

There are two kinds of multinational corporations, the multi-domestic corporation and the global corporation. The multi-domestic company pursues different strategies in each of its foreign markets. Each overseas subsidiary is autonomous. A company's management tries to operate effectively across a series of worldwide positions with diverse product requirements, growth rates, competitive environments, and political risks. Local managers are given the authority and control to make the necessary decisions; however, they are also held responsible for results. In effect, the company competes on a market-by-market basis. Honey-Well and General Foods are examples of two American companies that have operated well in this manner.

The global company, on the other hand, puts its entire resources against the competition in an integrated fashion. Foreign subsidiaries and divisions are largely interdependent on both operations and strategy. These "stateless" corporations standardize manufacturing, regularly offer innovative solutions to the market, and seek creative collaborations with other companies to merge complementary skills and gain access to new markets. The global company operates as though the world were one large market, not a series of individual countries. Since there is no one clear-cut way to organize a global company, three alternative structures are normally used:

(1) Worldwide product divisions, each responsible for selling its own products throughout the world;

(2) Divisions responsible for all products sold within a geographic area;

(3) A matrix system that combines elements of both these arrangements.

Many multinational companies already have structured their organization in a global fashion including IBM, Caterpillar, General Electric, Siemens, and Mitsubishi.

Most companies are realizing the need to take a global approach to managing their businesses. However, recognizing the need and actually implementing a truly global approach are two different tasks. For some companies, industry conditions dictate that they take a global perspective. The ability to actually implement a global approach to managing international operations, however, largely depends' on factors unique to the company. Globalization, as a competitive strategy, is inherently more vulnerable to risk than a multi-domestic or domestic strategy, due to the relative performance of the organizational structure once established.

In determining whether or not to globalize a particular business, managers should look first at gheir industry, market, economic, environmental, and competitive factors all influence the potential gains to be realized by following a global strategy. Factors constituting the external environment that are conductive to a global strategy are:

(1) Market factors

市场因素

Homogeneous market needs, global customers, shortening product life cycles, transferable brands and advertising and the ability globalize distribution channels.

(2) Economic factors

经济因素

Worldwide economics of scale in manufacturing and distribution, steep learning curves，worldwide sourcing efficiencies，rising product development costs，and significant differences in host-country costs.

(3) Environmental factors

环境因素

Improving communication，favorable government policies，and the increasing speed of technological change.

(4) Competitive factors

竞争因素

Competitive interdependencies among countries，global moves of competitors，and opportunities to preempt a competitor's global moves.

Many of the reasons given in the first part of the chapter as to why a domestic company should become a multinational can also be used to support the argument that a company should take a global perspective in doing so. In the past，companies had the option of remaining domestic or going multinational due to the separation of markets. This is no longer the case.

There are several internal factors that can either facilitate or impede a company's efforts to undertake a global approach to marketing strategies. These factors and their underplaying dimensions are：

(1) Structure

结构因素

The ease of installing a centralized global authority and the absence of rifts between present domestic and international division or operating units.

(2) Management processes

管理因素

The capabilities and resources available to perform global planning，budgeting，and coordination activities，coupled with the ability to conduct global performance reviews and implement global compensation plans.

(3) Culture

文化因素

The ability to project a global versus national identify，a worldwide versus domestic commitment to employees，and a willingness to tolerate interdependence among business units.

(4) People

人员因素

The availability of employable foreign nationals and the willingness current employees to commit to multinational careers，frequent travel，and having foreign superior.

Overall, whether a company should undertake a multi-domestic or approach to organizing its international operations will largely depend on the mature of the company and its products, how different foreign cultures are from the domestic market, and the company's ability to implement a global perspective. Many large brands have failed in their quest to go global. The primary reason for this failure is rushing the process. Successful global brands carefully stake out their markets, allowing plenty of time to develop their overseas marketing efforts and evolve into global brands.

Indeed, in many cases, companies do not undertake either purely multi-domestic or global approaches to marketing. Instead, a hybrid approach is developed whereby these global brands carry with them the same strategic positioning, and the same advertising. In addition, local characteristics are factored in. Regardless of the approach undertaken management and organizational skills that emphasize the need to handle diversity are the critical factors that determine the long-term success of any company's endeavors in the global marketplace.

6.3 Programs and Procedures for Global Marketing 全球市场营销程序和步骤

本部分主要讲述实施全球营销的程序和步骤，包括实施调研、制订产品战略和分销战略、价格、广告和促销，以及进入该目标市场的法人形式和经营模式。

In this section, the major areas in developing a global marketing program will be examined. As was mentioned at the outset, marketing manager must organize the same controllable decision variable that exist in marketing in the United States have not been able to duplicate their success in foreign markets.

6.3.1 Global Marketing Research 全球市场调研

Because the risks and uncertainties are so high, marketing research is equally important (and probably more so) in foreign markets than in domestic markets. Many companies encourage losing situations abroad because they do not know enough about the market. They don't know how to get the information or find the cost of collecting the information too high. To be successful, organizations must collect and analyze pertinent information to support the basic go or not—go decision before getting to the issue addressed by conventional market research. Toward this end, in attempting to analyze foreign consumers and markets, at least four original issues must be considered.

(1) Population characteristics

人口特征

Population characteristics are one of the major components of a market, and significant differences exist between and within foreign countries. If data is available, the marketing manager should be familiar with the total population and with the regional, urban, rural, and interurban distribution. Other demographic variables, such as the number and size of families, education, occupation, and religious are also important. In many markets, these variables can have a significant impact on the success of a company's marketing program. For example, in the United States, a cosmetics company can be reasonably sure of the desire to use cosmetics being common among women of all income classes. However, in Latin America the same company may be forced to segment it's market by upper, middle, and lower income women want highquality cosmetics promoted in prestige media and sold through exclusive outlets. In some rural and less prosperous areas, cosmetics must be inexpensive, in some rural areas, women do not accept cosmetics.

(2) Ability to buy

购买力

To assess the ability of consumers in a foreign market to buy, four broad measures should be examined:

① Gross national product, or per capital national income;

② Distribution of income;

③ Rate of growth in buying power;

④ Extent of available finance since each of these varies in different areas of the world, the market opportunities available must be examined closely.

(3) Willingness to buy

购买欲望

The cultural framework of consumer motives and behavior is integral to the understanding of the foreign consumers. If data is available, cultural values and attitude towards the material culture, social or organizations, the supernatural, aesthetics, and language should be analyzed for their possible influence on each factor as the group values concerning program. It is easy to see that the family, the position of men and women in society, and the various age groups and classes can have an effect on marketing, because each can influence consumer behavior.

6.3.2 Global Product Policy 全球产品战略

Global marketing research can help determine whether：

(1) there is an unsatisfied need for which a new product could be developed to serve a foreign market；

(2) there is an unsatisfied need that could be met with an existing domestic product，either as is or adapted to the foreign market. In either case，product planning is necessary to determine the type of product to be offered and whether there is sufficient demand to warrant entry into a foreign market.

Most multinational companies would not think of entering a foreign market without an extensive product planning. However，some markets have failed to do adequate product planning when entering foreign markets. An example of such a problem occurred when American manufacturers began to export refrigerator to Europe. The companies were the wrong size，shape，and temperature range for some areas and had weak in others，thus failing miserable. Although adaptation of the product to local conditions may have eliminated this failure，this adaptation is easier said than done.

The solution to this problem is not easy. In some cases，changes need not be made at all or，if so，can be accomplished rather inexpensively. In other cases，the sales potential of the particular market may not warrant expensive product changes. For example，Pepsi Radical Fruit line of juice drinks has been introduced without adaptation on three continents. On the other hand，U. S. companies wishing to market software in foreign countries must undertake painstaking and costly efforts to convent the embedded code from England and foreign languages. This undertaking severely limited the potential markets where individual software products can be profitably marketed. In any case，management must examine these product，related problem carefully prior to making foreign market entry decision.

6.3.3 Global Distribution Strategy 全球分销战略

The role of the distribution network in facilitating the transfer of goods and titles and in the demand stimulation process is as important in foreign markets as it is at home. Figure 6－2 illustrates some of the most common channels arrangements in global marketing. The continuum ranges from no control to almost complete control of the distribution system by manufacturers.

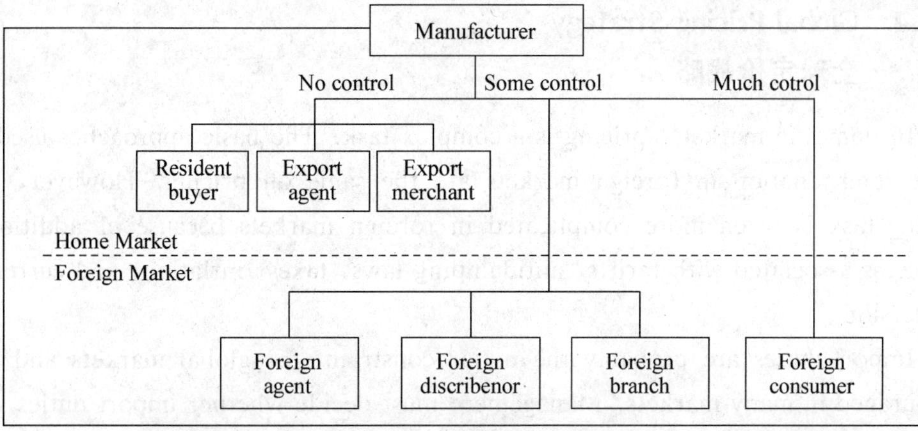

Figure 6 - 2 Common Distribution Channels for Global Marketing

The channel arrangements where manufacturers have the least control are shown at the left of Figure 6 - 2. These are the most indirect channels of distribution. Here manufacturers sell to resident buyers, export agents, or export merchants located in home country. In reality, these are similar to some domestic sales, since intermediaries assume all of the marketing functions.

Manufacturers become more directly involved and, hence, have greater control over distribution when agents and distribution located in foreign markets are selected. Both perform similar functions, except those agents do not assume titles to the manufacturers' products, while distribution does. If manufacturers should assume the functions of foreign agents or distribution and establish their own foreign branch, they greatly increase control over their global distribution system.

Manufacturers' effectiveness will then depend on their administrative organization rather than on independent intermediaries. If the foreign branch sells to outlier intermediaries, such as wholesale and retailers, as is the case with most consumer goods, manufacturers again relinquish some control. However, since the manufacturers are located in the market area, they have greater potential to influence those intermediaries. For example, Volkswagen, General motors, and P&G have each made substantial investments in building manufacturing facilities in Brazil. There investments allow the company to begin marketing direct sales to dealers and retailers in the country.

The channel arrangement that enables manufacturers to exercise a great deal of control is shown at the right of Figure 6 - 2. Here, manufacturers sell directly to organizational buyers or ultimate consumers. Although this arrangement is most common in the sale of industrial goods, some consumer goods companies have also pursued this arrangement.

6.3.4 Global Pricing Strategy 全球定价战略

In domestic markets, pricing is a complex task. The basic approaches used in price determination in foreign markets are the same on pricing. However, the pricing task is often more complicated in foreign markets because of additional problems associated with tariffs, antidumping laws, taxes, inflation, and currency conversion.

Import duties are probably the major constraint for global markets and are encouraged in many markets. Management must decide whether import duties will be paid by the Company, by the foreign consumers, or shared by both. This and similar constraint may force the company to abandon an otherwise creditable pricing strategy or may force the company out of a market altogether.

Another pricing problem arises because of the rigidity in price structures found in many foreign markets. Many foreign intermediaries are not aggressive in their pricing policies. They often prefer to maintain high margins at the expense of low sales volume rather than develop large sales volume by means of lower prices and smaller margins per unit. Many times this rigidity is encouraged by legislation that prevents retailers from cutting prices substantially at their own discretion.

6.3.5 Global Advertising and Sales Promotion Strategy 全球广告与促销战略

When expanding their operations into the world marketplace, most companies are aware of the language barriers that exist and realize the importanceof translating their messages into the proper idiom. However, there are numerous other issues that must be resolved, such as selecting appropriate media and advertising agencies in foreign markets.

There are many problems in selecting media in foreign markets. Often the media traditionally used in the domestic market are not available. For example, it was not until recently that national commercial TV because a reality in the former Soviet Union. If media are available, they may be so only on a limited basis or they may not reach the potential buyers. In addition to the problem of availability, other differences arise from the lack of accurate media available through out the world. Where data are available, their accuracy may be questionable.

Another important promotion decision that must be made is the type of agency used to prepare and place the company advertisements. Along with the growth in multinational product companies, more multinational advertising agencies are available. Among the top 15 global advertising agencies, less than half are U.S. owned. Alliance and take-over have served to stimulate growth in the formation of global agencies. For multinational companies, there are two major approaches to choosing an agency. The first is to use a purely local agency in each area where the advertisement is to appear. The rationale for this approach is that a purely local agency employing only local national can better adapt the company's message to the local culture.

Overall Political and Economic Conditions

总的政治和经济形势

(1) What is the foreign debt service expense as a percentage of hard currency foreign exchange earnings?

(2) What is the inflation rate? If hyper inflation exists, are appropriate fiscal and monetary policy being implemented to bring it under control?

(3) How substantial are raw material reserves that can be converted to hard currency?

(4) Are state subsidies, cheap credit, and tax concessions for state enterprise being phased out?

(5) Dose the government intend to sell stakes enterprises to foreign investors?

(6) Is there an emerging capital markets based on real interest rates?

(7) What progress is being made toward developing a code of company law?

(8) Is political decision, making authority centralized or fragmented?

(9) How rapid and sustainable is continued towards democracy and a free market economy? Is there any historical tradition to support such trends?

Climate for Foreign Investment

外国投资环

(1) What percentage of ownership may foreign companies have in joint ventures? Is government approval required, and if so, how long dose it take to obtain?

(2) Is private ownership of property recognized?

(3) Are intellectual property rights upheld?

(4) Can a foreign investor obtain premises easily? Can they own real estate?

(5) Can an initial capital investment by a foreign company be held in hard estate?

(6) Can a foreign investor sell its stake in a joint venture?

(7) Can hard currency be used to pay for important raw materials or to repatriate profits?

(8) What is the tax rate on business enterprise profits?

Market Attractiveness

市场吸引力

(1) What is the sales potential in this country?

(2) Do the company's geographical locations and relations permit it to serve as a gateway to other markets?

(3) How well developed are the necessary managerial and technical skills?

(4) Can continued supply of the raw materials requests for production be assured?

(5) What is the quality of the transportation and telecommunications infrastructure?

(6) To what degree have government officials developed a familiarity with international business practices?

The other approach is to implement the ad campaign. For example, the Coca-Cola Company uses one agency to create ads for the 80 nations in which diet coke is marketed. The use of these so-called super agencies is increasing (annual growth rates averaging over 30 percent in the last two decades). By using global advertising agencies, companies are able to take advantage of economies of scale and other efficiencies. However, global agencies are not without their critics. Many managers believe that small, local agencies in emerging markets take a more entrepreneurial and fresher approach to advertising than do global agencies. Much discussion has developed over which approach is best, and it appears that both approaches can be used successfully by particular companies.

The use of sales promotion can also lead to opportunities and problems for markets in foreign markets. Sales promotions often contain certain characteristics that are more attractive than other elements of the promotion mix. In less wealthy countries, consumers tend to be even more interested in saving money though price discounts, sampling, or premiums. Sales promotion can also be used as a strategy for bypassing restrictions on advertising placed by some foreign governments. In addition, sales promotion can be an effective means for reaching people who live in rural locations where media support for advertising is virtually nonexistent.

6.4 Entry and Growth Strategies
市场进入与成长战略

在充分考虑目标市场存在的机遇以及风险后，企业根据自身的实力，确定阶段性市场进入战略和成长战略。

A major decision facing companies that desire to enter a foreign market or pursue growth within a specific market relates to the choice of entry or growth strategy. What type of strategy to employ depends on many factors, including the analysis of market opportunities, company capabilities, the degree of marketing involvement and commitment the company is willing to mark, and the amount of risk that the company is able to take. A company can decide to:

(1) Make minimal investments of funds and resources by limiting its efforts to

exporting;

(2) Make large initial investments of resources and management effort to try to establish a long -term share of global markets; or Take an incremental approach whereby the company starts with a low-risk mode of entry that requires the least financial and other resource commitment and gradually increases its commitment over time.

All there approaches can be profitable. In general, there are six ways by which a company can initially enter a global market and, subsequently, pursue growth in the global marketplace.

6.4.1 Exporting
出口

Exporting occurs when a company produces the product outside the final destination and then ships it there for sale. It is the easiest and most common approach for a company making its first international move. Exporting has two distinct advantages. First, it avoids the cost of establishing manufacturing operations in the host country; second, it may help a company achieve experience in the market. By manufacturing the product in a centralized location and exporting it to other national markets, the company may be able to realize substantial scale economies from its global sales volume. This method is what allowed Sony to dominate the global TV market. The major disadvantages related to exporting include:

(1) The sometimes higher cost associated with the process;

(2) The necessity of the exporting company to pay import duties or face trade barriers;

(3) The delegation of marketing responsibility for the product to foreign agents who may or may not be dependable.

6.4.2 Licensing
许可证

Companies can grant patent rights, trademark rights, and the right to use technological processes to foreign companies. This is the most common strategy for small and medium-sized companies. The major advantage to licensing is that the company does not have to bear the development costs and risks associated with opening lip a foreign market, In addition, licensing can be an attractive option in unfamiliar or politically volatile markets. The major disadvantages are that:

(1) The company does not have tight control over manufacturing, marketing,

and strategy that is required for realizing economics of scale;

(2) There is the risk that the licensed technology may be capitalized on by foreign companies. RCA Corporation, for example, once licensed its color TV technology to a number of Japanese companies. These Companies quickly assimilated the technology and used it to enter the U.S. market.

6.4.3 Franchising 专卖权

Franchising is similar to licensing but tends to involve longer-term commitments. Also, franchising is commonly employed by service as opposed to manufacturing companies. In a franchising agreement, the franchiser sells limited rights to use its brand name in return for a lump-sum and share of the Franchisee's future profits. In contrast to licensing agreements, the franchisee agrees to abide by strict operating procedures. Advantages and disadvantages associated with franchising are primarily the same as with licensing except to a lesser degree. In many cases, franchising offers an effective mix of centralized and decentralized decision making.

6.4.4 Joint Ventures 合资企业

A company may decide to share management with one or more collaborating foreign companies. Joint ventures are especially popular in industries that call for large investments, such as natural gas exploration and automobile manufacturing. Control of the joint venture may be split equally, or one party may control decision-making. Joint ventures hold several advantages. First, a company may be able to benefit from a partner's knowledge of the host country's competitive position, culture, language, political systems, and so forth. Second, the company gains by sharing costs and risks of operating in a foreign market. Third, in many countries, political considerations make joint ventures the only feasible entry mode. Finally, joint ventures allow companies to take advantage of a partner's distribution system, technological know-how, or marketing skills.

The major disadvantages associated with joint ventures are that:

(1) A Company may risk giving up control of proprietary knowledge to its partner;

(2) The Company may lose the tight control over a foreign subsidiary needed to engage in coordinated global attacks against rivals.

6.4.5 Strategic Alliances 战略联盟

Although considered by some to be a form of joint venture, we consider strategic alliances to be a distinct entity for two reasons. First, strategic alliances are normally partnerships that entered into by two or more companies to gain a comparative advantage on a worldwide as opposed to local basis. Second, strategic alliances are usually of a much longer-term nature than are joint ventures. In strategic alliances, the partners share long-term goals and pledge almost total cooperation. Strategic alliances can be used to reduce manufacturing costs, accelerate technological diffusion and new product development, and overcome legal and trade barriers. The major disadvantage associated with formation of a strategic alliance is the increased risk for competitive conflict between the partners. Indeed, a recent study showed that strategic alliances have grown at a percent average annual rate, but the median life span of such alliances is only about seven years.

6.4.6 Direct Ownership 直接控股

Some companies prefer to enter and grow in markets either through establishment of a wholly owned subsidiary or through acquisition. In either case, the company owns 100 percent of the stock. The advantages of direct ownership are that the company has:

(1) Complete control over its technology and operations

(2) Immediate access to foreign markets;

(3) Instant credibility and gains in the foreign country when acquisitions are the mode of entry or growth;

(4) The ability to install its own management team.

Of course, the primary disadvantages of direct ownership are huge costs and significant risks associated with this strategy. These problems may more than offset the advantages depending upon the country entered.

Regardless of the choice of methods used to gain entry into and grow within a foreign marketplace, companies must somehow integrate their operations. The complexities involved in operating on a worldwide basis dictate that companies decided on operating strategies. A critical decision that marketing managers must make relates to the extent of adaptation of the marketing mix elements for the foreign country in which the company operates. Depending on the area of the world under consideration and the particular product mix, different degrees of standardization/adaptation of the marketing mix elements may take place. As a guideline, standardization of one or more parts of the marketing mix us a function of many factors that individually and collectively affect companies in their decision making. These factors and their resulting influences are:

(1) When markets are economically alike, standardization is more practical.

(2) When worldwide customs, not countries, are the basis for segmenting markets, a standardization strategy is more effective.

(3) The greater the degree of similarity in the markets in terms of customer behavior and lifestyle, the more effective a standardization strategy is.

(4) The higher the cultural compatibility of the product across the host countries, the more appropriate is standardization.

(5) When a company's competitive position is similar in different markets, standardization is more practical.

(6) When competing against the same adversaries, with similar share position, in different countries, standardization is more appropriate than when competing against purely local companies.

(7) Organizational and high-technology products are more suitable for standardization than consumer products.

(8) The greater the differences in physical, political, and legal environments between home and host countries, the greater will be the necessary degree of adaptation.

(9) The more similar the marketing infrastructure in the home and host countries, the more likely is the effectiveness of standardization.

The decision to adapt or standardize marketing should be made only after a thorough analysis of the product-market mix has been undertaken. The company's end goal is to develop, manufacture, and market the products best suited to the actual and potential needs of the local (wherever that may be) customer and to social and economic conditions of the marketplace. There can be subtle differences from country to country and from region to region in the ways a product is used and what customers expect from it.

6.5 Conclusion
结语

The world is truly becoming a global market. Many companies that avoid operating in the global arena are destined for failure. For those willing to undertake the challenges and risks necessary to become multinational corporations, long-term survival and growth are likely outcomes. The purpose of this chapter was to introduce the reader to the opportunities, problems, and challenges involved in global marketing.

The Chapter's Referential Questions:
本章参考性问题

1. Why should companies enter the global market?
   是什么原因使得企业走进全球市场?
2. Can you give some examples about the cultural differences in your region comparing with other places?
   就你所在的区域与其他区域比较,你能举出一些关于文化差异的事例吗?
3. Describe the procedures for organizing the global marketing.
   谈谈实施全球营销都有哪些步骤。
4. What do you have to do when conducting the global marketing research?
   实施全球营销调研,企业需要做哪些工作?
5. What are the advantages for companies doing direct ownership in overseas market?
   企业以直接控股形式进入海外市场具有哪些优势?
6. How many approaches could be applied for companies to enter the global marketplace?
   企业可以以哪些形式进入海外市场?
7. What are the disadvantages for companies to enter the overseas market in the way of joint ventures?
   企业以合资形式进入海外市场具有哪些劣势?
8. What are the Strategic Alliances? Can you provide some examples?
   什么是战略联盟? 请举例说明。

微信扫码查看

Chapter 7 Product Policies for World Markets

全球市场营销中的产品策略

Learning Objectives

本章学习目标

1. Stages of the international product life cycle
   国际市场产品生命周期的各个阶段
2. Operational objectives and market characteristics of each stage
   每个阶段的运营目标和市场特点
3. International product standardization and differentiation options
   国际产品标准化和差异化选择
4. Issues that need to be addressed when developing product strategies
   制定产品策略时需要注意的问题
5. The steps of international product development
   国际市场产品开发的步骤

Product is the heart of the marketing mix. If the product fails to satisfy the consumer and his needs, no additional expenditure and effort on any of the other ingredients of the mix will improve the product performance in the market place. A washing machine that fails to perform satisfactorily will not become more attractive to the buyer just because large sums have been spent on glossy advertisements extolling the virtue of the machine in question.

Similarly an airline whose planes are consistently late will not improve its "product" as a result of a television campaign which attempts to suggest that the airline is so punctual that any passer-by can virtually tell the exact time the minute he hears the plane's engines droning overhead. No communication message can in the long term improve the level of satisfaction emanating from a poor product.

In this connection one must remember that the word "product" encapsulates a host of components and attributes. They must add up to an assemblage that will provide the level of satisfaction that the company seeks to attain within its marketing objectives. Thus "product" includes such items as the functionality of the product, the ergonomics in use, the aesthetics of its design, the packaging, the longevity, the supportive literature, the instructions incorporated in the literature, the marker's warranty, after-sales service, etc.. The perfect product is the one that manages to incorporate all the attributes and qualities which in-depth research of consumers' needs and expectations has identified. The toy maker who designs an admirable model aircraft but incorporates in the package assembly instructions which are beyond the comprehension of reasonably intelligent children (and often of intelligent parents) can be accused of poor product design, although the written instructions are not part of the physical design itself. A motor car may be of such an excellent design that it would delight buyers and potential consumers. However, if the after-sales service proves to be of a most inferior standard, the car in question would be considered incomplete or unsatisfactory. The fact that the physical side of the design has been developed with extreme care and attention to detail will be offset by the lack of an acceptable level of service. A sound marketing effort presupposes that the company has researched the market to such an extent that all the supportive attributes of the product have been clearly detected. This task must be undertaken within a number of important dimensions:

(1) Within a time scale;

(2) Within the framework of the company's resources and goals;

(3) Within a specified market or segment environment.

The first of these points relates to the need to interpret research findings in a dynamic fashion and take cognizance of the changing tastes and demands of the consumer. The American Edsel car was a failure in spite of long and laborious research studies. The American Edsel car was a failure in spite of long and laborious research studies. The popular interpretation of the reasons for this failure was that by the time the car was designed and ready market conditions had changed sufficiently to make the product out-of-fate before it was launched. This is one of the trick aspects of modern marketing. One must endeavor to combine facts with a rapidly changing scene. It is almost like trying to hit a moving target in a fair ground. The skillful marksman aims ahead of the moving target to allow for the inevitable changing position.

The second point seeks to emphasize the importance of designing a product within the economic realities, resources and goals of the company. Whilst the aim is to attain the full satisfaction of the consumer and his specific and requirements, one must endeavor to undertake this task in such a way as to make a profit or attain the company's other objectives. This of course is not always easy in so far as the marketing objectives may be out of step with the financial and commercial realities of the situation. Thus a company distributing perishable food products chose to make daily deliveries to multiple stores located in the center of all major conurbations—a highly commendable marketing objective. The company soon discovered that the cost of such a service was totally unacceptable to the stores and to the customers. In other words the "product" in this instance, though highly desirable, was totally inappropriate within the resources framework of the company in question and its corporate objectives.

The third dimension refers to the need to design a product for a well-defined target group. The target group can be a very narrow segment or a very wide marketplace, like a whole country or a geographical region. What is important to remember when designing a product assemblage is that the job must be carried out with a definite buyer in mind. This point is particularly important in international marketing in so far as the product that has been designed for a domestic consumer may or may not be suitable for the international consumer. If it is suitable for the non-domestic buyer, so much the better, but this would be simply a stroke of good luck. Sound international marketing envisages a planned effort and not just lucky strikes. This is the essence of international marketing. If the company seeks to satisfy the needs of the international consumer the product should be designed accordingly. The product that has been designed for a home market and for which one discerns foreign opportunities is essentially an export effort rather than a fully-fledged global marketing effort. We shall see later the implications of this distinction in connection with product policy and planning problems.

7.1 The Product Life Cycle in International Marketing 国际市场营销中的产品生命周期

产品的生命周期概念至关重要，它不仅会影响到企业的投资策略，而且在不同的阶段需要实施不同的营销策略。因为不同的产品具有不同的生命周期。

7.1.1 General Principles 一般性原则

The product life cycle concept is well known to most marketers. Its impact on the company's marketing efforts that differ from company to company and from product to product. A manufacturer of pharmaceutical products has to pay very serious attention to this concept and plan in advance the various strategies that he proposes to adopt at each stage of the life cycle. On the other hand a house builder need not concern himself too much with the meaning of this theory because in practice each house he builds is a product and once erected and sold the transaction is finished (with the exception of the after-sales service commitment) and the ravages of the life cycle hardly apply; any change in taste or habits can be easily translated into the next product without substantial planning and investment. Nonetheless the concept is a useful one; it alerts the marketer to the fact that market dynamism affects not only the appearance and functionality of a product but also the effectiveness of the supportive marketing mix ingredients at each stage of a product's life. This is the aspect which is often overlooked by those who tend to describe the value of the product life concept as an impractical one.

Briefly the product life cycle concept can be summarized thus: every product has a life span of a limited duration. Some products live for many years, others have a short life. If the sales of the product are plotted over a period of time the result will be a curve as shown in Figure 7-1.

The curve, or life cycle is normally divided into five distinct periods-introduction, growth, maturity, saturation and decline. Whilst the shape of the curve will be more or less the same for most products, the time duration and the rapidity of change from stage to stage will vary enormously among products. The life cycle of the hula-hoop only lasted a few months; the life-cycle of the ballpoint pen has lasted many years although during those years the product has undergone fundamental marketing changes.

The significant point to remember in this connection is the fact that in most

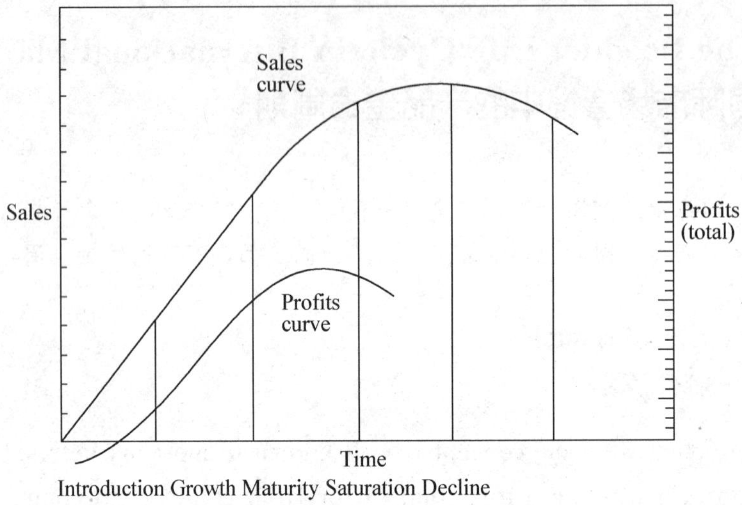

Figure 7 - 1 Product Life Cycle Pattern, Typical Sales and Profit Curves

instances the product's profits tend to follow a predictable pattern through the life cycle. Profits are either absent during the growth stage or reach a peak during the maturity stage. During the saturation stage they normally manifest signs of erosion and all but disappear during the decline stage. If we plot the profit performance on Figure 7 - 1(the scale shown on the right-hand side) it would become apparent that in typical circumstances peak profitability is reached before peak sales. The marketer who is aware of this situation seeks to overcome the problem by either differentiating the product thus giving it a fresh lease of life or by introducing new products in order to safeguard the company's overall profitability. When a car manufacturer introduces a "face-lift" to a well-established model that he seeks to "cheat old age" through differentiation. When he launches a new model he introduces a totally new product with a distinct life cycle curve in order to generate a new profit pattern which runs in parallel with the decaying product and eventually takes over the task of sustaining the company's performance. This can be demonstrated in Figures 7 - 2 and 7 - 3. The first shows how an endeavor is made through differentiation to give the product extra life where in normal circumstances it would enter the saturation stage. Figure 7 - 3 illustrates how a succession of products with their distinct life cycles helps the company to maintain a steady profit performance. The point to remember is that quite the difference between these two strategies is not as clear in practice as in theory. Is the Ford Cortina Mark II a new product or only a product differentiation forms the Mark I range? If a brewer decides to market beer in cans instead of bottles, does that constitute a newproduct or a differentiation strategy? In practice the distinction is subtle and need not give the marketer sleepless nights. On the other hand, it is useful to appreciate that differentiation often implies an endeavor to lengthen the life of an already "sick" product and to that extent it must be looked at as a salvage operation rather than a total life cycle policy. The realization of this aspect can be very helpful in planning the product strategy intelligently.

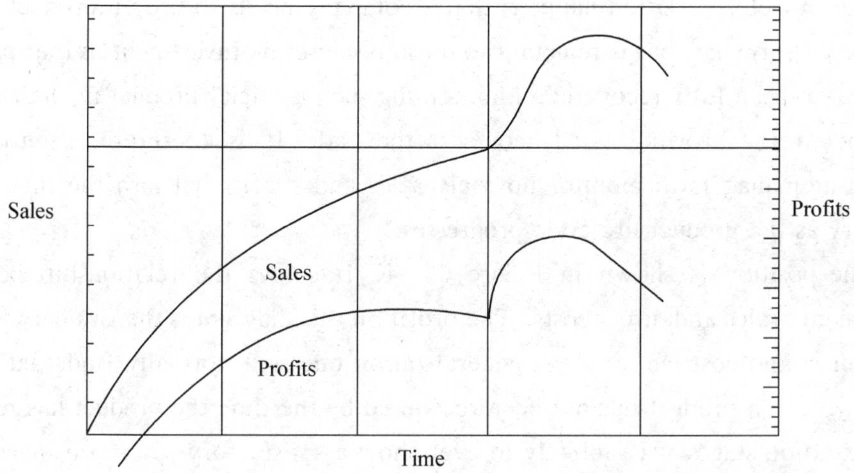

Figure 7 - 2 The Effect of Differentiation on the Product Life Cycle, Sales and Profit Curves

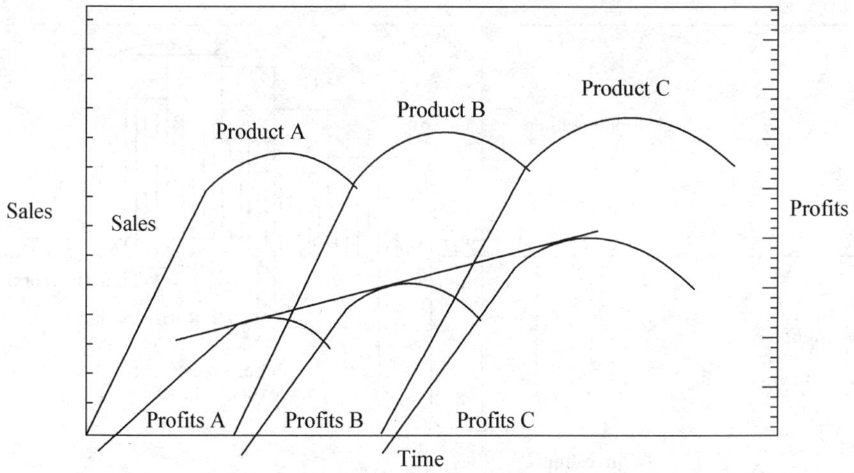

Figure 7 - 3 New Product Policy and Its Effect on Profit Performance

In this connection it is vitally important to remember that growth in sales and profitability is not necessarily a sign of long-term success. A product may well earn handsome profits for one, two or more years but may still represent a poor investment. A marketer must never overlook this aspect of the life cycle theory. A product is only successful in strategic terms when it is capable of earning sufficient returns during its total life cycle in relation to the investment made in it. In other words a product must be capable, first and foremost, to earn sufficient funds to recover the full investment that the company has incurred in it. It is only at the point of investment recovery that the question of returns and profits arises. Furthermore, when we talk in terms of investment we must include not only the cost of design, manufacturing and inventory but also the full cost of pre-launch marketing projects such as market research, promotion, sampling, physical distribution, etc.. It often happens that a company needs to drop a product owing to poor performance but is reluctant to do so because the investment in that product has not yet been fully recovered. Maintaining such a "sick" product in the range is tantamount to throwing good money after bad. It is therefore essential for marketing managers to monitor not only sales and profits but also the investment recovery as the product life cycle progresses.

The position is shown in Figure 7 - 4. It shows the relationship between investment, sales and direct costs. The profit on this diagram is the gap between the sales curve and cost curve. As a generalization one will normally find that if the investment in a product has not been recovered by the time the product has reached the saturation stage, it is unlikely to ever show a satisfactory return on investment over the life of the product. Of course this angle must not be overlooked when evaluation the future of aging products.

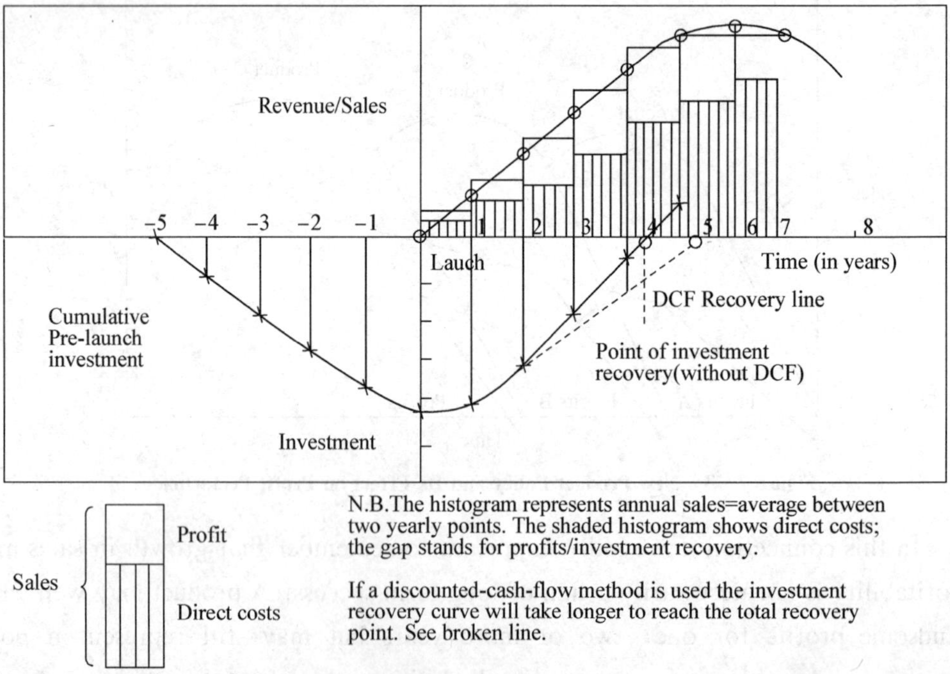

Figure 7 - 4 The Investment Recovery Process and Product Life Cycle

7.1.2 International Implications 国际的含义

The product life cycle concept has a significant relevance to international marketing. Historically most companies tended to operate in their domestic markets as long as such markets offered adequate commercial rewards. As soon as signs of sales and profit erosion started to manifest themselves the company would seek to fill the growing gap trough exports. This in turn meant that one could discern differing life cycle patters in different parts of the world. Figure 7 - 5 illustrates this point. This diagram shows how a product that has reached the decline stage in the domestic market is at the growth stage in country A, at the introduction stage in country B, whilst in country C it is still unknown. The fifth chart in this diagram shows the gap that one would expect to detect between the two extreme situations (excluding course these countries where the product has not been launched at all).

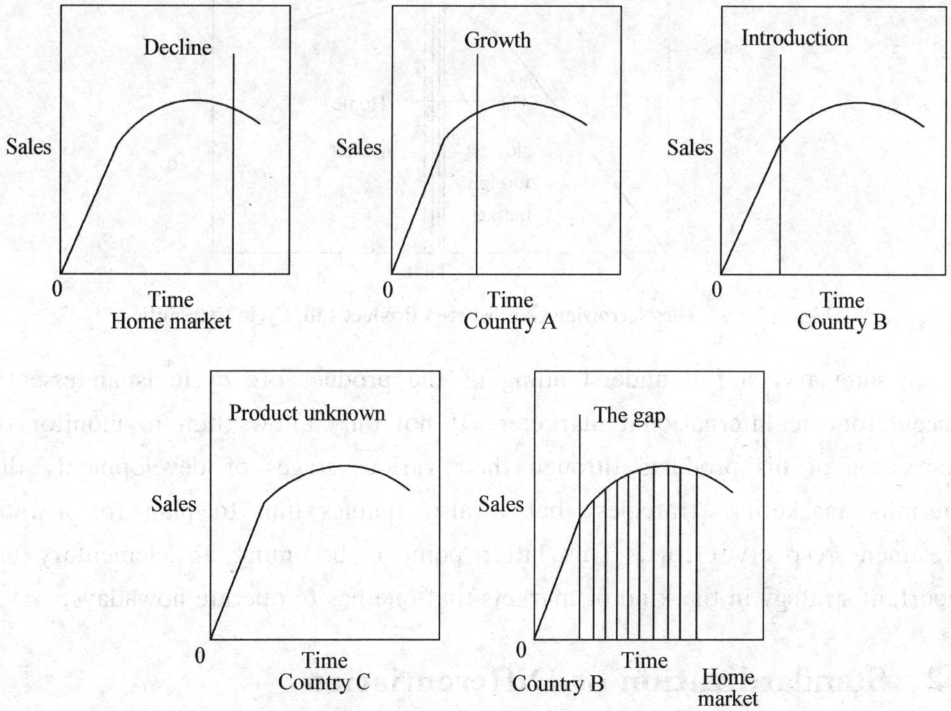

Figure 7 - 5 Variations in Life Cycle Performance in Different Countries

This represented a most comfortable routine. All a company had to do was to classify world markets in accordance with their economic development and launch declining products in quick succession and in a descending scale of sophistication in these groups of countries. One could always hope to find a number of markets which would absorb products which in ones domestic market had lost consumer interest.

Unfortunately, changes have been taking place in recent years in world markets which have upset this routine. The communication revolution has meant that the gap between the time when the home market reaches saturation and the last of the export markets reaches saturation has been narrowing. The total life span of the product over all its markets has become shorter and shorter. The trend, in fact, is for the pattern of the life cycle in a domestic market to become identical to the pattern in other markets. This change, illustrated in Figure 7 - 6 is the underlying philosophy that has made international marketing so different from the previous process of "selling abroad". This is one of the main reasons why the marketer of today must gaze at international markets simultaneously, with the view of planning a global launch. Failure to do so may in many instances mean that good opportunities will be lost.

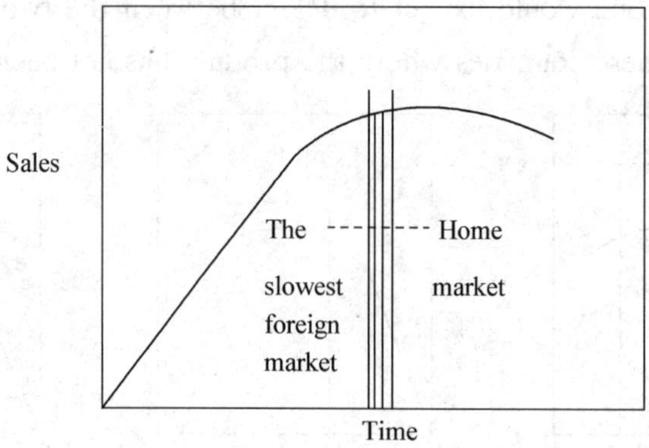

Figure 7 - 6 The Narrowing Gap between Product Life Cycle Extremities

In summary, a full understanding of the product life cycle is an essential concept for the international marketer. It not only allows him to monitor the progression of his products through their various stages of development, thus determine marketing strategies, but it also enables him to plan for a rapid investment recovery effort. This latter point is becoming an elementary and important strategy in the kind of markets that one has to operate nowadays.

7.2 Standardization or Differentiation
标准化还是差异化

面对巨大的市场诱惑，企业需要将其产品设计成适合所有地球人的，还是按照特定市场的特定需求而设计？产品自身的特点和使用价值起着决定性作用。

The international marketer cannot escape from the fundamental decision. Should he design a product which is standard for all markets or should he match the product to the special needs and nuances of each market? This is a problem. However, it gains a very practical importance in relation to the product itself. A decision taken at the product design stage can determine the pattern of the company's marketing effort for many years to come. A mistake at this early stage can make a major difference to the company's fortunes. Whilst it is always very tempting to seek to standardize the product, as every international businessman knows, it is not always possible to do so. On the other hand, as a general rule, to differentiate where market conditions allow for total or partial standardization is certainly a very extravagant policy. For Kodak to differentiate its range of cameras in different parts of the world would be a policy of indescribable wastage. At the same time it is difficult to see how a typewriter manufacturer can afford not to differentiate, in order to accommodate the special needs of language and script variations in different countries. It is unlikely that a typewriter that contains Germanic letters only would gain popularity in the French market.

The advantages of product Standardization can be summarized thus:

(1) Economy of scale in production, stock-control and servicing policies can be quite significant.

(2) Product standardization is an essential forerunner to the wider aim of developing a marketing mix standardization. Without a standard product the other ingredients of the mix do not lend themselves to such a policy.

(3) The chances of attaining a rapid investment recovery are greatly enhanced where a standard product exists throughout the world.

(4) A company that markets standard products internationally is invariably an easier company to manage both in terms of organization and control procedures. This is of course quite an attractive attribute to aim for.

On the other hand it is relevant to mention a number of disadvantages that a standardization strategy entails:

(1) Marketing flexibility is often lost in foreign markets through the inability to match the product to detailed local requirements.

(2) Standardization often discourages creativity and innovation especially among personnel of local companies. As their main role is to sell effectively they gradually lose the motivation to contribute ideas to product improvement and innovation.

(3) Linked with the above point one often finds that personnel in foreign subsidiaries tend to seek their fortunes in other companies where total marketing jurisdiction including product design is possible.

7.3 Considerations Determining International Product Policy 国际产品策略的思考

为国际市场提供产品绝不能掉以轻心，一个小失误就会导致损失惨重。因此，在企业进行国际市场开发的初级阶段，就应该及早认真设计产品策略。

It is thus apparent that product decisions relating to international markets must not be taken lightly. Errors can creep in without the company realizing the full implications. The difficulties that may occur can be very costly. To try to unravel a mess is much more expensive than taking one's time in planning a sound and systematic product policy at the initial stages of the company's development as an international company.

The main considerations that must be borne in mind in determining a sound product policy can be summarized thus.

7.3.1 Corporate Objectives 企业目标

This point is fundamental; a company that seeks to maximize profits regardless ofinternational market penetration goals is more likely to strive towards product standardization. By the very nature of such a strategy it is likely to generate, certainly in the shorter term, a better profit performance. However, this consideration must be looked at in juxta position to other and often equally important aspects to be discussed hereafter.

7.3.2 The Markets Needs 市场需求

Here we are concerned wit the nature of the product itself and the special requirements of the marketplace. We come back to the question of information and the basic "input" needed in this connection is the marketing profile analysis which we discussed at some length in earlier chapters. A profile analysis relating to the product itself can be undertaken. The "product" is dissected into its major components viz. Functional attributes, design, packaging and branding. Depending on the individual circumstances one can determine the exact nature and number of elements that one wishes to research. The important point to remember is that this is the kind of "input" which facilitates the decision as to whether a standardization policy is on the cards or not. Attempting to take a decision of this nature without the information that the profile analysis can yield is asking for trouble.

In other words, one of the major considerations which the marketer must explore when determining his international product policy is the real needs of the markets. He must ask himself: "Are the needs of the individual markets so different from each other that standardization will limit the use of our product to uneconomic levels?"

7.3.3 Company Resources 企业资源

Differentiation is a fairly expensive exercise. A company seeking to attain maximum satisfaction of foreign markets through a non-standardization policy must be aware of the fact that such a policy will absorb considerable investment in production resources, inventory, and, of course, in the various ingredients of the marketing mix. It is quite easy to drift into a differentiation strategy without fully realizing the financial consequences.

7.3.4 The Nature of the Product 产品性质

Here the marketer must have a good look at the product itself and try to consider the following points.

(1) Is the life of the product likely to be short?

If the answer is yes, differentiation is probably owing to the investment recovery principle explained earlier.

In this respect past history of the company's other products can be very helpful in providing a clue as to the kind of life cycle performance that one can expect to encounter in the future. Although as a generalization one can observe that there is a tendency toward a shortening of life cycle characteristics many companies will discover, on careful monitoring, that products do tend to behave in a fairly consistent way within a given industry.

(2) Is the product of universal appeal?

Some products, by their very nature, are capable of international acceptance without needing any differentiation. Japanese manufacturers of Hi-Fi equipment, for instance, have recognized that a well-designed piece of equipment is capable of attaining a substantial penetration of world markets. It would be a strategy of immense waste to endeavor to re-design the product for every market. The interesting point to remember is that ever in the case of Japanese electronics, total standardization is not possible, in so far as wiring standards, safety rules and regulations are laid down by the laws of individual countries and need to be fully satisfied. Nonetheless, if a company starts from the basic strategy of wanting to standardize the product, it can ensure that deviations from a standard product are kept to the absolute minimum viz. Those are demanded by the legal system of individual countries.

(3) What level of service shall be required?

Products requiring considerable technical service and attention—either before or after delivery to the customer—usually prescribe a higher level of standardization. A computer manufacturer would find the technical justification for a standard product or range of products a decisive factor in his product planning and approach. An aircraft manufacturer will also strive towards avoiding any kind of differentiation—partly because of the importance of service and partly because of the universal appeal discussed earlier.

Where a company has managed to develop an internationally accepted brand or trademark for a specific product the pressure would weigh against differentiation. Coca-Cola is an example; Kodak is another. Which comes first—the chicken or the egg? Has the company sought a single brand in order to be able to standardize? Or, is it now seeking to attain maximum standardization because such a powerful and well-established brand has been developed? In practice the likelihood is that a company that has consciously gone for standardization will start with international brands from an early stage of its internationalization process. Once such brands have developed the company would tend to continue to support a standardized product policy under the banner of these international trademarks. Thus the major oil distribution companies like shell and Exxon will frown upon any attempts at product differentiation under any of their internationally recognized and accepted brands. These brands act as a constraint on differentiation.

(4) Is the production easy or difficult?

It is not possible to dissociate product policy from production realities. A product requiring intricate manufacturing processes is less likely to support differentiation strategies than a product which can be manufactured with ease. This is of course an important consideration and in many cases production factors may outweigh the marketing benefits that differentiation may yield.

Detergent production is a relatively simple process; manufacturers often opt for local production to serve local markets. In such circumstances it is obviously simple and economic to think in terms of differentiation. At the other extreme, a sophisticated aero-engine is likely to be manufactured in one location and this will have a major influence on marketing decisions, especially where the questions of standardization and non-standardization are concerned.

(5) Are there any legal constraints?

Legal systems can have a major impact on the design of the product, its packaging the printed messages incorporated thereon. Thus, a packet of cigarettes sold in the UK must contain a warning about the health hazard of smoking. The same packet sold in Canada must contain a warning in two languages—English and French and the actual wording is different from the one prescribed in the UK. In other words the legal systems of the two countries virtually impose a differentiation policy. The law is not interested in the inconvenience that such regulations may impose on marketing personnel. Such variations in legal requirements are particularly troublesome in relation to weights, measures and contents of food products. Such legal requirements must be adhered to most scrupulously. The only way that partial standardization can be achieved in such situations is through the incorporation of multi-lingual messages, each complying with the rules and regulations of the country of destination. However it needs a very large label to be able to accommodate the legal requirements of eighty or more countries.

(6) Are there any Country-of-origin effect?

Country-of-origin effect (COE) can be defined as any influence that the country of manufacture, assembly, or design has on a consumer's positive or negative perception of a product. A company competing in global markets today manufactures products worldwide; when the customer becomes aware of the country of origin, there is the possibility that the place of manufacture will affect product or brand images.

Once the market gains experience with a product, negative country stereotypes can be overcome. Moreover, country stereotyping or "nation equity" can be overcome with good marketing.

7.4 Product Strategies for International Markets 国际市场产品战略

In domestic marketing one recognizes that sound product planning calls for the application of one or more of the following strategies:

(1) Development of new products;

(2) Deletion of old or weak products;

(3) Modification of existing products (differentiation) with a view to:

① improving the product performance;

② adjusting the product for new markets (segmentation).

The process of modifying the product may include up-trading, where the modification seeks to raise the appeal of the product to more exclusive and discerning segments of the market or down-trading, where the product is being modified to appeal to wider and possibly more popular parts of the consumer population. These strategies apply with equal validity to international markets. However, a number of important aspects pertaining more specifically to international decisions must be emphasized.

7.5 Conclusion
结语

Starting with a large number of ideas, and gradually moving through a systematic process of distillation, one ends with a very small number of products likely to show fair returns at the commercialization stage. This process is used of course also in domestic marketing: our purpose here is to highlight the special implications pertaining to sound product screening in a multinational environment.

The Chapter's Referential Questions:
本章参考性问题

1. Why is it said that the product is the heart of the marketing mix?
   为什么说产品是营销组合的核心?
2. How could you consider the product life cycle factor when making investments in foreign markets?
   在企业对海外市场进行投资决策时,应该如何考虑产品的生命周期?
3. What are the advantages and disadvantages of the standardization of products?
   标准化产品设计有哪些优缺点?
4. What are your major considerations when determining the international product policy?
   在制订国际产品策略时,企业通常会有哪些主要因素需要考虑?
5. What steps shall be taken when companies doing the classical screening process for new products normally?
   在设计新产品时,企业通常的传统做法有哪些步骤?
6. List some examples for multinational companies doing standardization or differentiation for their product strategies.
   列举在全球市场中跨国企业实施标准化和差异化产品策略的事例。
7. Define a global brand. Basted on out global brand, to discuss about how

important the global brand is?

根据一个熟知的全球品牌,谈谈全球品牌有多重要?

8. Define Country-of-origin effect. How can a company overcome this effect?

定义原产国效应。公司如何克服这种影响?

微信扫码查看

Chapter 8 International Pricing Strategy

国际市场价格策略

Learning Objectives

本章学习目标

1. Pricing-related internal challenges being faced by international firms
   国际企业需要面对的与订价相关的内部挑战
2. The factors that affect pricing
   定价的影响因素
3. How to make pricing decisions
   如何进行定价决策

Pricing is especially important in international marketing strategy decisions because of its effect on product positioning, market segmentation, demand management, and market share dynamics. The international pricing decision is complex. Variables internal to the firm, such as the location of production plants and factory utilization rates, as well as variables external to the firm, such as the economic climate, the price sensitivity of customers, and barriers to entry, must be evaluated before determining the final price of products and services. Pricing decisions are further affected by companies' experience in international markets, market share, exchange rates, tariffs, inflation, and government intervention in pricing.

This chapter addresses challenges that international firms face internally when setting prices. It also addresses the impact of the international competitive, political and legal, and economic and financial environment on firm pricing decisions. Finally, it evaluates pricing policies of firms for different international markets.

8.1 Pricing Decisions and Procedures 定价决策与程序

生产设备和设施的先进水平、工厂的位置以及对于成本的核算与管理是决定企业价格策略的主要因素。

Pricing decisions are determined by the location of production facilities and the companies' abilities to track costs.

8.1.1 Production Facilities 生产设备和设施

Production facilities are important internal(within the firm's control) decision making factors in international pricing strategy. The location of production facilities determines the extent to which companies can control costs and price their products competitively. Multinationals usually can afford to shift production to take advantage of lower costs and exchange rates, whereas small to medium-sized firms are often limited to exporting as the only venue for product distribution. Companies often price themselves out of the market in certain countries, especially if they do not shift production to a low-labor-cost, low-tax country. As an example, Marc Controls purchases raw materials in Korea, China, and India to lower the price of its products and ships them to the United States for manufacturing; its products are competitively priced when sold on the German market, but they are considered overpriced in most of Asia.

Important aspects related to firms' production facilities are factory capacity utilization, internal cost structures, and the market contribution rate.

(1) Factory capacity utilization: Firms with factories operating at full capacity are able to spread fixed costs over more units, and thus have more flexibility in their pricing strategies. On the other hand, Firms with factories operating at less-than-full capacity have high costs to contend with and do not have much price flexibility.

(2) Internal cost structures: Some firms have more advantageous cost structures than others. For example, firms with production facilities in countries that have an abundance of cheap labor have an advantage over firms with production facilities in countries that have no excess labor. Also, firms that exploit technological advantages have cost advantages that ultimately have an impact on their pricing strategies.

(3) Market contribution rate: This is the percentage of total firm profits from a particular product—this product will garner more attention than a less-lucrative product and thus affect pricing decisions.

8.1.2 Ability to Keep Track of Costs 掌握成本要素

Product components often are manufactured in different countries. Often, the final products are assembled in a particular country—which is usually not the company's home country—and then sold all over the word. It is consequently difficult for financial officers to keep track of product costs. However, with improvement in information technology and electronic data interchange (EDI) systems, which are increasingly coordinated throughout the supply chain, firms are better able to track product costs in emerging markets and even in lower-income countries.

8.2 Environment Related Challenges and Pricing Decisions 环境因素对定价策略的挑战

在国际市场所处的外部环境同样会影响企业的价格策略。因此,企业的价格策略必须随着环境的变化而变化,应对竞争,应对当地复杂的政治、法律和经济形势。

Pricing decisions are affected by all the external elements in a company's international environment. An international company must react effectively to changes in the competitive environment, in the political and legal environment, and in the economic and financial environment. Figure 8 - 1 addresses examples of different challenges in the international firm's environment that affect the firm's pricing decisions.

The Competitive Environment	Gray market/parallel imports as a competitive threat; Dumping as a competitive threat
The Political and Legal Environment	Transfer pricing; The price of protectionism
The Economic and Financial Environment	Inflationary pressures on price; Fluctuating exchange rates; Shortage of hard currency and countertrade

Figure 8 - 1 Environmental factors Affecting Pricing Decisions

8.2.1 The Competition
关于竞争

International and local competitions often pose serious concerns to multinational firms. Competitor's offerings, as well as the price sensitivity of customers, influence the pricing decisions of the firm. Also, if there is a high cost for consumers to switch from one product to another, firms have to price their offering low enough to have the customers switching to their brand. On the other hand, if the firm is operating where there is barriers to entry, such as non-tariff barriers, patents, or technological advantages are high, they can retain relatively high prices without fear of competition. Finally, if competition can keep product prices low by manufacturing in a low-labor-cost country, then the firm must meet this challenge and maintain a low price, potentially at a loss.

In retailing, and especially in service environments, companies often are challenged by local competitors offering legal copycat products at a much lower price. For example, Pizza Hut is challenged in every market in Poland by a local pizza chain that offers almost identical products, such as Neapolitan pizza, at a fraction of Pizza Hut's offering. Often, challenges at the retail level may be difficult to identify. Here's an example of such a challenge: firms operating in markets where retailers are likely to keep the price of their products under the even number of the banknote that would normally be used in purchasing those products so that the cashier can keep any change. For example, in Egypt, Romania, and Turkey, among others, retailers are unlikely to give back small changing, or even any change at all, to customers. In such an environment, a company using an even-pricing strategy will be at a disadvantage because retailers will choose to sell competitors' products. This is the case even if the company's prices are below competitors' prices.

8.2.2 Parallel Imports as A Competitive Threat 来自相同产品进口的威胁

A firm engaging in a differential pricing strategy could be vulnerable to competition from unauthorized channels. In fact, differential pricing (price discrimination) by the manufacturer has been identified as a main cause of parallel importing-diverting products purchased in a low-price market to other markets (parallel imports) by means of a distribution system not authorized by the manufacturer, otherwise known as a gray market.

A manufacturer may charge different prices in different markets for the same product:

(1) To meet the needs of target consumers who have a limited purchasing power;

(2) To keep the product price competitive in markets that are actively targeted by competition;

(3) Due to changes in the exchange rate in countries where the products are sold; the product is likely to be cheaper in the countries with the weakest currency;

(4) Due to the fact that it offers discounts to wholesalers buying higher quantities;

(5) Due to differences in wholesale prices in different markets, for example, wholesale prices for luxury goods are relatively high in the United States compared with wholesale prices in the rest of the world.

Gray markets or parallel imports are common in the United Kingdom and elsewhere in the world (see International Marketing Illustration 8-1).

8.2.3 Parallel Imports 关于平行进口

In the United Kingdom, one can buy Coke produced for the Middle East, Russian Head & Shoulders shampoo, South African Colgate toothpaste, and Brazilian Dove soap.

Tesco even purchased Levi Strauss jeans in the United States to sell them at a discount in its U.K. stores; the stores sold about 15,000 pairs of Levi's jeans a week for half the price charged in specialty stores approved by Levi Strauss. Levi Strauss filed a lawsuit at the European Court of Justice, which was joined by Zion Davidoff, the perfume marker. The Court ruled that selling Levi's jeans meant for

U.S. consumers was illegal. As a result of the Court's decision, Tesco and the public were outraged. Tesco was seen as attempting to level an uneven ground where jeans were sold as premium goods in Europe and as mass-merchandise in the United States, thus cheating U. K. consumers. Even attempts by Levi Strauss to explain that it is costly to sell jeans in the United Kingdom because of the limited availability of retail space were met with significant consumer skepticism. Levi Strauss subsequently agreed to introduce lower-priced jeans under the Signature brand name at Tesco, pricing it at about \$ 40 a pair—a fraction of the price of its regular jeans.

All in all, the international brand often speaks the wrong language in much of the world. Consumers may recognize that the brand looks somewhat different, but they are always glad to get a bargain: the brand name alone provides the guarantee. This debate will linger and, possibly, the only way to circumvent parallel imports is to closely control distribution Gucci, the upscale Italian clothing manufacturer, was practically destroyed by loose licensing and over exposure in discount retailers. However, it was able to take charge of its situation, ending contracts with third-party suppliers, controlling its distribution, and opening its own stores. This strategy worked so well that it is difficult to find discounted Gucci products today.

Anti-dumping policies differ somewhat from country to country. China, according to its Anti-dumping and Anti Subsidy Regulations set forth by the State Council, defines dumping as the subsidization of exports resulting in substantial injury, or the threat of substantial injury, to an established domestic industry, or substantially impeding the establishment of a comparable domestic industry. According to the Chinese, dumping is involved if a product is sold at a price below its normal value, where normal value may be based on production costs plus reasonable expenses and profit or on the comparable price in the exporting country for an identical or like product, if there is no comparable price for the product in the exporting country, reference is made to the price at which the exporter sells a similar product in a third country.

Similarly, the United States Department of Commerce, the government branch responsible for determining whether products are dumped on the U. S. market, considers that dumping takes place if products are priced only minimally above cost or at prices below those charged in the producing country. The European Commission, in charge of anti-dumping regulation in the European Union, has been particularly harsh on its trade partners: to obtain an anti-dumping penalty, an association of companies representing more than 25 percent of a sector must support an anti-dumping complaint and show that the alleged case of dumping has cut into their market share. However, the EU is planning to increase that percentage, perhaps to 40 percent. The EU is also planning to ask companies to publish changes in their market share to mark the penalty cases more transparent.

Dumpling challenges and charges abound. China, Japan, and South Korea have often been challenged for dumping products in the United States and Europe. China is currently fighting back, enforcing its anti-dumping legislation to protect local industry from international competition; one target of Chinese scrutiny is U. S. newsprint. Another point of contention centers on calculating product prices in non-market and transition economies, such as those of China and Russia. There is a strong disagreement on exactly how to determine product costs in a state-owned or directed economy; the U.S. Department of Commerce is attempting to address this unknown by marketing reference to tangible measures, such as product price in the products home country or in other markets.

As established by the World Trade Organization, after determining that price discrimination did indeed occur and that a particular local industry was injured by the dumping activity, governments are entitled to impose anti-dumping duties on the merchandise. Similar to these are countervailing duties, which are imposed on subsidized products imported into the country. Such subsidizing could, for example, take the form of government aid in the processes of production and distribution.

Enforcement of anti-dumping regulation is particularly intense when the economy is not faring well and when price competition is intense. In the recent past, the United States Department of Commerce and the International Trade Commission scrutinized numerous importers' pricing practices, using strict criteria to determine whether the importer had committed price discrimination and, if so, if it resulted in injury to a particular local industry. Electronics, textiles, and steel originating in countries from Japan and Russia to China and Mexico have been at the center of anti-dumping action in the past few decades. In the case of Mexico, the current U. S. administration has imposed prohibitive and unreasonable anti-dumping duties on imports of cement, in spite of the shortage of cement in the United States; instead, builders in the United States must rely on suppliers from Asia, who take on average 44 days to deliver the product at a U.S. port.

In spite of more-strict enforcement, companies continue to be affected by pricing actions of importers taking advantage of loopholes in the anti-dumping legislation. To avoid price discrimination charges, the importers modify their products slightly so as not to permit then to be directly compared with products sold in other countries at higher prices.

8.2.4 Dumping as a Competitive Threat 来自竞争对手倾销的威胁

Firms also can face challenges from companies dumping products in their target market. Dumping is an important factor affecting pricing decisions. A typical example of dumping involves a foreign company that enjoys high prices and high profits at home as a result of trade barriers against imports; the company uses those profits to sell at much lower prices in foreign markets to build market share and suppress the profitability of competitors with open home markets. According to the World Trade Organization, dumping should be condemned if it threatens to cause injury to an established industry in a particular market and if it delays the establishment of a viable domestic industry.

8.2.5 The Political and Legal Environment 当地的政治与法律环境

Governments regulate prices charged by multinational firms. Regulations and restrictions exist with regard to many pricing decisions, ranging from dumping to setting limits on wholesalers' gross margins and on the product's retail price. As mentioned in Chapter 10, "International Retailing" Wal-Mart has been challenged in the European Union for charging prices that are too low (just above cost) and that drive competition our of business. Price promotions are severely restricted, limiting the manufacturers' ability to boost sales in the short term and to help retailers renew their inventories.

Multinational companies also are affected by local government subsidies to local manufacturers—in particular, to producers of agricultural products and to exporting firms. Subsidies lower the price charged in international markers for products and challenge the competitive position of firms operating in the same industry. Finally, governments can also impose tariffs and other duties on products in certain industries, especially if those industries are in infancy in the respective countries. Governments defend such action under the infant industry argument, which permits setting high tariffs on imports that challenge emerging local producers.

In general, governments use numerous strategies in their attempts to restrict the repatriation of profits by multinationals and to tax or to encourage the reinvestment of profits. One way that companies can bypass such restrictions is through the use of transfer pricing.

8. 2. 5. 1 Transfer pricing

价格转让

Transfer pricing is a pricing strategy used in intra-firm sales: the pricing of products in the process of conducting transactions between units of the same corporation that are within or beyond the national borders of the parent company is known as transfer pricing and regarded as a legitimate business opportunity by transnational corporations. Developing countries often bring the issue of transfer pricing to the attention of international trade bodies as a strategy that could help a multinational company under-report profits and decrease its tax burden in countries where it has foreign direct investment, thus evading taxation. Instead of pricing products at cost, products can be priced at market level, known as market-based transfer pricing, where the price reflects the price products sell for in a particular market; at cost, known as cost-based transfer pricing, where the cost reflects not the cost incurred by the company, but the estimated opportunity cost of the product; or products can be priced using a combination of the two strategies.

8. 2. 5. 2 The price of protectionism

价格保护

Protectionism adds to the final price paid by consumers. In spite of the Uruguay Round Agreement on trade liberalization and the strides made subsequently by the World Trade Organization, protectionist actions continue to increase the costs of goods, and hence the price for the final consumer. Europe's economy, for example, is almost as protected as it was 10 years ago, and its costs are as high as 7 percent of the gross domestic product of the European Union—some $ 600 billion. To illustrate, the EU's banana-import restrictions cost European consumers up to $ 2 billion a year, or about 55 cents per kilogram of bananas. In other examples, European beef farmers receive large subsidies, while tariffs of up to 125 percent are imposed on beef imports; in addition, the EU has a ban on hormone-treated beef from the United States. The costs incurred by European beef consumers for subsidies, tariffs, and other restrictions amount to $ 14.6 billion a year in the form of higher prices and taxes, or around $ 1.60 per kilogram of beef.

These figures are high in the United States aswell, especially in service industries such as shipping and banking.

8.2.6 The Economic and Financial Environment 当地的经济和金融环境

8.2.6.1 Inflationary pressures on price 通货膨胀压力与价格

An inflationary environment places strong pressures on companies to lower prices; often, pricing competitively may mean that companies are not producing a profit. During inflationary periods, firms often find that they must decide between maintaining a competitive presence in a market and weathering the downside of the economic cycle or abandoning the market, which is a high-cost, high-risk proposition. Companies operating in Latin America in the 1980s and early 1990s often faced challenges posed by inflation. In the United States and Europe, inflationary fears emerged as a result of the rapid increase in gasoline prices in 2006 and 2007.

8.2.6.2 Fluctuating exchange rates 浮动汇率

Fluctuating exchange rates provide both challenges and opportunities to firms trading in the global arena. Companies that do not pay attention to fluctuations in exchange rates could find that their profits are greatly eroded during the time lapsed between contract negotiations and the actual product delivery. Including a percentage that covers exchange rate fluctuations when specifying the product price is one strategy companies use to address the unpredictability of such fluctuations

Traditionally, firms specified all transactions in a strong, stable, hard currency—usually the Dollar. Since the dollar's ups and downs in the 1970s and 1980s, however, other currencies have emerged as standards for exchanges. Increasingly, pricing decisions are facilitated by the advent of successful venues for regional integration, such as the European Union and the Southern Cone Common Market (MERCOSUR). Member countries have adopted a single currency, in the case of the European Union, or, in the case of MERCOSUR, they are attempting to peg the currency of member countries relative to each other. The advent of the Euro in the European Union has greatly facilitated transactions in the region.

8.2.6.3 Hard currency and counter-trade 硬通货与易货贸易

Developing countries face a significant shortage of hard currency reserves. Hard currency is currency that is accepted for payment by any international seller; soft currency is currency that is kept at a high artificial exchange rate, overvalued, and controlled by the national government. This situation, compounded by the inability to borrow from international banks or other sources such as the International Monetary Fund, has led developing countries to resort to counter-trade to remain active in international trade and to address the needs of local consumers. Moreover, as global markets are growing competitive, increasingly, the balance of power is shifting from sellers to buyers; in the process, buyers require sellers to engage in reciprocal purchases, known as counter-trade.

Counter-trade involves selling a product to a buyer and agreeing to accept, in return for payment, products from the buyer's firm or from the trade agency/institution of the buyer. Counter-trade has been traditionally associated with companies from countries in the former Soviet Bloc and from other countries with a tightly controlled soft currency. The classic counter-trade example is the one initiated by Pepsi with the former Soviet Union. In the late 1960s, Nikita Khrushchev, then president of the Soviet Union, was impressed by the taste of Pepsi and agreed to an exchange of Pepsi syrup and bottling equipment in return for Stolichnaya vodka. This exchange was an example of successful counter-trade conducted over decades. And counter-trade is on the increase worldwide; it is estimated that the percentage of the total world trade financed through counter-trade transactions is just more than 20 percent. Many developing countries rely heavily on counter-trade in their international trade activity; for example, as such as 70 percent of Russian industrial activity involves barter.

It should be noted that counter-trade is an important venue for firms in developed countries as well. For example, firms in the United States and Western Europe use counter-trade exchanges routinely.

8.2.6.4 The position of the U.S. government

美国政府的立场

The United States, in line with the mandates of the Would Trade Organization (WTO), has a policy that opposes government-mandated counter-trade. The U.S. government interferes only in the case of firms that operate with U.S. government financing or firms that have contracts with the U.S. government. In this case, the U.S. government could compromise the competitive position of U.S. firms, which are at a disadvantage in developing countries compared with their Japanese and European competitors. However, the U.S. government does not deter firms from engaging in counter-trade with private parties.

8.2.6.5 Counter-trade brokers

易货贸易经纪人

Often, counter-trade is conducted with the help of counter-trade brokers because it is rate that a perfect match can exist for product exchanges and because the exchanges are complex. Exchanges could range from paying sausages to rock stars for their performances, and bringing French high fashion to Russian consumers by selling quality Russian crystal to Saudi merchants. In the second example, the barter of French high fashion for Russian crystal is mediated by Saudi parties, who pay cash for the product to the French couturiers.

Numerous companies specialize in brokering barter deals. Located in many financial centers, such as London and New York, as well as in countries that have transactions of brokering barter agreements, such as Sweden, these brokers can put together intricate exchanges. Among the major U. S. corporate barter firms doing large-volume business are the firms of Argent Trading, Active International, Media Resources International, and Tradewell, Inc..

8.2.6.6 Advantages of counter-trade
易货贸易的优势

Counter-trade offers substantial advantages to the involved parties. Counter-trade allows firms from industrialized countries to sell their products in markets in the developing world that otherwise would not be accessible. Many countries that have a shortage of hard currency and that otherwise cannot secure bank loans to finance imports restrict the import of products considered nonessential by using foreign exchange controls and other barriers. Counter-trade can help an exploiting company bypass such restrictions.

In addition to offering an opportunity to many developing countries to participate in trade, counter-trade also offers individuals from developing countries access to consumer products. Ministries of Foreign Trade in many developing countries tend to favor heavy industry imports and to restrict light industry imports, especially imports of soft consumer goods. For example, counter-trade makes it possible for consumers in developing countries to have access to brand-name clothing and small appliances and to attend concerts of popular rock stars.

8.2.6.7 Disadvantages of counter-trade
易货贸易的劣势

Among the disadvantages of counter-trade are the following:

(1) Companies counter-trading with an indebted nation may find that foreign lenders have prior claim on goods offered as part of the counter-trading agreement;

(2) Counter-trade arrangements often restrict profit margins, and during negotiations, price setting is difficult because not all cost factors are known in advance;

(3) Counter-trade practices encourage economic inefficiency and are a cumbersome and time-consuming way of doing business;

(4) Prices are distorted as deliveries, which could take place over time, are made without reference to changes in technology, taste, quality, market structure, or competing products;

(5) Companies may receive inferior quality products as payment because rigorous quality control may not be a practice in the trading partner's enterprise;

(6) Exchange partners can, in the long terms, become competitor;

(7) Counter-trade agreements often require long and expensive negotiations.

Often, the goods firms receive as payment are unrelated to the products they sell, and the firms have no expertise in marketing these products; for example, Caterpillar Tractor received Algerian wine in exchange for its products but was unable to sell it in the U.S. market.

8.2.6.8 Types of counter-trade
易货贸易的种类

The different types of counter-trade usually involve monetary exchange to a certain degree. Barter is the only type of exchange that does not involve monetary exchange. Ar the next level are clearing agreements and switch trading, which involve the transfer of the currency, usually a mutually agreed-on hard currency. All other types of counter-trade are based on direct monetary exchange.

Barter(易货贸易): Barter can be traced back for centuries as a form of exchange. It involves a simple, non-monetized exchange of goods or services between two parties. Although no money is involved in the exchange, the parties calculate the value of the goods in a particular currency and attempt to achieve value party for the exchanged goods.

Clearing Agreement(清算协议): A clearing agreement, also known as a clearing account, is a somewhat complex form of counter-trade. Under this form of counter-trade, a third party, usually a barter agent or some other type of broker, creates clearing accounts that represent trade credits for the respective parties, and companies trade in and out as necessary. Under a clearing agreement, countries are likely to trade products up to a certain amount stated in a particular, mutually agree-on hard currency on within a given time frame. When an imbalance occurs and one country owes money to the other, swing credits are paid in an agree-on hard currency, known as the clearing currency.

Switch Trading(交换贸易): Switch trading involves buying a party's position in a counter-trade in exchange for hard currency and selling it to another customer. Professional switch trading firms purchase products that are not accepted by the seller as payment for products and, for a commission, sell them on the market at a discount.

Compensation(补偿贸易)：Compensation involves payment in products and in cash，usually in a mutually agreed-on convertible currency. The firms compensated using this system is at lesser risk—especially if the proportion of cash is higher than the firm that is entirely dependent on the sale of the products it receives from the trading partner.

Counter-purchase(易货采购)：Counter-purchase involves two exchanges that are paid for in cash；as such，counter-purchase involves two parallel contracts—hence，its name of parallel barter. The seller agrees to purchase products that usually are unrelated to its business from the buyer and sell them on international markets. The purchase could be for the total sum of the products sold or for a fraction thereof. The exporter agrees to buy goods from a shopping list provided by the importer；the list typically consists of light manufactures and consumer goods. In a few historical examples，Volkswagen sold 10，000 cars to the former East Germany and agreed to purchase over a period of 2 years，goods for the value of the automobiles，from a list of goods provided by the East German government. And，in another classic counter trade example whereby Pepsi sold its syrup to Russia in the late 1960s，the export agreement stated that Pepsi would subsequently import Stolichnaya vodka to be sold in the United States.

The advantage of counter-purchase is that，typically，the seller is paid up front，in cash；the seller also has a specified，limited period (usually no more than a year) to sell the goods obtained through the exchange. Many governments of developing countries mandate counter-purchase as a requirement for firms exporting products to them.

Offset purchase (抵消购买)：Offset purchases involve large hard currency purchases，such as the purchase of defense equipment，airplanes，telecommunications networks，railway or road building，and other expensive civil engineering projects，by a developing country. The seller agrees，in return for the sale of its offering，to purchase products that are valued at a certain percentage of the sale，ranging from 20 percent，which is quite typical，to as much as 100 percent for highly competitive deals. Among the advantages of offers are reduced currency requirements，increased economic activity，and increased sales volume of both the product for the seller and of corresponding other products for the buyer and improved technology development throughout the country. And，in addition to the direct economic benefit to the buyer，offset purchases also provide indirect economic benefit to the country，as the offset provides a vehicle to increase a country's technology base，allowing the country to develop a competitive position in a well-established international market.

Buyback agreements(回购协议): In a buyback agreement, the seller builds and provides a turnkey plant, as well as the manufacturing know-how, the necessary equipment, patents, and licenses necessary for production and distribution of the product. The seller is paid up front part of the cost of the plant in agree-on convertible currency, which is typically obtained by borrowing from international banks or the International Monetary Fund. The seller agrees to purchase specific quantities of the plant's output over an extended period of time. An advantages of this type of counter-trade to the seller is that it has the know-how in terms of marketing and distributing the products because the company operates in a similar business.

A buyback agreement that raised eyebrows was Royal Dutch Shell's Iranian deal. The company defied the U.S. government restrictions on trade with Iran and established a buyback agreement worth $ 10 billion with the National Iranian Oil Company to produce liquefied natural gas from the Iranian South Pars oil field.

8.3 International Pricing Decisions 国际定价决策

定价的技巧源于发掘当地消费者的不同需求、购买欲望和支付能力,还应当关注价格的弹性。目前,跨国企业的定价策略大部分已经下放给了当地的子公司。

8.3.1 Price Setting 定价

Setting prices internationally tends to be intuition and experience driven and highly decentralized. The skill in pricing lies in exploiting differences in consumers willingness to pay for products and services; consequently, it is important for marketing managers to be familiar with the price elasticity of their products in a particular international market.

Important determinants of the final price are currency fluctuations. Managers must decide what their reactions should be to currency fluctuations. Should they adjust their prices based on these fluctuations, or should they fix the prices on their home country currency or the currency in the country of production? Should they pass on price increases to customers or choose a lower profit? Due to the instability or currencies, many sales contracts have exchange rate fluctuations and exchange risk. Periodic examinations of exchange rate trends determine the adjustments necessary to align prices accordingly.

Additional important determinants of the final prices paid down the chain of distribution, in business-to-business transactions. In these transactions, buyers and sellers need to agree to the terms of sale on the terms of payment. The terms of sale determine what is and what is not included in the price quotation and when the seller takes possession of the goods. In a business-to -business environment, a buyer can correctly evaluate price deals on their face value only when fully taking into account the terms of sale and the terms of sale and the terms of payment offered by the seller. Consequently, these considerations constitute important competitive tools when quoting prices. It is helpful to be aware not only of the prices that competitors set, but also the terms of sale and terms of payment quoted. Moreover, it is important to note that businesses in certain markets may have a preference for one type or category of quote over another, and that certain markets may not be well equipped to handle a higher level of risk, for instance.

The terms of sale are stated using Incoterms, the International Commercial Terms. As a general trend, marketers tend to be more inclined to quote more inclusive terms—the terms.

Other important determinants of the final price are the terms of payment offered by the seller. Handling the payment is often one of the last items to be considered in the international transaction and, as a result, it is sometimes given less weight. The methods of payment are typically determined by the company's reasons for going international, the company's strategy in the respective market, and its expected return. The company needs to find out what forms of payment are preferred in a particular market and are acceptable for the buyer; this information will also shed light on the partner's financial strength.

In setting prices, companies need to examine existing competition, the labor marketand market and materials costs, the buying power of consumers, and the goal of the company with regard to the respective target market. The company may price products higher or lower in the home market; it could engage in aggressive export pricing, skimming, or penetration pricing; or it could use standardized pricing worldwide or local pricing. These strategies are described next.

8.3.1.1 Prices Higher in the Home Market

母市场价格更高

Setting prices higher in the home market than in the international market is justified by one or a combination of the following reasons:

(1) A lower labor or raw material cost in the international market;

(2) Strong local competition in the international market;

(3) A lower buying power of host-country consumers. relative to consumers in

the company's home market;

(4) A firm goal to increase market share by using a penetration pricing strategy in the international market.

8.3.1.2 Prices Lower in the Home Country

母市场价格更低

Setting prices lower in the home country, compared with company prices in the international market, is justified by one or a combination of the following reasons:

(1) There may be no cost advantages to producing overseas such as economies of scale and labor to justify a lower price;

(2) There may be few or no challenges from competition in the international market;

(3) The market potential might be limited;

(4) Buyers in the international market can afford the higher price;

One strategy used by multinational firms to penetrate an attractive international market is aggressive export pricing.

8.3.1.3 Terms of Sale

贸易术语

Incoterms apply both to domestic and to international transactions. They were first devised by the International Chamber of Commerce (ICC, based in Paris, France) in 1936 and, since then, have been updated a number of times, most recently in the year 2000. These terms of sale are also referred to as "Incoterms 2000".

The terms are further organized into E-terms, implying that the seller makes the goods available at the seller's plant, factory, or place of business. The E-term EXW—Ex Works (factory, warehouse, etc.)—states that the title and risk pass to the buyer from the seller's factory, plant, or warehouse. The seller's merchandise is not cleared for export, and the seller does not load merchandise on a vehicle. Ex Works in used for any mode of transportation, and it requires the minimum responsibility of the seller.

Prices are also quoted using F-terms, meaning that the seller delivers goods to the carrier that the buyer appoints. Among the F-terms are FCA-Free Carrier (a place after the origin point)—whereby the title and risk pass too the buyer at the point when the seller delivers goods that have been cleared for export to the carrier designated by the buyer. The seller loads the goods on the buyer's vehicle, and the buyer receives the seller's arriving vehicle unloaded. A product that is delivered FAS-Free Alongside Ship (at port, after all port charges)—requires the title and risk to pass to the buyer after the merchandise is delivered alongside the ship by the seller. This term is used for sea or inland waterway transportation. The sells are in charge of export clearance. FOB—Free on Board(port, after all port charges)—means that the title and risk pass to the buyer once delivered on board the ship by the seller—after the goods pass the ship's rail. This term is used for sea or inland waterway transportation. The seller is in charge of export clearance.

C-terms denote that the seller must arrange for transportation without assuming the risk of loss. CFR—Cast and Freight(destinationport)—means that the title, risk, and insurance cost pass to the buyer when delivered on board the ship by the seller. The seller pays transportation costs to the destination port. CIF—Cost, Insurance, and Freight(destination port)—means that the title, risk and insurance costs pass to the buyer when delivered on board the ship by the seller. The seller pays transportation and insurance costs to the destination port, CFR and CIF ate used for sea or inland waterway transportation. CPT—Carriage Paid To(pace at destination; includes all port charges)—means that the title, risk, and insurance costs pass to the buyer when delivered to the cattier or seller. The seller pays transportation and insurance costs to the destination port. A product delivered CIP—Carriage and Insurance Paid To (place at destination: includes all port charges)—means that title and risk pass to the buyer when delivered to the carrier or seller. The seller pays transportation and insurance costs to the destination port. Both CIP and CPT ate used for any mode of transportation, and the seller is obligated to clear the goods for export.

D-terms imply that the costs and risks to bring the goods to a location agrees on by the buyers. DAF—Delivered to Frontier(border of country)—means that the title and risk pass to the buyer who is responsible for import clearance. This term is used for any mode of transportation. DES—Delivered Ex Ship(on board ship to destination port)—means that the title, risk, and responsibility for vessel unloading and import clearance pass to the buyer when the seller delivers goods on board the ship to the destination port. DEQ—Delivered Ex Quay(Wharf). Duty Paid (destination port, includes duties and taxes but not destination charges and delivery)—means that the title and risk pass to the buyer when delivered on board the ship at the destination by the seller. The buyer clears the merchandise for import and pays for all formalities duties, taxes and other charges. The seller delivers goods on dock at the destination and clears merchandise for import. The terms DES and DEQ are use for sea or inland waterway transportation.

DDU—Delivered Duty Unpaid (destination; excludes all duties and taxes)—means that the title and responsibility for the vessel's discharge and import clearance pass to the buyer when delivered on board the ship at the destination point by the seller. Finally, DDP—Delivered Duty Paid (buyer's door includes all charges)—means that the title and risk pass to the buyer when the seller delivers goods to the destination. The terms DDU and DDP are used for any mode of transportation.

Now consider three identical shipments with identical prices for each shipment, quoted for EXW (Dieburg, Germany), CIF (Norfolk, Virginia), and DDP (Norfolk, Virginia) for merchandise shipped from Dieburg, Germany, to Norfolk, Virginia. The best deal for the buyer is the DDP (Norfolk).

8.3.1.4 Terms of Payment
付款方式

Buyers and sellers can agree to a number of methods of payment in international transactions:

(1) Cash in Advance—This is the most advantageous payment option for the sellers, but not foe the buyer. It is used for sellers' markers primarily or for high-risk buyer environments.

(2) Open Account—This method entails delivering goods or services without a guarantee of payment; the buyer and seller had conducted transactions in the past, and there is an expectation of continues business for both. The Basic Open Account entails payment reasonably soon after the shipment arrives or within an agreed on period. This method is risky for the seller, who must choose buyer well.

(3) Consignment with Open Account—Sellers can reduce risk with this type of Open Account because they still own the merchandise. However, the costs of recovering the goods are typically high in international transactions.

(4) Documentary Collection—With this method, title and possession pass to the buyer when the documents attesting to the title and the shipping documents pass as well. These documents can be a bill of lading, a commercial invoice, an insurance certificate, or a certificate of origin. The payment document, known as a bill of exchange or draft, requiring the buyer to pay immediately (sight draft) or at a specified time (time draft), is seat through the sellers' bank to the buyers' bank after the goods have been shipped the time draft, the documents are released to the buyer, and the buyer can take possession of the goods.

(5) Letter of Credit (L/C)—With this method the letter is drawn by the buyers' bank, which guarantees to pay the seller for the merchandise upon the presentation of documents stipulated in the letter that provide evidence of shipment, adherence to the purchase order, and even inspection, if so stipulated. The bank releases the funds when all the conditions of the sale are met. Most L/Cs are irrevocable. In the sense that neither party can change it without the consent of the other parties.

It should be mentioned that the risk of selling to international buyers, especially using cash in advance or on open account, can be alleviated by purchasing insurance using the many different sources.

8.3.2 Aggressive Export Pricing 来自出口价格的威胁

To gain market share and to remain competitive in international markets, companies often engage in aggressive export pricing. One example of aggressive export pricing is dynamic incremental pricing, whereby a company assumes that it will have certain fixed costs whether or not it exports its products overseas; as such, the company does not factor in its international price marketing and promotion costs or its full overhead for domestic distribution. The price is based on variable international marketing and motion costs or its full overhead for domestic distribution. The price is based on variable international marketing and promotion costs, which allows the company to be more competitive. The company allows for the produce cost to reflect only the variable cost of taking the product abroad(thus using variable-cost pricing), rather than the full cost of the product (that is, full-cost pricing). Companies from Japan, China Taiwan, and South Korea exporting semiconductor chips to the United States gained high marker share rankings using aggressive export pricing.

8.3.3 Standardized Pricing versus Local Pricing 标准定价和当地定价

Companies charge different prices for their products to meet the needs of consumers and to fit their purchase power and to account for differences in distribution systems, market position, and tax systems; this type of pricing is known as local pricing. In different markets, certain pricing traditions are followed. For example , in luxury markets in the United States, products are priced using even numbers—for example, $ 500 for a pair of Prada shoes. When those shoes go on sale, they are priced using odd pricing, such as $ 199. Alternatively, products in most discount outlets and in grocery stores are priced using odd pricing.

In Europe and Asia, odd/even pricing strategies are used increasingly, even though even pricing used to be preferred because it facilitated calculation. Strategies depend on the country, the currency, and even on the local price. To illustrate, in Japan, prices appear to be mostly even for non-luxury goods, as well as for luxury goods, and this might have to do with the currency—there are 133 yen to the dollar.

Similarly, products in China are mostly priced evenly, even though the currency there is on a closer parity to the dollar and the euro, at about 7 yuan to the dollar. Consumer research shows that consumers in high context, non-Western cultures were found to be less prone to the illusion of cheapness or gain created by odd price endings, and more likely offended by perceived attempts to "fool" them. Thus, Western firms need to be cautious when attempting to replicate odd ending practices in non-Western markets. Even pricing is thought to be a "safer" format for the Chinese at the Japanese.

On the other hand, and contrary to the pricing theory discussed earlier, in China Taiwan, odd prices appear to be predominant. Even in luxury markets, sales signs abound and information on price-cutting is everywhere.

Finally, odd prices are becoming popular in the European Union. At first, just after the adoption of the Euro, prices were pretty strange, with endings all over the place. European retailers wanted to prove to their consumers that they diligently transformed prices based on the original currency (Franc, Deutsche Mark, Lira) to the Euro. Subsequently, odd-pricing strategies became prevalent.

8.3.4 Penetration Pricing Strategies 价格渗透策略

Multinationals that have sales-based objectives, attempting to gain a high sales volume, are likely to use penetration pricing. Firms using this strategy price the product at first below the price of competitors to quickly penetrate the market at their competitors' expense. Compaq, which sells computers, was able to quickly capture the European market by using this strategy. In the Netherlands, for example, Compaq offered deals unmatched by any brand name competitor and coupled this pricing strategy with excellent warranties and support.

Alternatively, firms may have pricing objectives that are centered on generating a high profit and recovering the costs of product development quickly. Competitors thus use a skimming strategy, piecing the product above that of competitors, when competition is minimal. In general, consumers responding to skimming strategies are more concerned with quality, uniqueness, and status, rather than price.

The Chapter's Referential Questions: 本章参考性问题

1. What is dumping? Why do international companies use dumping strategies in select target markets?

什么是倾销？在选择目标市场时跨国企业为什么会使用倾销策略？

2. What are the different motivations behind a company when setting prices higher or lower in the home-country?

为什么企业在本国市场采用高价位（或者低价位）策略？是何用心？

3. What are the factors affecting the international market pricing?

影响国际市场营销中的价格策略的因素都有哪些？

4. What are gray markets? How do distributors using parallel imports affect a multinational firm's operations in the target market?

什么是灰色市场？目标市场上平行进口会怎样影响跨国企业的经营活动？

5. How should the Penetration Pricing Strategies be applied in international marketing?

在国际市场营销中怎样运用价格渗透策略？

6. Discussing the types of counter-trade.

谈谈易货贸易的种类。

7. Discussing about advantages and disadvantages of the counter-trade.

谈谈易货贸易的优势以及劣势。

8. Discussing about the position of the U.S. Government towards the international trade, especially when her new administration came to power led by Mr. Donald Trump.

谈谈美国政府对于国际贸易的立场，尤其是以特朗普为首的新政府上台以来。

微信扫码查看

Chapter 9 Distribution Decisions in International Marketing

国际市场营销分销决策

Learning Objectives

本章学习目标

1. The international marketing and distribution
   国际市场营销与分销
2. How to develop distribution channels
   如何开发分销渠道
3. How to manage the brokers
   如何对中间商进行管理

Distribution decisions are pretty difficult in domestic marketing; they are even more complicated in international marketing. The problem of selecting the right channels is simply multiplied by as many countries as one wishes to serve. Yet it is essential for companies which market their products internationally to be able to find their way through the maze of channels that are available or can be developed in each market.

The variations that exist in institutional availability are very extensive indeed and no one person can ever hope to become aware of the details of the channel options in every country. Further more, environmental and legal constraints play an enormous role in the choices that can be made and the distribution strategies that can be explored.

It is important to remember that the best product in the word may prove a commercial disaster if the channels of distribution selected are incapable or unwilling to provide the "utility of place" and the "utility of time" which the local consumer expects. The expectation of the consumer is ultimately the criterion of effectiveness and therefore failure to satisfy the consumer means a poor marketing effort.

This chapter deals with two interrelated aspects of the distribution process:

(1) Channels of distribution on world markets;

(2) Physical distribution (logistics) for the international manufacturer.

9.1 Channels of Distribution in World Markets 全球市场中的分销渠道

不同的跨国企业在选择分销渠道方面有不同的做法。一个生产型企业非常可能在国外选点建厂且注重物流和后勤保障;而一个营销型企业会更注重分销渠道,并会根据分销渠道的格局建立生产线。

An international company can have a number of bases from which channel decisions originate. A manufacturing orientated company would have a number of plants located around the world and distribution decisions will probably stem from logistics rather than marketing considerations. On the other hand, a marketing orientated company will look at the problem differently; it will identify the best marketing opportunities, determine distribution patterns and then seek to recommend locations for manufacturing facilities which could best serve the marketing objectives.

The difference is fundamental insofar as the marketing orientated company may come to the conclusion that one manufacturing unit in one centrally located place is perfectly adequate to be able to serve world markets. A production orientated company seldom wishes to recognize the validity of such an approach. To the production and technical personnel such an approach is much too parochial and they refuse to acknowledge that in certain circumstances it may be much more profitable too build a company's international trade from one manufacturing base. There may, of course, exists very compelling legal and commercial reasons for establishing local manufacturing plants in various parts of the world. However, to the marketing orientated company such decisions must be fully justified by marketing and commercial realities. In this connection the way the Japanese industry has developed its penetration of world markets is good example of this approach.

It is useful to remember that a company that has been proliferated its production facilities in many countries is gradually ceasing to perform an international marketing task. For all intents and purposes such a company is approaching a situation where the company is becoming a collection of domestic units, operating under one corporate flag. In such an extreme situation each member of the group has a normal domestic marketing task to perform, knowledge of international marketing ceases to be an essential quality of an effective management. The channels of distribution selected in each market in such circumstances would be purely a domestic matter for the local management and in accordance with locally defined criteria of choice.

Our objective here is to deal with a situation where a marketer operating on an international scale has to lay downdistribution policies in a number of countries. We are not concerned here with the problem of selecting channels in a single domestic market. Our aim to assist the marketer who has to select, or help others to select, distribution channels in a number of international markets of differing marketing ecologies.

9.2 Main Considerations for Selecting Channels 选择分销渠道时应主要考虑的问题

分销渠道对于企业的影响是长期的，会对产品、价格和促销都产生影响。因此，选择分销渠道时要格外慎重。分销渠道决定了企业对于一个特定市场能否实施有效开发。

It must be borne in mind that channel decisions may have a long-term effect on:

9.2.1 Every Ingredient of the Marketing Mix 营销组合中的所有成分

An early, albeit well intentioned, mistake may affect the company's position in a given market for many years. Alternatively, it may cost substantial amounts of money to extricate the company from undesirable commitments. Thus a British company that chose to distribute its decorative products through a chain of supermarkets in Switzerland, on an exclusive basis, discovered that it had very little control over the price of the product. The distributor, in this situation, opted to use the product in question as part of his leadership's price strategy, with the result that the retail price eroded to levels that could not be justified within the supplying company's pricing objectives and policies. Inevitably the pressure on prices had to follow suit in other markets, where the supply was being made by manufacturer's own marketing subsidiaries.

9.2.2 To Control the Effective Exploitation of the Given Markets 对于特定市场有效开发的控制

Channel decisions normally involve the company in legal commitments of a longterm nature. The cancellation of such arrangements can be highly problematic in certain instances. National legislation differs significantly from country to country as to what constitutes a just cause for the termination of distribution agreements, and as to the supplier's obligations in such case. An, agreement, entered at a stage when the company is trying to introduce itself into foreign markets, may prove a serious obstacle at a future point when the company will wish to launch a major penetrative strategy in the same market. Ignoring the pitfalls at the beginning can be very costly later on.

The following considerations should be explored in some depth prior to taking channel decisions.

9.2.2.1 The International Marketing Objectives 企业国际市场营销的目标

This is fundamental. One cannot determine a distribution policy until the international marketing objectives have been clearly defined. In extreme situations, the selection of channels is totally inappropriate in certain markets, in so far as the markets in questions may be outside the company's objectives in relation to their size, development or longer term viability. Further more, the kind of objectives which have been defined for the company's international marketing effort will determine whether the channels to be selected should be long (indirect) or short (direct).

9.2.2.2 Other Corporate Considerations

其他考虑事项

The choice of distribution in a multinational environment is often determined by the size of the company, the way it is organized and the managerial resources availableto it. Given comparable market considerations, some companies are better equipped than others to have shorter channels or even opt for a direct distribution approach to the ultimate consumer or user. In this connection the main considerations are:

(1) Managerial resources and their experience

管理人员及其经验

The management of distribution channels depends to a great extent on the experience those vests in the company's managers. A company that is entering international operations for the first time, normally lacks the expertise that is required to be able to choose and control short channels or the company's own local subsidiary. Obviously, companies with limited international marketing know-how would prefer to turn the job to middlemen. Even well established companies often seek the help of middlemen in cases involving new products or new segments calling for the acquisition of a new type of experience. It is therefore essential that a company identifies its strengths and weaknesses in this area; mistakes can be pretty costly.

(2) Company's international organization

企业的国际化程度

The way the international company is organized is also very relevant. The company that has opted for a macro-pyramid structure is likely to look at each marketwith a cold and factual approach with the view of maximizing the opportunities of each market. Such a company will endeavor to identify the markets which are likely to yield 80 per cent of the company's revenue and sales, both in the short term and in the longer term, and pour its managerial and financial resources into the best opportunities thus identified. This is seldom the case with companies adhering to the "umbrella structure". The fact that strategic authority has been delegated to the local management means that channels of distribution, as well as other important decisions, will be taken at local level. In the "umbrella situation" it is inevitable that the financial success of the local market will prevail over the international marketing considerations. In the extreme situation, as discussed earlier, the local company becomes a purely domestic company which just happens to belong to an international company. In such a case the meaning of international marketing and its value case to apply.

(3) Company's image

企业形象

A company must consider the effect that its distribution choice may have on its international image. This means, that among other factors, it must probe carefully into the questions of middlemen's respectability and the way in which the world at large would view the arrangement reached with a given channel of distribution. Any arrangement which is made with a middleman, whose image is dubious, can have a long-lasting and far-reaching impact on the company's image throughout the world. Competitors will be quick to capitalize on such an error of judgments.

Furthermore in reaching a distribution decision one must consider the effect on neighboring countries. A decision to sever the company's relationship with a local wholesaler, in order to set up one's own subsidiary, is bound to create a fear of repetition in neighboring markets, and nothing is more harmful to the middleman's performance than the feeling that his security of tenure is limited.

(4) Distribution arrangements in each market

市场中的营销渠道设置

A multi-product company may have existing distribution arrangements in many markets although the nature of the products is such that different channels are required for each product line. It is important that those responsible for selecting channels in a given country pay attention to other arrangements that already exist there. In other words, before one starts looking for totally new relationships, it would be wise to explore the usefulness of existing channels; they may prove better than one expects. They may be capable of further development. In any event a marketer must not generate unhappiness among existing channels, in spite of the fact that he himself may never have to work with them. The international marketer must be sensitive to any achievements and goodwill that other parts of the company have attained in each market.

(5) Timing

时间

The speed with which a company has to penetrate each market is a vital consideration when one is choosing channels of distribution. The need to act fast and achieve results may force the hand of the marketer to select channels which in the longer term may not be ideal. However such a decision must be taken with one's eyes wide open as to the longer-term implications.

9.2.2.3 Channels Availability

可利用的分销渠道

This is of course a major consideration. You cannot expect toselect a specific type of channel in a given country if:

(1) Such a channel does not exist;

(2) It belongs to a competitor;

(3) It is fully committed to other suppliers;

(4) It does not wish to distribute your product.

It must be borne in mind that channels of distribution are independent and harnessing their help is not always an easy task. Furthermore, each country has developed over the years different patterns of distribution, coupled with supportive institutions, and it is hazardous to assume that because the Netherlands possesses a specific type of distribution method the same occurs in Belgium. This indeed is one of the difficulties and subtleties of international marketing and this is where the marketing profile analysis is an invaluable tool.

9.2.2.4 Financial Considerations

财务方面的考虑

Cost of different marketing channels. Before selecting channels of distribution the international marketer must be analyzed in detail the relative costs of different channels. Such a study must bring into consideration the fact that in the initial stages costs are distorted by the start-up expenditure. These costs are in the main of a non-recurring nature. Furthermore, the cost evaluation must be geared to the expected market performance that one can forecast for the various channels. In other words, the fact that through direct marketing one could achieve a cost ratio of 6 percent to sales can be meaningless if at 8 percent ratio, based on indirect distribution (viz. using middlemen), one can expect to achieve three times the volume of sales. It is the total business coupled with the final pay-off to the company that must be appraised.

In this connection the following elements must be investigated:

① The cost of staffing and training local personnel;

② The comparative administrative costs;

③ Possible expenditure resulting from moving personnel from head office to the local subsidiary;

④ Cost of canceling current arrangement with a local distributor;

⑤ Cost of incorporatinga company and any additional costs involved in complying with the legal obligations of the market in question, having to have local directors, keeping books, etc. ;

⑥ The cost of promotion to be incurred in direct distribution as against indirect distribution;

⑦ Cost of registering patents and/or trademarks;

⑧ The difference in cost of duty; in the case of a subsidiary importing there often exist complications;

⑨ Tax difference based on the nature of the revenue received;

⑩ Physical distribution costs including warehousing;

⑪ Start-up costs and the length of time needed to break-even.

The cash flow effectiveness of the channels under consideration.

For many international marketers it is often vital to ensure that the channels selected for distributing the company's products are capable of generating a quick cash recovery. This in turn means that the company's cash resources must not be over-stretched through the inevitable level of credit that one has to grant to one's direct customers. In most instances middlemen provide the cash cushion that a company with limited cash resources requires. Indeed, the provision of early cash recovery is one of the important tasks of a distribution channel. A company must balance its margin objective with the cash flow needs before deciding whether to choose short(or long) channel arrangements.

9.2.2.5 Capital factors

资本因素

Closely linked with the above consideration the marketer must explore the financial and capital implications of choosing a channel of distribution to the exclusion of another one. Examples of this aspect are:

(1) Can one raise local capital easily?

(2) Is the local currency stable or convertible?

(3) Can earnings be remitted out of the country and capital repatriated?

(4) Are there any borrowing restrictions on foreign companies?

(5) Is the local government likely to offer substantial capital support to a domestic firm in order to protect the country's balance of payment?

9.2.2.6 The market and its characteristics

市场及其特征

The market itself, its state of development and special needs, constitute a very important "input" in determining the kind of distribution choice that should be made. Once again the marketing profile analysis should prove a very valuable tool in identifying the appropriate elements in this respect. Relevant factors are:

(1) The medium and longer-term economic health of the country;

(2) The extent to which a channel selected may be vulnerable to political change;

(3) The size of the market in term of personal disposable income, income distribution etc. ;

(4) The potential growth for the company's products or similar ones;

(5) Special trade arrangements such as cartels or trade associations;

(6) The market's receptiveness to new and sophisticated products, specific habits of the consumer which preclude the possibility of by-passing traditional channels;

(7) Marketing techniques which depend on third parties such as merchandising agencies.

9.2.2.7 The Specific Needs of the Product

产品的具体需要

The product itself may have a major influence on the type of channels that the company can choose for achieving distribution goals. Points to remember are:

(1) A product calling for extensive pre-sale or after-sale service is normally best handled by the company's own distribution facilities provided of course it can be achieved economically.

(2) Bulky items can often justify direct marketing. Thus a company distributing tankers requires only one or two representatives in a whole region to perform an effective distribution effort.

(3) Sophisticated products such as computers or electronic equipment installations are more likely to justify a direct distribution approach than fast moving consumer goods. The client normally expects an intimate knowledge of the intricacies of the product which is more likely to be available among the company's own employees.

(4) The unit value of a product also influences channel decisions. Obviously if the product has a high value more funds can be derived from each unit sold thus permitting the luxury of short channels.

(5) Perish-ability is another significant factor in international distribution development. The fact that product subject to physical or fashion perish-ability must be speeded through channels to the ultimate consumer often forces the manufacture to choose short channels. This is particularly common in the fruit and vegetable trade.

(6) Products which are custom-made will probably be distributed direct to the ultimate consumer or user. Too much personal contact has to exist between the manufacturer and the buyer to allow for middlemen. Nonetheless, even in such

situations, one often encounters active agents who collect an introductory commission for identifying and bringing opportunities to the notice of the manufacture.

In the previous few sections we attempted to summarize a number of important considerations that ought to be explored in some depth before channel decisions can be taken in relation to international markets. Most of these points are based on simple commonsense. Unfortunately when a marketer is faced with a myriad of markets, with conflicting needs and conditions, he tends to lose sight of what is the best course of action in a given set of circumstances. One cannot overemphasize the value of a carefully assembled marketing profile analysis. Other questions can be added in order to make the checklist more comprehensive and more relevant to a particular marketing project. This method id extremely useful not only in ensuring that all relevant facts are assembled but also in helping the marketer to look at all markets in a rational and systematic way. With these two ingredients he is more likely to take sound distribution decisions.

9.3 The Management of Middlemen
对于中间商的管理

企业对于中间商管理的重视程度应等同于企业内部的销售人员，无论这个中间商是企业子公司的雇员，还是作为独立法人同时服务于几家企业。应该重视对于分销企业的培训和管理。

Middlemen must be managed with the same care as one normally applies to a company's own sales force. Whether the intermediaries are the employees of the company's subsidiary or whether they are totally independent there is a mutual interest between the supplying company and its channel's personnel. And it is important that the best principles of man management are applied to the management of personnel working in the distribution process. Assuming that the channels selected were right in the first place one has to manage them in such a way as to:

(1) Create distributor's loyalty;

(2) Ensure that distributors are adequately remunerated;

(3) Train and develop distributors and their personnel;

(4) Determine standards of performance;

(5) Evaluate performance against standards;

(6) Maintain an efficient communication system with every distributor.

9.3.1 Creating Distributor Loyalty 培养分销商的忠诚度

In order to achieve distributor loyalty it is important that he does not feel at any stage that his relationship with the supplying company is a temporary one. A company that is able to demonstrate that throughout its international activities it has treated its distributor fairly and reasonably is more likely to earn the loyalty of its foreign agents and distributors.

The task of building distributor's loyalty should be shared with the public relations department; in the absence of such a department the marketer should employ some of the principles of the public relations function. In this connection one may find that house magazines have an important role to play. Similarly, organizing visits to factories for the best performers and their families tends to develop a feeling of belonging. Such a sentiment is the foundation of a happy and fruitful relationship with people who are not directly under the company's managerial jurisdiction. Other ways that have been found useful in an attempt to build loyalty among the company's foreign distributors can be summarized as follows:

(1) Provide prizes, medals, plaques, cash bonuses to excellent performers and generate sufficient publicity among the international community of distributors so that others will strive to join those honored in previous years.

(2) Arrange for senior personnel of the parent board to visit periodically distributors in their own country and on their home ground. It is important that such visitors are alerted to the cultural idiosyncrasies of each territory to be visited. Nothing is more harmful to a distributor relationship than a rumor that the chairman of the company visited a certain country and refrained from making contract with the local agent or distributor.

It may I certain instances be very helpful to invite the son or daughter of the distributor to come to the company's head office or regional headquarters for a period of training.

The point to remember is that although the distributor is trying to maximize his profit out of the company's products, he is a vital link in the route to success and his monetary reward, however high, must not be looked at by the company's own personnel with pusillanimous envy. It often happens that unnecessary friction develops between an agent and principal's staff for no better reason than the latter resent the level of success that the former has achieved. Good management in international marketing calls for the kind of generosity that enables a person to regard the personal success of a distributor as a pleasant evidence of the company's achievement in the specific market. This approach does indeed help in most cases to develop a long-lasting and genuine loyalty.

9.3.2 Remuneration of Distributors 分销商的薪酬管理

Middlemen must be rewarded in such a way that they are motivated to do an effective job. In those countries where channel traditions exist the level of remuneration is probably well accepted by everybody concerned. The difficulties start in those markets where the product to be marketed is new and no precedents exist as to what constitutes an acceptable 'package'. The package normally consists of commission, contribution towards promotion, discounts for prompt payment, and other financial incentives. There is no hard and fast rule as to what constitutes a perfect level of remuneration in every situation. The point to remember is that a distributor can be as easily over-remunerated as under-remunerated. Those responsible for reaching a distribution arrangement with the foreign middleman must strike a happy medium between the two extremes, whilst maintaining at the same time equity vis-à-vis middlemen in other territories and the company's own objectives. Over-remuneration can of course generate the right incentive among the distributors but is bound to affect the ultimate profit; under-remuneration may lead to minimal effort on the part of the middleman.

The biggest problem arises when a company entering the international marketing scene indulges in distribution/agency arrangements with different remuneration terms in each deal. Whilst this can work for a while, complications are sure to follow. Middlemen whose level of remuneration is lower than others will react strongly when they discover such deviations and the results can be quite unpleasant. Trying to keep special arrangements secret seldom work insofar as the slightest clerical error may bring the house down. It is sufficient for a commission statement to be inserted in error in wrong envelope for the information to become public knowledge and a source of general aggravation.

Remuneration therefore must be worked out in detail and in accordance with a logical plan with the view of keeping all the middlemen happy. Ideally one should aim to develop a standardized remuneration package, in the same way as one is always trying to work in accordance with a salary grading system; anomalies must be capable of an explanation should the situation arise.

9.3.3 Training Middlemen and Their Staff 对中间商及其员工的培训

Distributors and their staff need training and development as much as any company's personnel. It is very much in the interest of the supplying company to ensure that such training is actually undertaken, because in the final analysis competent personnel with perform a more effective job and that in turn will mean better sales in the market and hopefully better profits.

A well-planned program of training held either at the Center or at some neutral venue can not only help distributors and their personnel to improve their effectiveness, but can contribute enormously to the feeling of loyalty that the company wishes to foster. Furthermore, it may serve as a communication forum where distributors form different countries can exchange views and compare distribution methods and practices. Training programs could include:

(1) Knowledge of the company and its products;

(2) Knowledge of the specific products which the distributor handles should be developed in some depth;

(3) The above should include specific details about servicing complicated products;

(4) Selling skills—these must of course be adaptedby the trainer to the specific needs of each market. To that extent a strong communication must exist between the trainer and local management;

(5) Communication skills including report writing, and effective presentations.

9.3.4 Determining Standards of Performance 为中间商定制工作服务标准

Once again distributors and agents have to be managed in the same way as one normally tries to manage one's own personnel, with the major exception that such middlemen do net actually work for the company and should therefore be treatedwith considerable tact and diplomacy. At the same time there is a great merit, even form the middleman's point of view, to know what amounts in the eyes of his principal to a good performance and what constitutes a poor result.

It is important, however, that standards of performance ascribed to each middleman are fair and based on a sound assessment of what is an attainable target in each market. Setting standards of performance which are neither realistic nor achievable can do more harm good. A particularly useful approach is to have the supplying company and the distributor develops jointly standards for the latter's performance. Jointly agreed norms are always more palatable than are those imposed from above. Standards of performance should include:

(1) Sales volume objective;

(2) Market share in each market;

(3) Inventory turnover ratio;

(4) Number of accounts per area;

(5) Growth objective;

(6) Price stability objective;

(7) Quality of publicity;

(8) In the case of distributors who carry other lines the percentage of floor space allocated to the supplying company's products can be defined in standards terms;

(9) General image of the middleman in the market place.

These are only a few standards that one normally encounters in international distribution. Others can be defined to meet the requirements of specific arrangements and locations. Standards must be meaningful in the sense that the middleman is able to understand what is expected of him. If they are too complicated or couched in jargon the likelihood is that the distributor will wash his hands of the whole matter and ignore the standards thus set for him.

9.3.5 Evaluation Performance 对中间商的服务评价

Where standards of performance have been defined and communicated to distributors it is relatively easy to monitor achievement. Such an evaluation should be carried out at periodic intervals and the results should be discussed with the distributors with the view of identifying weaknesses and dangerous trends. It must be made clear to distributors that such procedures are aimed at monitoring performance and if necessary form the basis of remedial help. They are not just an instrument of bureaucracy and red tape. Distributors aboard are normally happy to go along with the former, they deeply resent the latter.

Many companies operate evaluation forms especially where the company has a large number of agents and distributors. It must be emphasized that in each marketing area one must identify the most important parameters to be achieved. What is applicable in pharmaceuticals is not necessarily applicable in the produce trade. Further more there is no point including an evaluation dimension in the procedures unless it is relevant and measurable. Thus there is little point in including details of market share if neither the company nor the distributor possesses information about market share performance in a given market. Similarly, if the product is such that the price behaves in a commodity fashion and the distributor is unable to control price behavior, it is futile to include price details in the evaluation procedures. The evaluation method must be based on standards which are directly relevant to what constitutes good or bad performance and very little else. The items measured must be such that consistently poor returns may cost the distributor his right to handle the companies products in the future. Anything else is quite irrelevant and must be avoided in such procedures.

9.3.6 Maintaining an Efficient Communication 保持有效的沟通

Good communication between the supplying company and its international distribution network is an essential condition for a successful marketing effort with middlemen scattered all over the world and with major language and cultural differences. Developing a sound communication system with one's international distributors is certainly one of the major tasks of the international marketer. This is equally true whether the company is small and is entering the international arena for the first time or whether the company is a well-established multinational company with years of experience. Communication can be effectively maintained through:

(1) Ensuring that letters are promptly answered and such correspondence is carried out in very clear and sympathetic style.

(2) Information sheets and/or house magazines.

(3) Periodical visits to each distributor. Such visits must be well planned with clearly defined objectives.

(4) Invitations to distributors to visits head office and/or regional headquarters.

(5) Occasional conferences held in a central point or at some resort where all distributors can get together and discuss major issues of mutual interest.

(6) The establishment of the Distributor Consultative Council as discussed earlier.

9.4 Conclusion 结语

Most companies embarking on the path to internationalization go through a classical pattern of evolution in relation to distribution policies. They commence their overseas development by means of an export effort. They appoint agents or distributors in foreign countries and motivate them towards hard and effective selling. At a certain point the company comes to realize that the contribution form a certain market is sufficiently high to justify a wholly-owned subsidiary company. The agent or distributor in such a country has to be bought out or dismissed and a subsidiary company established to handle the selling on behalf of the parent company. The full contribution belongs mow to the parent company. Depending on the success of the subsidiary and the size of the market, one starts considering the establishment of manufacturing or assembly plants. At this stage an intricate international structure comes into being and a fully-fledged multinational company is born.

Some companies opt for license agreements instead of building their own operating subsidiaries. With technologically advanced companies this approach can prove highly rewarding especially where the company seeks to maximize profits rather than sales.

This description oversimplifies the real situation in as much as the modern multinational often operates through a myriad of arrangements. In a number of markets it will operate through subsidiaries. In other markets it will work through agents. Yet, in other countries it may opt for license arrangements. A hybrid situation like this is fairly common and inevitably presents the international company with intricate management and control problems.

The internationalization process is usually carried out in an evolutionary way. Thus, for example, Northern Telecom, the Canada based multinational company commenced its overseas activity almost entirely by direct exports. It has then followed by an increasing investment to cope with the growth in sales volume which finally led to the gradual establishment of overseas manufacturing facilities. This is a fairly normal pattern with most international companies.

The Chapter's Referential Questions:
本章参考性问题

1. Describe the possible major channel options in each market.
   谈谈每一个特定市场中可能存在的主要分销渠道。
2. What are the main/minor considerations for selecting channels?
   在选择分销渠道时,哪些是重要或者次要的考虑因素?
3. How could you manage middlemen effectively and efficiently?
   怎样才能对中间商进行有效的管理?
4. Comparing with domestic marketing, how much more complicated the

distribution process could be in international marketing?

与国内市场分销相比,国际市场的分销有多复杂?

5. How could a good communication between the company and its international distribution network be ensured?

在企业与分销渠道之间怎样保持有效沟通?

6. How could the company evaluate middleman's performance?

企业怎样对中间商的服务进行评价?

7. How could the company determine standards of performance for middleman?

企业如何为中间商定制工作服务标准?

8. How could the company provide training for middleman?

企业如何为中间商定制培训计划?

微信扫码查看

Chapter 10 International Marketing Promotion

国际市场促销策略

Learning Objectives

本章学习目标

1. International promotional mix and international communication process
   国际促销组合和国际沟通过程
2. The forms and practices of advertising on a global scale
   全球范围内的广告形式和实践
3. The advertising strategy and budget, and some examples of international applications
   广告战略和预算，以及国际应用实例

Promotion and, as an element of promotion, advertising are omnipresent in all countries of the world. Promotion has become part of the world landscape, framing highways, lighting crowded down-towns, projecting glamour on walls of slums, and shading street cafés. It reaches consumers in high-income and low-income countries alike, on their doorsteps, in mail or E-mail, and via blasting stereos or drumbeats: Promotion is daily life in the markets of Dar es Salaam, in the blazing Shanghai skyline at night, and on the famous avenues of wanton consumption in Buenos Aires and Manhattan.

Worldwide, promotion is condemned for creating consumption desires for products that consumers cannot afford or do not need, and celebrated for its creativity and for setting new trends. See the following example on Dove's "Evolution" ad.

Case Studiles: Dove's Campaign 多芙广告

"Evolution," Dove's famous viral video, and other new media ads were the big winners at the Cannes Lions International Advertising Festival in 2007. Dove's spot, from Ogilvy, Toronto, was a 60-plus-second spot that barely qualified for the category: it first went viral on the Web and garnered more attention than a Super Bowl ad. Dove had the foresight to run the ad just once on TV, so it qualified for the Lions award. The Lions award also reflects a change in the realm of promotion: most of the wards went to new media (Internet) ads.

The "Evolution" video shows a woman undergoing a complete makeover, from human to billboard model. It presents a succession of stylists poking and lining the face and teasing the hair and a computer elongating the neck and enhancing the eyes for a billboard-ready look. The ad is part of Dove's "Campaign for Real Beauty". The campaign fights the definition of beauty that use narrow, stifling stereotypes and tries to build an acceptance that real beauty comes in many shapes, sizes, and ages. The tool the campaign uses is advertising that inspires women and society to think differently about what is defined as beautiful.

In the campaign, for the Unilever company the Dove compaign specializing in skin, body cleansing, and hair care products—uses the "Evolution" video, as well as other advertisements using television, magazine, and Internet advertising to portray women older than 50 as beautiful whether they are nude or dressed up or down. The company Web sites in most of Europe, Australia, and New Zealand, as well as in Japan, South Korea, Chile, Canada, and the United States, portray women of all sizes, ethnic-cities, and ages, with wrinkles, moles, pimples and all. In the

Romanian Web site, the Dove campaign asks women to submit a photo that indicates how beautiful they are for a contest where, if selected, they win a cruise on the Mediterranean. The site lists the winner's names as well.

The previous Doves example illustrates Unilever's creative approach to promotion, from advertising to sales promotion to public relations. This chapter discusses the international promotional mix and the international communication process. Of the mix items, the chapter focuses on advertising and illustrates advertising formats, practices, and infrastructure-related issues around the world.

10.1 The International Promotion Mix 国际促销组合

国际市场促销组合的组成部分包括国际广告、对国际促销人员的培训和管理、公共关系以及大众传媒的运用。

The components of the international promotional mix are international advertising, international sales force management, international sales promotion, and public relations and publicity (see Figure 10 - 1). Companies use the promotional mix to communicate with international consumers about their products and services. In the process of expanding internationally, companies are faced with numerous challenges to their plans for communicating with the world's consumers.

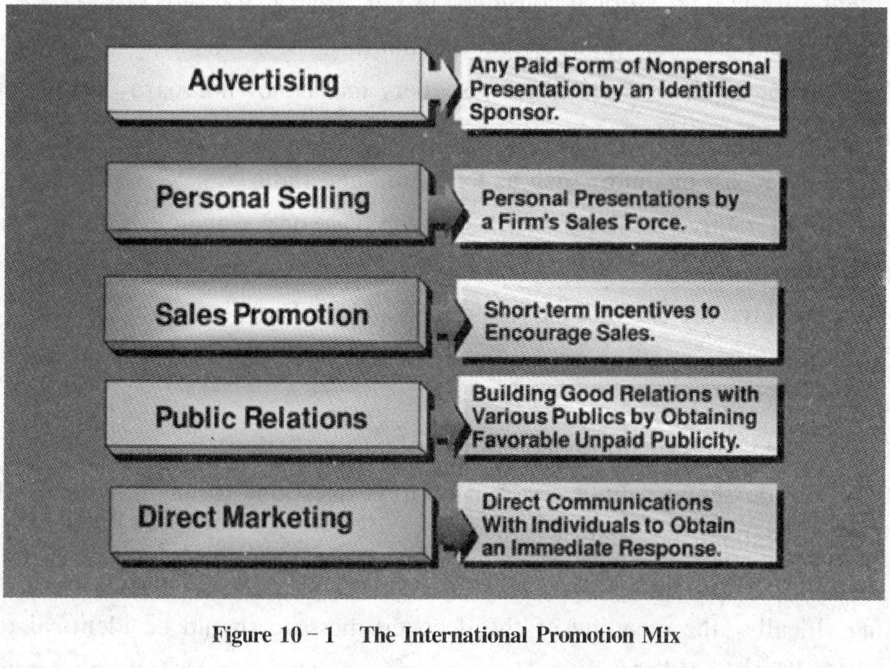

Figure 10 - 1 The International Promotion Mix

Many of the challenges are attributed to differences in culture. As described in previous chapters, "Cultural Influences on International Marketing", understanding the norms, motivations, attitudes, interests, and opinions of the target market is crucial to company success in marketing to and communicating with different cultures around the globe. Companies also must be prepared to handle the challenges presented by the local media, local advertising infrastructure, and the different layers of government regulating all aspects of communication with the target market.

10.2 The International Communication Process 国际营销沟通过程

国际营销沟通过程是指,由于促销组合整体发挥的作用,信息由国际委托机构发出,通过沟通渠道,国际消费者最终接收到该信息。

The international communication process involves using the entire promotional mix to communicate with the final consumer. Regardless of the elements of the promotional mix involved, the communication essentially has the same format. The international sponsor(sender), usually represented by an advertising agency, encodes a message into words and images. The message is then translated into the language of the target market and transmitted through a channel of communication, or medium, to the international consumer in the target market(receiver).

The medium may be a non-personal medium:

(1) A print medium, such as a newspaper, magazine, billboard, pamphlet, or a point of-purchase display;

(2) A broadcast medium, such as television and radio;

(3) An interactive medium, such as a Web page or a computer terminal on the retailer's premises.

Alternatively, the channel may be a personal medium:

(1) A salesperson calling on a supplier or a door-to-door salesperson calling on consumers;

(2) A telemarketer calling on consumers(telemarketing);

(3) A trade show, where one can address questions to an individual who is knowledgeable about the product.

The international consumer(receiver) receives the message and decodes it into meaning. Ideally, the meaning of the decoded message should be identical to the meaning of the encoded message. However, noise—all the potential interference in the communication process, particularly noise attributed to cultural differences—may impede communication. During the message transmission and delivery processes, noise may interfere with proper message reception. The sponsor(sender) collects and relies on information regarding the effectiveness of the message (feedback) to evaluate the success of the promotional campaign; such information may be provided by sales data or by advertising research evaluating message recall rates.

Each step of the international communication process presents challenges to the message sponsor beyond those encountered when marketing to home-country consumers. First, when encoding the message, the source determines whether the attitudes, interests, and motivations of consumers in the international target market are different from those in the home-country target market. Manufacturers of Peugeot bicycles in France selling their product in Belgium and the United States need to be aware that consumer motivations behind the purchase differ. In Belgium, the main purpose of using the Peugeot bicycle is transportation. Major cities have bicycle paths on the sidewalks, and pedestrians and automobiles are not allowed to block them; bicycle paths also have their own signals at intersections. In the countryside, paths, in parallel with the main roads or highways, are reserved for bicycles. A Belgian consumer who purchases a Peugeot bicycle wants a product that is reliable and can perform optimally, regardless of weather. Communication about the product, then, should stress durability, reliability, and quality. In the United States, a Peugeot bicycle is used primarily for recreation. Communication about the product is more likely to be successful if it focuses on a weekend recreational activity and on performance.

Similarly, Pizza Hut in the United States and the United Kingdom is a staple family restaurant for busy families who do not have time to cook. Pizza Hut advertising focuses on deals for the entire family. In Poland, Pizza Hut is the in-place for dinner accompanied by techno music before consumers descend to the downstairs disco in the city of Wroclaw. It is also the place for business lunch in Warsaw's prestigious Marriot building, located strategically between stores selling haute couture. Consequently, communication about Pizza Hut in Poland should not limit itself to a family focus.

When encoding the message, one must ensure that the message is appropriately translated. In the process of translating the message, one should note that language is closely related to advertising strategy. For example, English requires less space in print and less airtime for broadcast advertising (this is one of the reasons it is widely used in advertising). Translated into German, Dutch, or French, the headline, body copy, and tag line require more space for a print advertisement and more airtime for a broadcast ad.

From product name to the entire marketing communication, all must be monitored to ensure that the meanings intended are the meanings conveyed. There is an explosion of naming consultancies, set up as offshoots of advertising agencies, which develop product names that are intended to work worldwide; because consumers travel everywhere, it is important that brand names are consistent in any country where they are sold. From names such as Vauxhall's Nova automobile, meaning "no go" in Spanish, to airlines claiming that one will fly "naked" (as opposed to "on leather") in first class, companies have made many mistakes when communicating with international consumers.

Sending the message through the appropriate channel is often a challenge; the media infrastructure might be such that the most appropriate medium cannot be successfully used. In countries where mail is less reliable, such as India and Mali, it is advisable not to send direct mail containing samples. In other countries where the mailing system is reliable, such as Saudi Arabia, mail might not constitute a traditional medium for sending samples, and a direct mail package might be perceived as suspicious. In Rwanda and Burundi, the only broadcast medium available is the radio; however, international brands are rarely advertised on this medium. To reach the mass market in these two countries, the only appropriate communication medium is the billboard. Furthermore, it is preferable that the advertisement has few words and relies on pictorials to convey the message because many target consumers are illiterate.

All this competition, including other noise, such as audience inattention, from other channels of communication and from programming could negatively affect the decoding process, such that the target consumer does not fully comprehend the communication. To lessen the impact of these communication impediments, companies do the following:

(1) Hire research firms to evaluate the message in multiple international environments.

(2) Evaluate the effectiveness of the communication in attracting target market attention, using recall tests and other memory-based procedures.

(3) Evaluate the effectiveness of the communication in getting consumers ropurchase the product.

The company then uses this feedback in modifying or designing future communication strategies.

10.3 International Business Advertising 国际商业广告

国际商业广告被定义为，一种通过公认的发送者在国际间开展的使用广播、电视、印刷品、交互式媒体的、有商业目的的非人员沟通方式。国际商业广告正在日趋复杂化。

International advertising is becoming increasingly complex; more local and international companies are competing for consumers who are increasingly sophisticated and demanding. International advertising is defined as a non-personal communication by an identified sponsor across international borders, using broadcast, print, and/or interactive media.

10.3.1 The Media Infrastructure 媒体基础设施

The media infrastructure provides different challenges in countries of different levels of economic development. And, even though the media structure is essentially the same in most industrialized countries, challenges still arise in terms of business practices: A medium might not be considered appropriate for advertising. For example, newspapers might not constitute the right medium for advertising a particular product in one country, whereas, in other countries, advertising a particular type of product or service might be restricted or prohibited in other media-for instance, television.

Media infrastructure challenges are discussed below. However, one additional caution is in order: It is not just the infrastructure that poses challenges in a target market, but also the status of promotion and the extent to which management considers promotion to be an important strategic tool.

Case studies: Advertising in Germany 德国的广告业

Germany's advertising market is the third largest in the world, behind the United States and Japan. However, German companies hold advertising in low regard: there, business strengths are linked to technical talent rather than to marketing talent. And, when the economy does not perform well, the first thing to go is advertising expenditures. As a result, ad agencies had to change their management styles. For example, executives at Leo Burnett in Frankfurt started becoming more involved in the agency's daily business, participating in al client meetings and even attending focus groups, to express their commitment to their clients. Also, the advertising companies have become more selective about the accounts they take on instead of going after every potential business.

10. 3. 1. 1 Media Challenges

源于媒体的竞争

Some of the challenges that firm's encounters on the media front are availability, reliability, restrictions, and costs.

(1) Media availability

媒体的可用性

An important issue facing the international marketing manager is media availability,the extent to which the media needed for a particular communication exist locally, and if they do exist, how they can be used as intended for the company communication. Certain types of media simply might not be available in a company's target markets. In many countries in sub-Saharan Africa, for example, there are no local television stations and access to television programming is possible only via satellite. Alternatively, there may be one or two government-owned or government-controlled stations that do permit advertising or that limit advertising to certain times. Although some television owners might have access to international satellite and cable television, especially in the emerging markets in Asia and Latin America, may more cannot afford a satellite dish or a subscription to cable television. Access to these consumers, then, is limited. And, even though more and more consumers have access to Internet advertising worldwide, such access primarily favors consumers form more developed countries, or wealthy consumers and government employees from developing countries. See the following example of media in the Democratic Republic of Congo and Angola.

(2) Media reliability

媒体可靠性

Media Reliability, the extent to which the existing media reliably reach the target consumer in the intended format and within the intended time frame, is also an important consideration. In some cases, media may be unreliable. Magazine or newspaper issues might not be printed on time, or publishers might accept more advertisements than they can print. The quality of the medium itself may be questionable. Local newspapers might not be of a high enough quality to print advertising for a global brand. Television stations might go off the air indefinitely at inopportune times, such as when a company's advertisement is scheduled to air. This often happens to small television stations that compete with government stations for viewer's attention.

(3) Media restrictions

媒体限制性

Media Restrictions refer to the different limitations that existing the media pose on the sponsor. For example, the media could limit the types and number of advertisements aired or published. As mentioned in Chapter 3, "Cultural Influences on International Marketing", advertising in a number of Islamic countries might not permit the portrayal of woman, whereas in other countries(China, for instance) the media do not readily encourage the advertising of feminine hygiene products. Airtime might be limited; for example, the European Union allows only 12 minutes per hour for advertising on each television station.

Advertising also might be clustered and separated from editorial content in newspapers or magazines or from television programming. Many television stations in Europe, as well as in South America (Brazil, for instance), broadcast television advertising only between programs, in clusters. Consumers typically choose to engage in other activities in the home during that time. In these countries, a better venue for firms that need to send their messages using visuals in broadcast media is movie advertising. In Europe, cinema advertisements are typically shown before films to a captive audience; usually, viewers see about 25 minutes of product and service advertising and just 5 minutes of movie trailers. Films also have an intermission, when viewers are urged to purchase products that the movie theater offers (soft drinks, popcorn and the like). In many developing countries where literacy rate is low, advertising is primarily limited to billboards that do not display words other than the company logo and brand name.

Media scheduling also constitutes a restriction. Lag times between the submission of the advertisement and printing could reach as much as 1 year for some publications, primarily due to space restrictions allotted to advertising. Also, a contract that requires a publication or a television station to print or air an advertisement on a particular data is mot backed by guarantees in many countries.

(4) Media costs

媒体费用

Media Costs differ greatly between countries, and even within a particular country. Factors that account for this difference range from income per capita of a target market and competition for media by advertisers, to firm status (a local firm is charged less than an international firm in Eastern European countries, China, Cuba, and Vietnam).

Costs are high in countries where the advertising campaign must be translated into multiple languages. India is an interesting case in point. A campaign aimed at a more educated consumer can be communicated effectively in either Hindi or English. To each the masses in southern India and penetrate this target market, however, translating the advertisements into Malealam, Tamil, and Telegu would be important.

10.3.1.2 Media Formats, Features, and Trends around the World

世界范围的媒体机构、特征和趋势

(1) Advertising posters on kiosks and fences

报亭和栅栏广告

Advertising posters appear on kiosks and fences in the United States to a more limited extent than in much of the rest of the world. In the United States, some kiosks display neighborhood announcements, and construction fences in larger cities display advertisements for plays, concerts, and art exhibits. In much of the rest of the world, especially in developing countries, kiosks display advertisements for the international products they sell. Kiosks are valuable and relatively inexpensive communication venues for multinationals: they are typically required to have posters displayed in exchange for having the rights to carry particular brands. Fences and other display structures are omnipresent in international capitals and small towns alike. In France, the movement of modern art is displayed in major museums worldwide, used layers of posters that had been displayed for decades and then torn of walls and placed on canvas.

(2) Advertising on the sides of private homes

住户外墙广告

Typically located in high traffic areas, homes from Bangladesh to Bulgaria display advertising for international brands. This advertising constitutes a substantial source of revenue for the homeowners and owners of larger commercial buildings.

(3) Advertising on plastic shopping bags

购物袋广告

Although retailers and manufacturers often display their brand names on shopping bags, another phenomenon is quickly spreading in developing countries: the use of bags (that consumers actually have to pay for) to advertise popular television programs. The individual portrayed in sells shopping bags with characters from the U.S. soap operas Dynasty and Dallas in a Bucharest market.

(4) Advertising on outdoor umbrellas

户外雨伞广告

In the United States, outdoor umbrellas, if they contain any information at all, typically display the name of the restaurant where they are located. In other locations worldwide, umbrellas display international brand names, such as Marlboro, Coca-Cola, Pepsi, and others.

(5) The omnipresent billboard

路边广告牌

Although billboards are quite common in the United States, in other parts of the world they dominate the landscape. Examples of billboard advertisements include elegant advertisements for Coca-Cola in Russia and for the same brand at the railway station in Barcelona, Spain; ads for new housing developments that promise the good life in Shanghai, where they are allowed (in Beijing, the mayor is attempting to ban them); or for a new movie in Beijing, just outside the movie theater where it is playing. An especially interesting development is the fact that, increasingly, local ads are of comparable quality and compete effectively with ads of multinational firms. This new development is attributed to the proliferation of computer technology and lower technology costs.

Public services use billboards extensively as well. For example, a public service advertisement for train service replacing a retailer advertisement in a train station in southern Germany.

10.3.1.3 The Dominance of Global Media

跨国媒体的实力

Late-night talk show host Jay Leno's jokes are a staple around the world, as are Conan O'Brien's. CNN and Bloomberg broadcast all over the world, including in sub-Saharan Africa. CNN is a popular television station in Ethiopia for those who can afford a television set; in fact, Addis Ababa, its capital city, often has a more accurate forecast of the next day's weather in China Hong Kong from the CNN satellite than for drought-prone regions in Ethiopia itself. European television stations have competitors such as CNN Europe, Sky, and NBC. Asian stations compete with global companies such as CNN, MTV, NBC, Turner Broadcasting, Walt Disney/Capital Cities ABC, and the Cartoon Channel. ESPN Asia broadcasts American basketball in the Philippines and baseball in China Taiwan, and millions of Chinese viewers watch badminton and U. S. National Basketball Association games. Rupert Murdoch alone owns Star Plus, Star Plus Japan, Star Chinese Channel, and Star Movies in Asia, and has, among other media interests, resonant media companies such as Fox Broadcasting, 20th Century Fox, 20th Century Television, as well as investments in BskyB, Vox Channel, El Canal Fox, Australia's Channel 7, and 130 newspapers worldwide. All these stations can sell international brands to consumers all over the world.

Magazines such as Glamour, Cosmopolitan, and Mademoiselle are published in languages ranging from Mandarin and Italian to Polish and Japanese. These magazines are vehicles for global, regional, and local advertising campaigns of multinational companies.

(1) Infomercials and television shopping networks

商业信息和电视购物网络广告

Infomercials and television shopping networksonce were a North American phenomenon. Currently, infomercials and television shopping channels exist in much of the industrialized world and in many emerging markets. Not only have QVC and the Home Shopping Network expanded in Europe, Latin America, and Asia, but also local competition is growing rapidly.

(2) English in local advertising

当地英文广告

It is stressed some of the benefits of using English for advertising. Other reasons for using English, particularly in advertising by local firms to local consumers, are to stress a cosmopolitan attitude and to endow a product or service with status. Words such as "very quick" are used in advertising for a tire inflation service (vulcanizacion) in Ecuador and "super wonderful" to describe the travel bags sold by a company in Poland. This is true also for product and service brand names-for example, the Romanian-American University and American Gold for brand of gold-plated jewelry—when the products or services really have nothing to do with the United States, Canada, or Mexico.

(3) Product placement

产品植入

Product placement involves placing brands in movies with the purpose of promoting the products to views. Studies have found that product placement can produce a greater level of advertising recall than television advertising. Year after year, films exported by the United States have swept the globe and, as a result of the world dominance of Hollywood films, product placement is likely to be a venue providing high exposure for international brands.

However, there are restrictions against product placement. The most restrictive has been the European Union (EU), where, until recently, product placement had been illegal in many EU countries. And, in spite of changes in EU law in 2007, Hollywood's product-placement countries are problematic.

(4) Product placement in the European Union

欧盟对产品植入的要求

In 2007, the European Union's(EU) national governments approved sweeping changes to the bloc's television-broadcasting rules, extending the amount of advertising allowed and allowing product placement in TV shows. The rules now allow product placement, although only under certain conditions: for example, the products featured must not be too prominent and must come with repeated disclaimers to viewers. In addition, they are banned from children's programs, news programs, and documentaries. These restrictions apply to all EU programming, including shows created outside the EU, which means it would be difficult or even illegal for broadcasters to show many U. S. programs, which are often laden with product placements.

EU film and TV companies have lobbied hard against product placement, and, in general, for tough limits on Hollywood imports. Of additional concern to European television broadcasters is that the EU had instituted no Internet regulations, and now the broadcasters are facing increased competition from services such as YouTube and mobile-multimedia companies, which places them at a competitive disadvantage.

10.3.1.4 Advertising Regulations

广告管理条例

Advertisers encounter numerous restrictions in their efforts to deliver communication to consumers worldwide. Most regulations are imposed by national (host-country) governments. Alternatively, local firm have established traditions and self-imposed regulations that must be observed by newcomers to the local advertising scene. Among advertising restrictions are the following:

(1) Comparative advertising

比较式广告

In the past, continental Europe condemned comparative advertising as denigration and unfair competition. However, Directive 2006/114/EC of the European Parliament and of the European Council of 12 December, 2006, acknowledges that comparative advertising, when it compares material, relevant, verifiable, and representative features and is not misleading, may be a legitimate means of informing consumers of their advantage. Considerations of comparative advertising should determine if the advantaging is detrimental to competitors, distorts competition, or have an adverse effect on consumer choice. Comparative advertising should take EU trademark law into consideration: as such, firms are not allowed to use competitors' trademarks and other copyrighted materials.

Worldwide, comparative advertising is typically not used, even if laws allow it, and consumers have difficulty understanding comparatives ads. For example, a company that engages in comparative advertising in the Arab world may be taking a risk, because the Arabic consumer is not accustomed to it. This lack of exposure to comparative ads, and not a lack of sophistication, may lead to confusion between the advertised brands.

(2) Advertising to children

针对儿童的广告

This is a contentious issue in high-income countries, but a non-issue in developing countries and emerging markets. In the EU, the European Union Directive Concerning Television Broadcasting does not permit advertising that directly exhorts minors to buy a product or a service, that directly encourages minors to persuade their parents to purchase the goods advertised, that exploits the trust minors place in adults, or that shows minors is dangerous situations. Local law restricts advertising to children further: French law limits the use of children as endorsers in advertising and prohibits the use of children's heroes as endorsers.

(3) Advertising vice products

广告与产品

The European Union Directive Concerning Television Broadcasting prohibits television advertising for tobacco products and prescription drugs.

(4) Other regulations

其他要求

The French have regulations requiring advertisers (and all broadcasters) to keep the language pure and not to use English terms or anglicized French terms (Franglais). Singapore does not permit advertising that is sexual in nature; the use of sex in advertising is also banned in most Islamic countries. Other challenges are posed by the need to copyright the advertising message in different languages in countries where multiple languages are spoken.

One of the most restrictive marketing regulations in Europe ended in December 2006: a ban on television advertising by supermarkets, hypermarkets, department stores, and other merchants. In January 2007, retailers responded like shoppers, rushing to advertise on television. The purpose of the ban was to safeguard advertising revenue for French local newspapers and to protect small retailers from advertising blitzes by large chains. In 2004, the European Commission forced France to drop the restriction on retailers. France continue to uphold a restriction regarding the television advertising of films; this restriction is intended to protect French movie producers from big-budget Hollywood marketing.

Before this regulation expired, retails spent 38 percent of their budget on print ads, 34 percent on radio ads, and 23 percent on outdoor advertising. Television advertising by retailers will have a negative impact on the other media. The print media, however, may retain a competitive edge: to protect them from a free-fall of advertising revenue, advertisers are allowed to include detailed information on product prices and sales in newspapers ads but are prohibited from mentioning prices or sales in their television advertisements.

10.3.2 The Advertising Infrastructure 广告基础设施

10.3.2.1 Advertising Agencies 广告机构

The approach to advertising varies from one company to another, and the strategies used by different companies are numerous. Advertising decisions may be determined based on the product strategy. In one example, Henkel, a leading German manufacturer on household and cleaning products, uses a Pan-European approach to advertising. The company attempts to achieve efficiency in advertising production and advertising impact by identifying how a particular product addresses target market needs (for consumer in Europe or a large area); by assigning that specific need or benefit to one product with one brand name; by assigning that brand to one brand manager and to one advertising agency to develop and market; and by not permitting the use of that individual brand's benefit, name, or creative campaign for any other brand in the company. This strategy results in the use of multiple advertising agencies, depending on the brand involved. Alternatively, the choice of the advertising agency in international markets may be based on a long-standing relationship with a particular agency in the home market; an advertising agency could follow a leading global brand anywhere in the world. This had been the case of McCann Erickson, the advertising agency that has been handing the Coca-Cola account in 60 countries since 1942 until recently-it has been replaced in a number of markets with its competitor, Leo Burnett.

A company can approach its international advertising strategy using one or more of the following options: developing local ads for the international markets in-house; developing ads using local advertising agencies, home-country agencies, or international advertising agencies with local offices; or using a combination strategy. The home-country agency and the in-house options by themselves are not likely to allow for local participation if they are located away from the target market.

The most common types of relationships between international corporations and the agencies providing advertising support are as follows:

(1) Hiring local advertising agencies;

(2) Hiring international advertising agencies;

(3) Hiring local advertising agencies to implement international agency messages.

10. 3. 2. 2 Hiring Local Advertising Agencies

雇佣本国广告机构

A company that uses a localized strategy, targeting each individual market, is more likely to hire a local advertising agency. Hiring a local advertising agency is appropriate, especially when knowledge of the market is important. The Swedish furniture company IKEA, for example, engaged in a branding campaign aimed at the San Diego market. The company left it up to the San Diego IKEA franchise to hire a firm to build the IKEA brand in the San Diego market; it hired AM Advertising, a Los Angeles firm boasting top local talent.

In a relatively uniform market, such as the Latin American market, advertisers often use Spanish and Portuguese to communicate with consumers. When a company advertises to 25 countries of Latin American and the Caribbean, however, it is preferable to translate into each country's regional dialect to avoid presenting the company as an outsider. A local agency could better design the campaign for each individual market. In addition to its knowledge of the local market, a local agency also offers the advantage of being capable of facilitating interaction with local media and government.

On the negative side, the quality of advertising is not at the level offered by a large international advertising agency. With the proliferation of technology, local companies, even in developing countries, are increasingly able to provide higher quality graphics, comparable to those produced by lager international advertisers. Nevertheless, if a company decides to hire local advertising agencies, it will not be able to coordinate a global, standardized advertising campaign.

10. 3. 2. 3 Hiring International Advertising Agencies

雇佣国际广告机构

In general, if a company uses a standardized (global) strategy for its products or services, it is more likely to use an international agency with local offices that can manage advertising in the respective markets. Most of leading advertising agencies have branches in important international markets. In Eastern Europe, companies such as Saatchi & Saatchi, Leo Burnett, Young and Rubicam, and Ogilvy & Mather are represented in practically every capital city. Other companies select primarily markets of interest to their clients. For example, J. Walter Thompson is present as J. Walter Thompson/ARK Communications in Prague, the Czech Republic; as Partners J. Walter Thompson Budapest in Hungary, and as Scala JWT Advertising in Bucharest, Romania.

The list of top advertising agency groups worldwide is led by Dentsu, the Japanese ad firm. Dentsu is followed by seven Madison Avenue, New York firms:

McCann Erickson, BBDO, DDB, Ogilvy &Mather, Young & Rubicam, TBWA, and JWT, followed by the French agency Publications, and Leo Burnett in Chicago.

International advertising agencies benefit from access to the parent company's experience and talent, as well astechnology and research capabilities. They also can take advantage of local representatives' expertise and relationships with the media and government. Increasingly, international advertising agencies are present with more than one type of agency in important markets. For example, Rapp Collins Worldwide, the third largest marketing services agency by non-U. S. revenue, opened an office of its interactive arm, Rapp Digital, in Brazil; because Latin America is advanced from the point of view of technology, the market has high potential for interactive services. Grey Global Group is present in Europe with Grey Direct, its direct marketing arm; Grey Desire, a London-based customer relationship management consultancy for Europe; Grey Interactive, GCI (one of the largest public relations firms in the world); and Grey Worldwide, the company's advertising arm.

10. 3. 2. 4 Local Advertising Agencies & International Agency Messages 雇佣本国广告机构,播放国际广告内容

Hiring an international advertising agency with local offices does not preclude the use of local advertising agencies. For example, although Coca-Cola uses leading global agencies to design its messages for advertising worldwide, it also encourages each country office to appoint local agencies to implement the brand message; in fact, Interpublic generates ideas at a global level, which are then translated by local marketers as part of Coke's "think global, act local" strategy. International Marketing Illustration 10 - 1 offers insights into the agency choice of one of the corporate sponsors of advertisements, McDonald's.

Table 10 - 1 The Top Ten Advertising Agencies in the World

Rank	Company	Headquarters	Worldwide Revenue(s)
1	Dentsu	Tokyo	2,487.0
2	McCann Erickson Worldwide	New York	2,127.4
3	BBOO Worldwide	New York	2,09.8
4	DDB Worldwide Communications Group	New York	2,077.8
5	Ogilvy & Mather Worldwide	New York	1,714.1
6	Young & Rubicam Brands	New York	1,588.3
7	TBWA Worldwide	New York	1,523.1
8	JWT	New York	1,496.7
9	Publications Worldwide	Paris	1,243.8
10	Leo Burnett Worldwide	Chicago	1,185.0

Source: *Top* 10 *consolidated Agency Networks*, Advertising Age, April 26,2007. http://adage.com.

10.3.3 The Advertising Strategy 广告策略

10.3.3.1 Standardization versus Localization 标准化,还是当地化

One of the most important decisions of firms designing their international promotional mix is whether to standardize (globalize) their promotional strategy (standardization of the advertising strategy), to adapt their promotional mix to each country or market (adaptation of the advertising strategy), or to create local campaigns. Practitioners are divided on this issue. Sponsors, as well as advertising agencies, agree that using a standardized strategy worldwide presents substantial advantages. This is most obvious from a cost perspective: cost is reduced considerably if companies do not need to duplicate the creative effort and the resultant communication campaign in each market. In addition, as product life cycles shrink, companies are pressured to accelerate worldwide roll-out of new products; developing communication strategies for each market would delay launch. Moreover, world consumers are developing common product preferences and increasingly share similar frames of references with regard to products and consumption because they are exposed to the same sources of influence (broadcast and print media, in particular, as well as blockbuster films and tourists, among others).

10.3.3.2 McDonald's a Global Advertising Campaign 麦当劳及其广告代理的真实案例

McDonald's surprised the agency world by selecting a small advertising agency to lead its worldwide campaign. It hired the fifteenth largest agency in Germany, Omnicom's Heye & Partner, a company with a reputation for lacking creativity. But Heye, led by chief executive Jurgen Knauss, was able to gain the trust of McDonald's. McDonald's was also ready to take greater risks in its international advertising because its brand outside the United States is relatively young. Today, Heye & Partner is so closely associated with the chain that it is often referred to as the McDonald's agency. Heye also has as clients other top multinationals, such as Johnson & Johnson and Esso (Exxon), but McDonald's, one of the largest ad spenders in the world, is its top client. To best serve this client, Heye employees eat at McDonald's on a regular basis and even work behind the counter.

Going against the German tradition, which shuns humor in advertising, the Heye ads show a man stuck in traffic and a kid in another automobile marketing faces at him. The man, in revenge, holds up McDonald's fries and cats them demonstratively. This ads is used for most world markets, with the exception of the United States. Heye also won the McDonald's competition between several agencies for a tag line—"I'm lovin' it"—and it is used for all the company's ads in English. In another ad, aliens are shown ready to eat humans standing in line at McDonald's, with one urging the other to wait until the humans have eaten the burgers because they taste better afterward. The ads are funny and emotional—and it is difficult to imagine that a German company came up with them. The ads campaign communicates a youthful spirit and the idea that something is changing at McDonald's—something that its franchisees are not especially keen on.

High-profile advertisers, including Mercedes-Benz, Hewlett-Packard, Walt Disney, and Coca-Cola, have started, or announced plans to start, worldwide ad campaigns. Some of these marketers have previously eschewed global campaigns or have gone back and forth between local and regional approaches. Now, however, there is clearly a shift in the strategy of multinational firms. Standardization versus adaptation decisions come down to a battle between marketing and sales: marketing emphasizes a global approach, whereas sales insist on being local.

Typically, marketers end up in between, with a consistent overall image, but tailoring the ads for perceived local differences. McDonald's, in the earlier example, has been using this strategy since 2003, with its theme "I'm lovin' it". The campaign, however, adapts to appeal to local markets, assuring consumers that McDonald's products are local.

Other companies whose brand identities had become fragmented through regional or country—specific advertising have also moved toward global campaigns. Coca-Cola, for example, has moved to unify its advertising under the theme, "The Coke side of life." The auto industry, which has for many years rejected this approach, is changing as well at the insistence of local sales branches: Mercedes hired the advertising agency BBDO to develop a single global ad campaign for its new C-Class. Hewlett-Packard rolled out the first global advertising campaign for its personal computer division in 2006, and Disney started a global campaign for its theme parks. This approach makes sense, as it costs less for one ad agency to create a single global ad campaign than it does for multiple agencies to create separate campaigns. Moreover, new technology makes it easier to adapt a global campaign for individual markets, and procurement officials know this, putting further pressure on agencies to cut costs. Most big marketing campaigns now include a substantial online presence, and the enormous popularity of social networking and video-sharing Web service means ads and videos quickly zip across borders.

In the case of Mercedes-Benz, it introduced that new C-Class in 2007 using a comprehensive integrated marketing campaign, with the slogan "C—for Yourself", developed by the advertising agency BBDO France. The campaign attempted to convince customers based on the world of qualities of the new C-Class sedan, its design, comfort, agility, and safety. Interestingly, Mercedes decided that all communication measures for the C-Class should be geared toward direct contact with customers and potential buyers. Specifically, magazines and newspapers with high circulation featured ads inviting customers to test-drive the sedan.

In Germany, a 30-/40-second television commercial was launched on all prominent public and commercial stations, featuring the Formula 1 world champion race car driver Fernando Alonso; at the end of the ad, Alonso, who drives for the Vodafone McLaren Mercedes Formula 1 Team, symbolically hands over the keys to a new C-Class to the audience at home, inviting them to test-drive the vehicle. Mercedes coupled this campaign with the more local "Exclusive Driving Experience" campaign, which allowed 80 consumers from all over Europe to experience the C-Class. In Barcelona, participants drove an off-road course-and King Juan Carlos of Spain and founding partner of Mercedes-Benz attended the event. Vacationers at Robinson Club Resorts and Westin Hotels & Resorts facilities in Germany, Austria, Scotland, Italy, Spain, Portugal, and Greece between May and September 2007 were also offered the opportunity to test-drive the new C-Class.

In addition to its traditional advertising strategies, Mercedes combined direct communication at driving events with interactive films on the Internet. The online presentation at www. mercedes-benz. com/c-class allowed viewers to select the vehicle of their choice and see it displayed against realistic backdrops. The site also offered several interactive films featuring individuals describing details of the new C-Class as they took the vehicle for a drive.

Different between countries, however, might render standardization a challenge, or even impossible. The following are barriers to advertising standardization:

(1) The communication infrastructure is one barrier: a particular medium might be inappropriate or not available for advertising.

(2) International advertising agencies might not serve a particular market.

(3) Consumer literacy level constitutes another major barrier: consumers might not be able to read the body copy or the advertisement, so the information conveyed to the consumer should be visual.

(4) Legal restrictionsand industry self-regulation might also impede standardization: comparative advertising is not permitted in many countries, whereas, in others—Korea, for example—Confucianism forbids the public criticism of others.

(5) Values and purchase motivations differ across countries and cultures, as illustrated in Chapter 3, "Cultural Influences on International Marketing". Targeting consumers with a campaign that stresses the good life, exemplified by driving a luxury car and having a blonde on one's side, might be inappropriate in countries where consumers are living a subsistence existence and just as improper in highly developed, cultured environments. Consumers form collectivist cultures will also question the values suggested by such ads. The decision of whether to standardize is most often contingent on the degree of cultural similarity between the sponsor and the target market: Standardization of communication is recommended when similarity exists between senders and receivers in the communication process.

(6) Attitudes toward the product or service country of origin create another barrier, especially in environments where is some level of hostility toward the United States and its economic and cultural dominance, it might be best to change an advertising campaign that stresses the product's country of origin.

(7) The elements of the promotional mix—particularly advertising—are especially difficult to standardize because communication is language and culture specific.

10.3.3.3 Budgeting for International Advertising Campaigns

国际广告预算决策

Companies use the following approaches to advertise spending decisions:

(1) Objective-and-task method

目标决算法

Companies using the objective-and-task method first identify advertising goals in term of communication goals such as target audience reach, awareness, comprehension, or even purchase. As a next step, research is conducted to determine the cost of achieving the respective goals. Finally, the necessary sum is allocated for the purpose.

This method is the most popular one used by multinational corporations in the process of deciding on their advertising budgets because it takes into consideration the firms' strategies. A comprehensive international study suggests that this method is more frequently used by firms form Canada and Singapore and less frequently by Swedish and Argentinean firms.

(2) Percent-of-sales method

销售额比例决算法

The percent-of-sales method determines the total budget allocated to advertising based on past or projected sales. This method is difficult to adopt for firms entering new markets, which are more likely to benefit form budgeting methods such as competitive parity or objective-and-task. The problem with this method is that it causes advertising expenditures to decline as sales decline; at this point, the company should increase advertising spending.

For firms that have been in a particular international market for some time, this method is used by almost half of the respondents in the study on transnational advertising practices. This study found that the percent-of-sales method is most popular in Brazil and China Hong Kong and less popular in Germany.

(3) Historical method

历史决算法

Firms using the historical method base their advertising budget on past expenditures, usually giving more weight to more recent expenditures. The percent-of-sales method uses the historical method as a first step, if the percentages allocated to advertising are based on past, rather than projected, sales. This method is not recommended for firms that operate in unstable economic, political, or competitive environments.

(4) Competitive-parity method

竞争决算法

The competitive-parity method uses competitors' level of advertising spending as benchmarks for a firm's own advertising expenditure. This approach is not recommended for a firm entering a new market and whose brands are not known locally. Moreover, this method suggests that a firm's goals and strategies are identical with those of competitors, which, most likely, is not the case.

(5) Executive-judgment method

管理者决算法

In the executive-judgment method, executive opinion is used in determining the advertising budget. A third of the responding firms queried in the study on transnational advertising practices reported relying on executive judgment.

(6) All-you-can-afford method

孤掷一注决算法

Most small and medium-sized enterprises entering a new market do not have the large budgets of multinational corporations. The all-you-can-afford method best suits the financial limitations of these firms. Unfortunately, this approach completely ignores strategic issues.

With the exception of the year 2001, advertising expenditures worldwide have increased since 2000. U.S. advertising spending used to account for more than half of world totals—that is, however, no longer the case. According to the *Advertising Age*, the largest top 100 media spenders boast $ 98.27 billion in global media spending. The top spender, by far, is Procter & Gamble Co. with $ 8.19 billion, followed by Unilever, at $ 4.27 billion; General Motors Corp., at $ 4.17 billion; and Toyota Motor Company, at $ 2.8 billion. The top 100 spent $ 47.46 billion in the United States—or 48.2 percent of the total—followed by Europe, at $ 30.17 billion or 30.7 percent. Noteworthy is also China, where media spending has been growing at more than 35 percent per year, or 15.8 percent of total spending ($ 15.57 billion) (See Table 10 - 2).

Table 10 - 2 The Top 10 Global Marketers

Rank	Company	Headquarters	Media Spending ($ in millions)
1	Procter & Gamble Co.	Cincinnati	8,190
2	Unilever	London/Rotterdam	4,272
3	General Motors Corp.	Detroit	4,173
4	Toyota Motor Corp.	Toyota City, Japan	2,800
5	L'oreal	Clichy, France	2,773
6	Ford Motor Co.	Dearborn, Michigan	2,645
7	Time Warner	New York	2,479
8	Daimler Chrysler	Auburn Hills, Michigan Stuttgart, Germany	2,104
9	Nestle	Vevey, Switzerland	2,033
10	Johnson & Johnson	New Brunswick, New Jersey	1,968

Source: *Top 100 Global Marketers*, Advertising Age, November 20, 2006.

10.4 Conclusion 结语

The components of the international promotional mix are international advertising, international sales force management, international sales promotion, and public relations andpublicity. The international communication process involves the sender encoding a message and sending it via a medium to the receiver, who then decodes the messages; the goal is to have the message sent be identical to the message received. In an international communications context, the process is complicated by interferences (noise) injected by cultural and language differences between the advertiser, sponsor, and the target audiences.

International advertising defined as a non-personal communication by an identified sponsor across international borders, using broadcast, print, and/or interactive media-faces many international challenges. The primary challenge is attributed to the lack of uniformity in media infrastructure, formats, and practices accepted in different markets. Among such challenges are media availability and reliability issues, such as media's inability to work with company deadlines and television going off the air frequently. The media could limit the types and the number of advertisements aired or published, or they might not permit the portrayal of women or advertising of certain products. They also might isolate advertising from programming or from editorial content. Media costs, formats, features, and trends may differ around the world.

Advertising worldwide is dominated by U. S. advertising agencies; however, that fact is quickly changing. Firms form the United Kingdom and Japan are competing with large full-service agencies from the United States, and boutique advertising agencies worldwide are winning important accounts and awards for quality advertising. Multinationals today have increasing advertising agency choices. Depending on availability of local talent and capability, companies advertising in international markets have a choice between advertising using a local agency, using an international agency, or using a local agency to advertise international agency messages.

An important decision facing international firms is whether to use a standardized message worldwide or to adapt the message to local markets. Standardization would lead to great economies of scale and cost savings; in reality, standardization may not be possible because of variations in the advertising and media infrastructures due to differences in consumer literacy, motivations, or consumer interests, and due to difference in advertising legislation. Advertising budgeting may involve one of the following methods: objective-and-task, whereby marketing managers set objectives and then calculate the cost for reaching the objectives; percent-of-sales, whereby the advertising budget is set as a percent of sales; historical, whereby spending is based on past expenditures; competitive-parity, whereby spending is based on competitors' spending; executive-judgment, whereby the firm's executives make the decisions; and the all-you-can-afford method.

The Chapter's Referential Questions:
本章参考性问题

1. What are the important traits of the international media infrastructure that are likely to affect local advertising strategies?
   国际媒体基础设施有哪些重要特征可能会影响当地的广告策略?
2. Describe how the local media format, features, and trends differ around the world.
   谈谈世界各国媒体在广告形式、特点和发展趋势方面有何不同。
3. How do multinational firms determine their budget for advertising?
   跨国企业是怎样制定其广告预算的?
4. What is your understanding about the different contributions of the promotion tools towards selling a product?
   你怎样理解在产品销售方面不同的促销工具产生不同的经济效益?
5. What factors do you have to consider when making advertising decisions?
   在进行广告决策时需要考虑哪些因素?
6. List the methods for multinational companies budgeting for their international advertising campaigns.
   列出跨国公司制定国际广告预算决策的几种方法。
7. Discuss about China's Advertising Regulations and the advertising restrictions.
   谈谈中国政府颁发的广告管理条例中对于商业广告的限制性规定。
8. Discuss about McDonald's a global advertising campaign.
   谈谈麦当劳及其广告代理的真实案例。

微信扫码查看

参考文献

[1] Warren J. Keegan. Global Marketing Management[M]. 北京：清华大学出版社，2001.

[2] 药朝诚. International Marketing & Global Strategy[M]. 北京：中国财政经济出版社，2003.

[3] 郭国庆，钱明辉，陈栋，袁宏福. Principles of Marketing[M]. 北京：清华大学出版社，2007.

[4] 达娜-尼科莱塔・拉斯库(Dana-Nicoleta Lascu). International Marketing[M]. 北京：机械工业出版社，2010.

[5] 玛丽・吉利(Mary C. Gilly). International Marketing[M]. 北京：中国人民大学出版社，2013.

后　记

习近平总书记在做关于杭州 G20 会议的总结时强调，“参与全球治理需要一大批熟悉党和国家方针政策、了解我国国情、具有全球视野、熟练运用外语、通晓国际规则、精通国际谈判的专业人才。”经济一体化已经成为世界经济发展的大趋势，企业走向国际化则是世界经济一体化的必然结果。随着中国经济的蓬勃发展和中国企业的日益壮大，中国企业跨出国门加入国际化的行列中，是参与国际竞争和争取更大发展空间的重要战略之一。但是，由于不熟悉跨国企业营销手段和相关战略，我国的企业在跨国经营方面相对落后于西方的竞争对手。因此，进一步学习和研究国际市场营销对于培养熟练运用外语、通晓国际规则、精通国际市场营销的专业人才具有十分重要的现实意义。

《国际市场营销双语教程》是专门为大学本科相关专业（如国际经济与贸易、市场营销、企业管理、经贸英语），MBA 学生以及相关专业人员用英文编写的一本教材，教材的编写尤其考虑了三本经济类学生的特点和需求。

编写本书的目的在于：

(1) 以现代市场营销的理论为基础，通过对一些跨国公司的成功营销实践和案例的介绍，使学生能够超脱“理论说教”的束缚而得到一个国际视野和思维空间。

(2) 通过直接使用英文教材和实施双语教学，使学生的专业知识和英语更紧密地联系在一起。

(3) 通过对于跨国公司营销活动的熟悉和研究，在学校、学生和跨国企业之间建立起合作的纽带，从而为学生就业创造机会，为跨国公司输送高质量的营销人才。

本书的参编人员有保罗·詹森（前言）、药朝诚（第一、二、五、十章）、江永洪（第三、四、六、七、八、九章）。全书的校对和修改、前言的中文翻译由药朝诚完成。

编　者

2017 年 2 月 28 日

于陕西·西安